TITUS LIVIUS

ETRUSCI

SABINI

AEQUI

Cremera Fl.

Tiberis Fl.

Veii

Crustumerium

Fidenae

Anio Fl.

Roma Gabii

L. Regillus

Pedum

Praeneste

Labici

Tusculum

Corbio

HERNICI

LATINI

Ostia

Aricia

Lavinium

Corioli

Velitrae

Signia

Cora

Norba

Longula

VOLSCI

Satricum

Suessa Pometia

Antium

Caeno

Paludes Pomptinae

AURUNCI

Circeii

LATIUM

MILES

0   5   10   15   20   25

LIVY
Book II

Edited with Introduction,
Notes and Vocabulary by

J.L. Whiteley, M.A. Ph.D.

Bristol Classical Press

First published by Macmillan & Co. Ltd in 1963

Reprinted in 1995 by
Bristol Classical Press
an imprint of
Gerald Duckworth & Co. Ltd
The Old Piano Factory
48 Hoxton Square, London N1 6PB

A catalogue record for this book is available
from the British Library

ISBN 1-85399-456-0

Available in USA and Canada from:
Focus Information Group
PO Box 369
Newburyport

Printed & bound by Antony Rowe Ltd, Eastbourne

FOREWORD

THIS edition of *Livy, Book II*, has been prepared on the same principles as previous volumes in the *Modern School Classics* series, i.e. a reliable[1] and clearly printed text, and notes that give much more practical help in translation than was usual in the annotated editions of the last hundred years—all in the hope that today's students will not only find the story of the beginning of the Roman Republic interesting, but also save himself or herself much valuable time in the preparation of the passages set by their teachers.

J. L. W.

LONDON, 1963

[1] The text used is that of the *Oxford Classical Text, Titus Livius, Book II*, by permission of The Clarendon Press, Oxford.

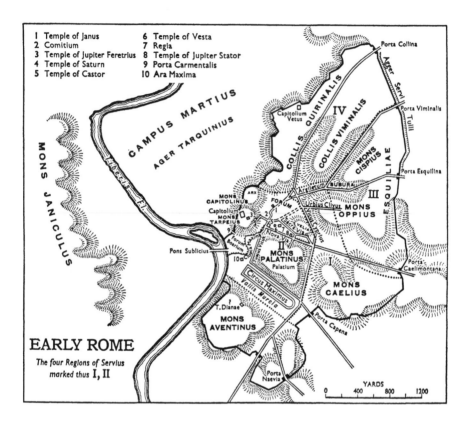

1 Temple of Janus   6 Temple of Vesta
2 Comitium   7 Regia
3 Temple of Jupiter Feretrius   8 Temple of Jupiter Stator
4 Temple of Saturn   9 Porta Carmentalis
5 Temple of Castor   10 Ara Maxima

CAMPUS MARTIUS

AGER TARQUINIUS

MONS JANICULUS

Tiberis Fl.

Porta Collina

Porta Viminalis

Agger Servi Tulli

COLLIS QUIRINALIS

Capitolium Vetus

IV

COLLIS VIMINALIS

MONS CISPIUS

Porta Esquilina

ESQUILIAE

MONS CAPITOLINUS

ARX

SUBURA

Argiletum

III

Urbius Clivus

MONS OPPIUS

Capitolium

FORUM

MONS TARPEIUS

Nova Via

Porta Caelimontana

Pons Sublicius

Forum Boarium

Vallis Murcia

II MONS PALATINUS

I

Palatium

10

MONS CAELIUS

Circus Maximus

T. Dianae

MONS AVENTINUS

Porta Capena

EARLY ROME

*The four Regions of Servius
marked thus* I, II

Porta Naevia

YARDS

0   400   800   1200

CONTENTS

INTRODUCTION

I. LIFE AND WORK OF LIVY

WE know very little of Livy's life, and what information we have can be stated in a few sentences.

Titus Livius lived from 59 B.C. to A.D. 17 and was a native of the north Italian town of Patavium (the modern Padua), an important and prosperous place with a reputation for strict morality. Many writers have suggested that it was from such a background of puritanism and simplicity of manners that Livy derived his dislike of the luxury and immorality that existed in Rome.

Livy tells us in his preface that he preferred to turn his eyes away from the miseries of the dying Republic and to fix them on all that was great and noble in the history of his nation. He seems, therefore, to have taken no active part in the politics of his own day, although we gather from his work that his sympathies were on the side of the senatorial party. Moreover, we learn from Tacitus (*Ann.* iv. 34) that his senatorial bias was so clear in the treatment of the Civil War that Augustus called him a ' Pompeian '.

As far as we can tell, Livy probably settled in Rome about the age of thirty and spent the last forty years of his life in the composition of his great history, a work which had the support of Augustus and his friends and immediately gave him an assured place at the imperial court and in literary circles.[1]

Jerome, who is the authority for the dates of his birth and death, tells us that at the end of his life he returned to his native Patavium.

The traditional title of the work is *Ab urbe condita libri*. Of the books, which originally numbered 142, we now have only 1–10, 21–45, of which 41 and 43 are imperfect. For all the books, however (except 136, 137), summaries have been preserved and enable us to form some conception of the general scheme and the treatment accorded to different periods from the earliest times down to the death of Drusus in 9 B.C.

2. LIVY AS AN HISTORIAN

If we criticised Livy as an historian in the light of modern historical research, we should have no difficulty in building up a strong case against him. It could easily be shown that Livy disregarded original sources that were available and accessible, that he often neglected to verify his facts and topography, that he used his sources with too little discrimination, that he was not interested in sifting his information and in making valid deductions from it, and that, finally, he allowed his patriotism to make him ungenerous towards his country's enemies. All this and more could be said against him.

But most of this criticism ignores the conditions under

---

[1] Cf. the story of the man from Cadiz who travelled to Rome merely to see Livy, and, having seen him, returned home immediately.

which and the ideals with which an historian of the ancient
world worked. Today, the historian is supported in his
work by a tradition that has been slowly built up in our
universities over the last hundred years and soundly based
on the scientific method which has revolutionised the
technique of modern scholarship as it has the world of the
natural sciences. Today the historian has access to
libraries and record offices, to archives and the journals of
learned societies, all of which did not and could not exist
until comparatively recently. Finally, the historian is
aided today by many fellow-workers, all of whom have
been trained in and inspired by the same historical methods
in our universities.

In a word, Livy is not a modern historian, but a writer
of the 1st century B.C., who had well defined aims in
writing the history of Rome which he undertook. He
sought, first, to emphasise in his story the traits in the
national character which had made Rome great, the firmness, the discipline, and the political wisdom of the founders
of the nation's greatness, and, secondly, to impress upon
his readers that Rome had developed into the mistress of
a great empire under divine guidance and leadership. It
was, therefore, his purpose that we should learn noble
lessons from the great heroes of the Republic. In both
these aims, Livy uses with great literary skill and artistry
all the technique of the rhetorician and the poet. Thus
Livy may be called an artist rather than a scientific
historian, a poet who wrote in prose. Every critic has
praised his power of graphic descriptions, his dramatic

contrivance, his imaginative skill in the composition of the
speeches, his details of character, and finally his language
which rarely fails in nobility and pathos to match the
events and character of his story. Livy's history is full of
noble rhetoric,[1] examples of which can be found in the
stories of Porsenna, Horatius Cocles, Mucius Scaevola,
Cloelia, and Coriolanus, stories which were in the first
place derived from family tradition, then handed down
orally to form part of the laudatory speeches delivered at
the funerals of distinguished members of noble families.

3. LIVY'S SOURCES

As Livy's history is altogether of the study and of the
arm-chair that is usually found in it, we do not expect him
to have travelled widely either to examine battle-sites, or
to decipher ancient monuments or inscriptions, or to
rummage among ancient records. In fact, we now know
that there was a considerable amount of documentary evidence available which he could have consulted, but did not,
e.g. the *annales maximi* which formally set out year by year
the chief events of the State, *libri lintei* in the temple of Juno
Moneta which contained lists of magistrates, decrees of the
senate (*Senatus consulta*) which were available in book form
in Livy's day, copies of laws (in the treasury), copies of
important treaties, and the archives of private families.

Livy did have, however, the work of several historians
on which he could draw in his work, e.g. of the earliest

[1] Quintilian, the Roman critic, refers to ' his eloquence beyond all description '.

Roman historian Q. Fabius Pictor (200 B.C.), who wrote annals of Rome in Greek and whom Livy often quotes (cf. Ch. 40, l. 39). If Fabius relied in his work chiefly on the legendary records of noble families, Livy probably borrowed much of his story of the Fabian clan (Chs. 48–50) from him. Then there was L. Calpurnius Piso, consul 133 B.C., who wrote annals of Rome in Latin from its foundation to his own day. He is named frequently by Livy in his history, invariably as an addition or as an alternative to the main account. The surviving fragments of his work show his ethical interests in that he praised the ancient virtues of simplicity and honesty mainly through lively anecdotes. In addition Valerfus Antias (first half of the 1st century B.C.), who wrote a history of Rome in 75 books, was also frequently used by Livy in his first decade, although he is not actually mentioned by name in this, the second book. Valerius Antias is noted for his patriotic bias and gross exaggeration which at times earned for him the reproof of Livy.

Other historians whom Livy consulted and sometimes used were Licinius Macer (middle of the 1st century B.C.) whose work reflected democratic and family bias and quoted original authorities, especially the *libri lintei*, and Aelius Tubero, a contemporary of Livy, and author of a history of Rome in 14 books.

4. LIVY AS WRITER AND STYLIST

Cicero, who had developed the Latin period to the pitch of perfection in his speeches, philosophical treatises and letters, died in 43 B.C. Livy, who was born in 59 B.C., may have begun his work about 26 B.C. During that interval of twenty years, the Latin language, as written and spoken by the educated Roman, must have changed to some extent, and it is, therefore, natural that we should find in Livy some characteristics which are similar to the age of Cicero, and others which no doubt reflect the use of language common to the educated people of his day.

On the one hand, the period, or long and elaborate sentence, which was brought to perfection by Cicero, was adapted by Livy to historical narrative. Many good examples in Book II will illustrate the usual framework: ablative absolute, **cum** and pluperfect subjunctive, nom. of perfect participle of deponent verb, ablative absolute with dependent clauses, sometimes another **cum** clause, and finally the main verb. On the whole, as one would expect in an author who wrote to be read rather than to be heard, the periods of Livy tend to be more elaborate than those of Cicero.

On the other hand, if we use the extant works of Cicero and Caesar as a criterion, we find in Livy usages, some of which reflect the natural development of the language, while others are the result of the author's attempt to introduce variety and colour into his work. Ciceronian prose with its symmetry and balance could not have sustained the weight of such a long historical work without becoming monotonous and tedious.

It is interesting to note that in any discussion on Livy's style, many scholars and editors have been greatly influenced by the work of S. G. Stacey who in 1895 produced a study of the development of Livy's style, the main point of which is to show that in the writing of the First Decade, the content being mostly legendary, Livy deliberately mingled a poetic style with a prose one and introduced many words and idioms which in his day were considered mainly poetic; but that, as he progressed in his later books, realising that this or that linguistic use was not ' Ciceronian ', he consciously returned to the ' Ciceronian ' ideal.

This view has been attacked by Konrad Gries in his work *Constancy in Livy's Latinity*. Two of his most important arguments are: (i) Livy must have used the language of the educated classes of his day and this cannot be criticised by Ciceronian standards, for a language is continually developing. (ii) We have not enough of Cicero's works extant to allow us to use them as the sole criterion of what is poetic or not.

It may be useful to readers, however, to note how in this book Livy differs from the usage of Cicero as we know it.

1. The Verb. (*a*) The subjunctive is used with **pridie quam,** even when there is no additional idea of purpose or action anticipated (4, l. 17).

(*b*) The subjunctive is used in a frequentative or iterative sense in temporal and relative clauses (16, l. 15).

(*c*) The strict use of the sequences of tenses is not followed and there is frequent alternation of secondary with primary tenses of the subjunctive in indirect speech (39, l. 35 and often). The following notes are taken from Professor Conway's Appendix to his edition of Book II.

He shows that, with a few exceptions, Livy usually retains
the tense of direct speech wherever practicable. But since
this is impossible with the imperative, future, and future-
perfect indicative, he changes these into secondary tenses
of the subjunctive.

2. Adverbs and prepositional phrases are used attribu-
tively, **deinceps** (1, l. 5).

3. The modal use of the gerund or gerundive is very
common (2, l. 41 and often).

4. The local ablative occurs without a preposition in 7,
l. 22.

5. The use of adjectives as nouns, especially in oblique
cases is common, **in plano** (11, l. 3).

6. Prepositions are used with names of towns, **ab
Inregillo** (16, l. 12).

7. A simple verb often does duty for the compound,
ferret=**offerret** (13, l. 7), **mittere**=**dimittere** (24, l. 14),
and cf. **sed**=**sed etiam** (2, l. 32).

Finally, worthy of note is Livy's fondness of the verbal
noun in –**tor**, for by using it he is able to give the meaning
of a whole clause, e.g. of purpose in 6, l. 35; 12, l. 17; 18,
l. 20; 24, l. 6, etc.

5. The History of the Period

When Book II begins, the royal house of Tarquin has
been expelled and a republic instituted with the royal
power shared by two annually elected consuls (or praetors
as they were first called) drawn from the patricians. They
took over the threefold duties of the kings, i.e. chief

general, chief judge, and chief priest, although the latter office was soon entrusted to a *rex sacrificulus*,[1] or *rex sacrorum*. They were thus the chief executives of the state. Unlike the kings, however, who ruled alone and for life, the consul had a colleague with the power to veto his actions, and held office for twelve months only. Amongst the insignia of the kings which the consuls possessed was the privilege of being preceded in single file by lictors on all occasions, each one carrying on his left shoulder the *fasces*, a bundle of rods from which an axe protruded,[2] symbols of the power to flog and execute.

The consul's power was further controlled by the *lex Valeria de prouocatione* which tradition ascribed to Publius Valerius, consul in the first year of the republic 509 B.C., a statute which gave every citizen the right to appeal if condemned to death for any offence, to the whole people. This right, regarded by the Romans as the cornerstone of their liberty and citizenship, was suspended only during a dictatorship or a similar emergency such as that proclaimed by a senatorial decree. Scholars are suspicious of the dating of this statute, as they are of many other facts in the early days of the republic—facts which owed much to the family loyalties and patriotism of the annalists.

The Senate, originally the council of co-opted elders of the kings, survived their expulsion, and grew in power and prestige under the republic, as it provided continuity of government, was recruited from ex-consuls, and acted both as a moral support for the executive and a check on those

---

[1] See Ch. 2, l. 3. [2] See the note on Ch. 18, l. 25.

consuls who might prove too ambitious or too wild.[1] In
times of national danger or emergency, a dictator could be
appointed for six months by the consuls with absolute
power and an assistant called *magister equitum*. All political
and most of the economic power was in the hands of the
patricians at this time, for they alone became consuls and
senators, bore the brunt of the fighting with their retainers
(*clientes*), and had a dominant position in the two Assemblies of the whole citizen body, the *Comitia Centuriata* (by
centuries), an assembly organised on a basis of wealth and
traditionally ascribed to Servius Tullius,[2] with the power
to pass laws, elect consuls and declare war or peace. It
met in the *Campus Martius* outside the city boundaries and
provided a means of mobilisation. As time went on this
Assembly superseded the older *Comitia Curiata* (by wards).

The political history of the years which followed the
institution of the republic is concerned mainly with the
struggle of the plebeians to obtain, first, protection from
and then equality with the patricians, in the first instance
in the economic field where they demanded to be released
from the harsh laws of debt and to have a fair share of the
apportionment of public land, i.e. land confiscated from a
defeated enemy. Much of this book is concerned with this
struggle, although Livy's account may be strongly shaped
by the agrarian problems which faced Rome from 133 B.C.
and ushered in the period of revolution. The plebeians
also sought political equality, and their first victory in

[1] Cf. their restraint of Appius Claudius in Ch. 57.
[2] Many scholars prefer a later date.

both these fields was the consciousness of their rights and the power to extort them by going on strike—the secession or withdrawal from the body politic. Whether or not the five such secessions recorded by tradition between 494 and 287 B.C. are historical or not, there is no doubt that this was the method the plebeians used and that it was successful. It must be remembered that at this time and for many years to come Rome and Latium were mainly agricultural. What industry there may have been under the Etruscan domination associated with the Tarquins languished after the fall of the monarchy and its failure to re-establish itself. There is no doubt that the farmers were desperately short of land and the capital and tools to develop what they had. The harsh laws of debt, the military levies, the devastation caused by frequent enemy raids, and the occasional bad seasons all aggravated a difficult situation in which at times there was a serious shortage of food. Cf. this book (Ch. 34). It was not only the high rates of interest but also the obligation of giving his person as security that oppressed the small-holder, who often found himself depressed in status, and reduced to serfdom, until he had worked off his debt.

Amid such agitations, the plebeians formed a state within a state with their own assembly (*concilium plebis tributum*) and officers whom they compelled the patricians eventually to recognise. It speaks much for the tolerance and good sense of both sides that these struggles, bitter and fierce though they must have been, passed off without bloodshed and revolution. Livy tells us in this book of the

First Secession in 494 B.C., of the famous parable of
Menenius Agrippa which persuaded the plebeians to return,
and of the institution of the tribunes, officers of the people,
sacrosanct in the eyes of all citizens and with the power to
give aid to anyone in distress. Again, these traditional
accounts are disputed by modern historians, and two
theories have been put forward for the creation of the
tribuni plebis: either that originally they were tribal leaders
and became annually elected magistrates who championed
the people; or that they may have come from the wealthier
farmers who were not patricians, but as men of intelli-
gence and initiative, had risen in position to voice the
grievances of the plebeians.

We now turn to the relationship of Rome with her
neighbours. During the Etruscan domination of Latium
which had culminated in the Tarquin dynasty at Rome,
the rude peasantry of Rome and the neighbouring territory
had been disciplined, organised and educated according to
Etruscan standards. But after Etruscan power had been
first repulsed and then broken by Aristodemus the tyrant
of Cumae[1] at Aricia in 505 B.C., Rome and the Latins[2]
fought a war—probably because the Latins refused to
recognise Rome's suzerainty—and met in a battle at Lake
Regillus in 494 or 496 B.C., which the Romans claimed as a

[1] Italy's first Greek colony, founded *c.* 750 B.C., became very wealthy
and powerful between 700 and 450 B.C.
[2] The Latins, inhabitants of the plain of Latium, had by this time
(500 B.C.) grouped themselves into a league (of Ferentina), centred on a
shrine of Diana in Arician territory. Here the representatives of the
thirty cities met on equal terms and decided on their officers and federal
policy.

glorious victory, but the *foedus Cassianum*[1] which resulted from it suggests a different interpretation. About this treaty, which lasted until 380 B.C., scholars agree: (i) it is genuine, (ii) it helped to establish peace throughout Latium, (iii) it was a treaty between equal partners (Rome and Latium), although Livy naturally tends to conceal this, (iv) it arranged for mutual military aid and assistance with equal share of the booty, and possibly military command alternately between the two signatories, (v) it established a community of private rights between them— a principle, as Scullard[2] says (p. 65), of fundamental importance in Rome's later unification of Italy. See also C.A.H. (1) pp. 487–493, 549.

A few years later (486 B.C.), the Romans formed another alliance with the Hernici, a league of peoples in the Trerus valley in Central Italy lying between the Aequi to the north-east and the Volsci to the south-west, two peoples whose names occur so frequently in this book as to produce a feeling of monotony. This treaty was naturally attributed to Spurius Cassius, but although we may be sceptical as to its author, there is no doubt of its historicity or of its strategic importance to the Romans, for they had now formed a kind of Triple Alliance (Romans, Latins and Hernicians) with a united front and had driven a wedge between the Aequi and Volsci who were now pressing so hard from Central Italy and the foothills into the plain of Latium, a very tempting prize with its prosperous farms and cities.

[1] See Ch. 33.   [2] *A History of the Roman World, 753–146 B.C.*

In spite of garbled and prejudiced accounts from the Roman annalists, we can see from Livy's narrative that the Volsci gained so many successes that it was only with the utmost difficulty that Rome held her own, even though much of the fighting must have fallen on her Latin allies. As for the Aequi, a tough and primitive people from the highlands, they proved even fiercer enemies than the Volsci. In spite of their much inferior numbers, they managed to secure a firm hold on the Alban hills from which they made many successful raids into Roman and Latin territory. It was not until 431 B.C. that they were finally brought under control.

The Sabini were a people who lived to the north-east of Rome in the Apennine hill-tops. They had had close contacts with the Romans from the earliest times, and some of them may have helped to form part of the early settlers in Rome. But the many campaigns with the Sabines, mentioned by Livy and Dionysius, were not so serious as those waged by the Volsci and Aequi; they probably represented cattle-rustling raids and forays rather than serious inroads by organised forces of invasion. From Ch. 6 of this book, we gather that some members of this people were incorporated into the Roman community.

TITI LIVI

AB URBE CONDITA

LIBER II

*At the end of Book I, the royal house of the Tarquinii has been
expelled, and the first consuls, L. Junius Brutus and
L. Tarquinius Collatinus, elected 509 B.C. Livy dis-
courses on the nature of this new political freedom, with
the annually elected consuls, on the determination of the
citizens (bound by oath) not to allow a king to rule in Rome,
and on the composition of the senate.*

1   **1.** Liberi iam hinc populi Romani res pace belloque
gestas, annuos magistratus, imperiaque legum potenti-
2 ora quam hominum peragam. Quae libertas ut
laetior esset proximi regis superbia fecerat. Nam
priores ita regnarunt ut haud immerito omnes deinceps 5
conditores partium certe urbis, quas nouas ipsi sedes
ab se auctae multitudinis addiderunt, numerentur;
3 neque ambigitur quin Brutus idem qui tantum
gloriae superbo exacto rege meruit pessimo publico
id facturus fuerit, si libertatis immaturae cupidine 10
4 priorum regum alicui regnum extorsisset. Quid enim
futurum fuit, si illa pastorum conuenarumque plebs,
transfuga ex suis populis, sub tutela inuiolati templi
aut libertatem aut certe impunitatem adepta, soluta
regio metu agitari coepta esset tribuniciis procellis, 15
5 et in aliena urbe cum patribus serere certamina,

priusquam pignera coniugum ac liberorum caritasque
ipsius soli, cui longo tempore adsuescitur, animos
6 eorum consociasset?   Dissipatae res nondum adultae
discordia forent, quas fouit tranquilla moderatio 20
imperii eoque nutriendo perduxit ut bonam frugem
libertatis maturis iam uiribus ferre possent.
7   Libertatis autem originem inde magis quia annuum
imperium consulare factum est quam quod deminu-
8 tum quicquam sit ex regia potestate numeres.   Om- 25
nia iura, omnia insignia primi consules tenuere; id
modo cautum est ne, si ambo fasces haberent, dupli-
catus terror uideretur. Brutus prior, concedente collega, fasces habuit; qui non acrior uindex libertatis
9 fuerat quam deinde custos fuit.   Omnium primum 30
auidum nouae libertatis populum, ne postmodum
flecti precibus aut donis regiis posset, iure iurando
10 adegit neminem Romae passuros regnare. Deinde quo
plus uirium in senatu frequentia etiam ordinis faceret,
caedibus regis deminutum patrum numerum primori- 35
bus equestris gradus lectis ad trecentorum summam
11 expleuit, traditumque inde fertur ut in senatum
uocarentur qui patres quique conscripti essent:
conscriptos uidelicet [nouum senatum] appellabant
lectos. Id mirum quantum profuit ad concordiam 40
ciuitatis iungendosque patribus plebis animos.

A ' king of Sacrifices ' is appointed and made subordinate to
the pontifex maximus—an action, indicative of the ner-
vousness of the new republic about the title ' king ' and the

royal family, as is well illustrated in the banishment of Collatinus, one of the consuls, merely because he bears the name Tarquinius and is a cousin of Tarquinius Superbus.

1 **2.** Rerum deinde diuinarum habita cura; et quia quaedam publica sacra per ipsos reges factitata erant, necubi regum desiderium esset, regem sacri-
2 ficolum creant. Id sacerdotium pontifici subiecere, ne additus nomini honos aliquid libertati, cuius tunc 5 prima erat cura, officeret. Ac nescio an nimium undique eam minimisque rebus muniendo modum excesserint.
3 Consulis enim alterius, cum nihil aliud offenderet, nomen inuisum ciuitati fuit: nimium Tarquinios regno adsuesse; initium a Prisco factum; regnasse 10 dein Ser. Tullium; ne interuallo quidem facto oblitum, tamquam alieni, regni, Superbum Tarquinium uelut hereditatem gentis scelere ac ui repetisse; pulso Superbo penes Collatinum imperium esse. nescire Tarquinios priuatos uiuere: non placere 15
4 nomen, periculosum libertati esse. Hinc primo sensim temptantium animos sermo per totam ciuitatem est datus, sollicitamque suspicione plebem Brutus ad
5 contionem uocat. Ibi omnium primum ius iurandum populi recitat neminem regnare passuros nec esse 20 Romae unde periculum libertati foret; id summa ope tuendum esse, neque ullam rem quae eo pertineat contemnendam. inuitum se dicere hominis causa, nec dicturum fuisse ni caritas rei publicae uinceret:
6 non credere populum Romanum solidam libertatem 25 reciperatam esse; regium genus, regium nomen non

solum in ciuitate sed etiam in imperio esse; id officere,
7 id obstare libertati. ' Hunc tu ' inquit ' tua uoluntate, L. Tarquini, remoue metum. Meminimus,
fatemur: eiecisti reges; absolue beneficium tuum, 30
aufer hinc regium nomen. Res tuas tibi non solum
reddent ciues tui auctore me, sed si quid deest
munifice augebunt. Amicus abi; exonera ciuitatem
uano forsitan metu; ita persuasum est animis cum
8 gente Tarquinia regnum hinc abiturum.' Consuli 35
primo tam nouae rei ac subitae admiratio incluserat
uocem; dicere deinde incipientem primores ciuitatis
`9 circumsistunt, eadem multis precibus orant. Et
ceteri quidem mouebant minus: postquam Sp.
Lucretius, maior aetate ac dignitate, socer praeterea 40
ipsius, agere uarie rogando alternis suadendoque
10 coepit ut uinci se consensu ciuitatis pateretur, timens
consul ne postmodum priuato sibi eadem illa cum
bonorum amissione additaque alia insuper ignominia
acciderent, abdicauit se consulatu rebusque suis 45
11 omnibus Lauinium translatis ciuitate cessit. Brutus
ex senatus consulto ad populum tulit ut omnes
Tarquiniae gentis exsules essent; collegam sibi comitiis centuriatis creauit P. Valerium, quo adiutore
reges eiecerat. 50

*Agents of the royal family, in Rome to discuss the return of royal
property, persuade some disaffected young nobles to conspire for the king's restoration.*

1 **3.** Cum haud cuiquam in dubio esset bellum ab

Tarquiniis imminere, id quidem spe omnium serius
fuit; ceterum, id quod non timebant, per dolum ac
2 proditionem prope libertas amissa est. Erant in
Romana iuuentute adulescentes aliquot, nec ii tenui 5
loco orti, quorum in regno libido solutior fuerat,
aequales sodalesque adulescentium Tarquiniorum,
3 adsueti more regio uiuere. Eam tum, aequato iure
omnium, licentiam quaerentes, libertatem aliorum
in suam uertisse seruitutem inter se conquerebantur: 10
regem hominem esse, a quo impetres, ubi ius, ubi
iniuria opus sit; esse gratiae locum, esse beneficio;
et irasci et ignoscere posse; inter amicum atque
4 inimicum discrimen nosse; leges rem surdam, in-
exorabilem esse, salubriorem melioremque inopi 15
quam potenti; nihil laxamenti nec ueniae habere, si
modum excesseris; periculosum esse in tot humanis
5 erroribus sola innocentia uiuere. Ita iam sua sponte
aegris animis legati ab regibus superueniunt, sine
mentione reditus bona tantum repetentes. Eorum 20
uerba postquam in senatu audita sunt, per aliquot
dies ea consultatio tenuit, ne non reddita belli causa,
6 reddita belli materia et adiumentum essent. Interim
legati alia moliri; aperte bona repetentes clam
reciperandi regni consilia struere; et tamquam ad 25
id quod agi uidebatur ambientes, nobilium adules-
7 centium animos pertemptant. A quibus placide
oratio accepta est, iis litteras ab Tarquiniis reddunt
et de accipiendis clam nocte in urbem regibus conloquuntur.   30

The conspirators, led by the brothers Vitellii and Aquilii, are
denounced by a slave and summarily arrested.

1   **4.** Vitelliis Aquiliisque fratribus primo commissa
res est. Vitelliorum soror consuli nupta Bruto erat,
iamque ex eo matrimonio adulescentes erant liberi,
Titus Tiberiusque; eos quoque in societatem consilii
2 auunculi adsumunt. Praeterea aliquot nobiles 5
adulescentes conscii adsumpti, quorum uetustate
3 memoria abiit. Interim cum in senatu uicisset
sententia quae censebat reddenda bona, eamque
ipsam causam morae in urbe haberent legati quod
spatium ad uehicula comparanda a consulibus sump- 10
sissent quibus regum asportarent res, omne id tempus
cum coniuratis consultando absumunt, euincuntque
instando ut litterae sibi ad Tarquinios darentur:
4 nam aliter qui credituros eos non uana ab legatis
super rebus tantis adferri? Datae litterae ut pignus 15
5 fidei essent, manifestum facinus fecerunt. Nam cum
pridie quam legati ad Tarquinios proficiscerentur
cenatum forte apud Vitellios esset, coniuratique ibi,
remotis arbitris, multa inter se de nouo, ut fit, consilio
egissent, sermonem eorum ex seruis unus excepit, qui 20
6 iam antea id senserat agi, sed eam occasionem, ut .
litterae legatis darentur quae deprehensae rem coar-
guere possent, exspectabat. Postquam datas sensit,
7 rem ad consules detulit. Consules ad deprehenden-
dos legatos coniuratosque profecti domo sine tumultu 25
rem omnem oppressere; litterarum in primis habita
cura ne interciderent. Proditoribus extemplo in

uincla coniectis, de legatis paululum addubitatum
est; et quamquam uisi sunt commisisse ut hostium
loco essent, ius tamen gentium ualuit. 30

*The royal property is given to the people as spoil, and the royal
domain becomes the Campus Martius. Amongst the traitors
who are flogged and beheaded are the sons of Brutus, the
consul, who, by virtue of his office, has to watch the execution
of his own children. The slave informant is rewarded with
freedom, citizenship and money.*

1 **5.** De bonis regiis, quae reddi ante censuerant, res
integra refertur ad patres. Ibi uicit ira; uetuere
2 reddi, uetuere in publicum redigi. Diripienda plebi
sunt data, ut contacta regia praeda spem in perpetuum cum iis pacis amitteret. Ager Tarquiniorum qui 5
inter urbem ac Tiberim fuit, consecratus Marti,
3 Martius deinde campus fuit. Forte ibi tum seges
farris dicitur fuisse matura messi. Quem campi
fructum quia religiosum erat consumere, desectam
cum stramento segetem magna uis hominum simul 10
immissa corbibus fudere in Tiberim tenui fluentem
aqua, ut mediis caloribus solet. Ita in uadis haesitantes
4 frumenti aceruos sedisse inlitos limo; insulam inde
paulatim, et aliis quae fert temere flumen eodem in-
uectis, factam; postea credo additas moles manuque 15
adiutum, ut tam eminens area firmaque templis
quoque ac porticibus sustinendis esset.
5 Direptis bonis regum damnati proditores sumptum-
que supplicium, conspectius eo quod poenae capien-

dae ministerium patri de liberis consulatus imposuit, 20
et, qui spectator erat amouendus, eum ipsum fortuna
6 exactorem supplicii dedit. Stabant deligati ad palum
nobilissimi iuuenes; sed a ceteris, uelut ab ignotis
capitibus, consulis liberi omnium in se auerterant
oculos, miserebatque non poenae magis homines 25
7 quam sceleris quo poenam meriti essent: illos eo
potissimum anno patriam liberatam, patrem libera-
torem, consulatum ortum ex domo Iunia, patres,
plebem, quidquid deorum hominumque Romanorum
esset, induxisse in animum ut superbo quondam regi, 30
8 tum infesto exsuli proderent. Consules in sedem processere suam, missique lictores ad sumendum supplicium. Nudatos uirgis caedunt securique feriunt,
cum inter omne tempus pater uoltusque et os eius
spectaculo esset, eminente animo patrio inter pub- 35
9 licae poenae ministerium. Secundum poenam nocen-
tium, ut in utramque partem arcendis sceleribus
exemplum nobile esset, praemium indici pecunia ex
aerario, libertas et ciuitas data. Ille primum dicitur
10 uindicta liberatus; quidam uindictae quoque nomen 40
tractum ab illo putant; Vindicio ipsi nomen fuisse.
Post illum obseruatum ut qui ita liberati essent in
ciuitatem accepti uiderentur.

*Two Etruscan towns, Veii and Tarquinii, roused by Tarquin-
ius, make war upon Rome. Arruns, Tarquinius' son, and
Brutus the consul slay each other. The fighting ends
indecisively.*

1   **6.** His sicut acta erant nuntiatis incensus Tarquinius non dolore solum tantae ad inritum cadentis
spei sed etiam odio iraque, postquam dolo uiam
obsaeptam uidit, bellum aperte moliendum ratus
2 circumire supplex Etruriae urbes; orare maxime 5
Veientes Tarquiniensesque, ne ex se ortum, eiusdem
sanguinis, extorrem, egentem ex tanto modo regno
cum liberis adulescentibus ante oculos suos perire
sinerent: alios peregre in regnum Romam accitos:
se regem, augentem bello Romanum imperium, a 10
3 proximis scelerata coniuratione pulsum. eos inter
se, quia nemo unus satis dignus regno uisus sit,
partes regni rapuisse; bona sua diripienda populo
dedisse, ne quis expers sceleris esset. patriam se
regnumque suum repetere et persequi ingratos ciues 15
uelle. ferrent opem, adiuuarent; suas quoque
ueteres iniurias ultum irent, totiens caesas legiones,
4 agrum ademptum. Haec mouerunt Veientes, ac pro
se quisque Romano saltem duce ignominias demen-
das belloque amissa repetenda minaciter fremunt. 20
Tarquinienses nomen ac cognatio mouet: pulchrum
uidebatur suos Romae regnare.
5   Ita duo duarum ciuitatium exercitus ad repeten-
dum regnum belloque persequendos Romanos secuti
Tarquinium. Postquam in agrum Romanum uentum 25
6 est, obuiam hosti consules eunt. Valerius quadrato
agmine peditem ducit: Brutus ad explorandum cum
equitatu antecessit. Eodem modo primus eques
hostium agminis fuit; praeerat Arruns Tarquinius

filius regis, rex ipse cum legionibus sequebatur. 30
7 Arruns ubi ex lictoribus procul consulem esse, deinde
iam propius ac certius facie quoque Brutum cognouit,
inflammatus ira ' Ille est uir ' inquit, ' qui nos extorres expulit patria.. Ipse en ille nostris decoratus
8 insignibus magnifice incedit.   Di regum ultores 35
adeste.' Concitat calcaribus equum atque in ipsum
infestus consulem derigit. Sensit in se iri Brutus;
decorum erat tum ipsis capessere pugnam ducibus;
9 auide itaque se certamini offert; adeoque infestis
animis concurrerunt, neuter dum hostem uolneraret 40
sui protegendi corporis memor, ut contrario ictu per
parmam uterque transfixus duabus haerentis hastis
10 moribundi ex equis lapsi sint. Simul et cetera equestris
pugna coepit, neque ita multo post et pedites superueniunt. Ibi uaria uictoria et uelut aequo Marte 45
pugnatum est; dextera utrimque cornua uicere,
11 laeua superata.   Veientes, uinci ab Romano milite
adsueti, fusi fugatique: Tarquiniensis, nouus hostis,
non stetit solum, sed etiam ab sua parte Romanum
pepulit.   50

*Portents, however, declare the Romans to be the victors, and the
other consul, Valerius, returns in triumph to Rome and
conducts his colleague's funeral. Losing his popularity
and being accused of aiming at the royal power, he successfully defends himself at a public meeting.*

1   **7.** Ita cum pugnatum esset, tantus terror Tarquinium atque Etruscos incessit ut omissa inrita re

nocte ambo exercitus, Veiens Tarquiniensisque, suas

2 quisque abirent domos.   Adiciunt miracula huic
pugnae: silentio proximae noctis ex silua Arsia 5
ingentem editam uocem; Siluani uocem eam credi-
tam; haec dicta: uno plus Tuscorum cecidisse in

3 acie; uincere bello Romanum. Ita certe inde abiere,
Romani ut uictores, Etrusci pro uictis; nam postquam inluxit nec quisquam hostium in conspectu 10
erat, P. Valerius consul spolia legit triumphansque

4 inde Romam rediit.   Collegae funus quanto tum
potuit apparatu fecit; sed multo maius morti decus
publica fuit maestitia, eo ante omnia insignis quia
matronae annum ut parentem eum luxerunt, quod 15
tam acer ultor uiolatae pudicitiae fuisset.

5   Consuli deinde qui superfuerat, ut sunt mutabiles
uolgi animi, ex fauore non inuidia modo sed suspicio

6 etiam cum atroci crimine orta. Regnum eum adfec-
tare fama ferebat, quia nec collegam subrogauerat in 20
locum Bruti et aedificabat in summa Velia: ibi alto

7 atque munito loco arcem inexpugnabilem fieri. Haec
dicta uolgo creditaque cum indignitate angerent
consulis animum, uocato ad concilium populo submissis fascibus in contionem escendit. Gratum 25
multitudini spectaculum fuit, submissa sibi esse
imperii insignia confessionemque factam populi
quam consulis maiestatem uimque maiorem esse.

8 Ibi audire iussis consul laudare fortunam collegae,
quod liberata patria, in summo honore, pro re publica 30
dimicans, matura gloria necdum se uertente in in-

uidiam, mortem occubuisset: se superstitem gloriae
suae ad crimen atque inuidiam superesse; ex liberatore patriae ad Aquilios se Vitelliosque recidisse.
9 'Nunquamne ergo' inquit, 'ulla adeo uobis spec- 35
tata uirtus erit, ut suspicione uiolari nequeat? Ego
me, illum acerrimum regum hostem, ipsum cupidi-
10 tatis regni crimen subiturum timerem? Ego si in ipsa
arce Capitolioque habitarem, metui me crederem
posse a ciuibus meis? Tam leui momento mea apud 40
uos fama pendet? Adeone est fundata leuiter fides
11 ut ubi sim quam qui sim magis referat? Non obsta-
bunt Publi Valeri aedes libertati uestrae, Quirites; tuta
erit uobis Velia; deferam non in planum modo aedes
sed colli etiam subiciam, ut uos supra suspectum me 45
ciuem habitetis; in Velia aedificent quibus melius
12 quam P. Valerio creditur libertas.' Delata confestim
materia omnis infra Veliam et, ubi nunc Vicae Potae
aedes est, domus in infimo cliuo aedificata.

*Valerius introduces the Lex Valeria de prouocatione and wins
the title of the 'People's Friend'. His colleague Horatius
dedicates the temple of Jupiter in the Capitol, in spite of
the attempt of Valerius' friends to hinder the ceremony.*

1 **8.** Latae deinde leges, non solum quae regni suspicione consulem absoluerent, sed quae adeo in con-
trarium uerterent ut popularem etiam facerent; inde
2 cognomen factum Publicolae est. Ante omnes de
prouocatione aduersus magistratus ad populum 5
sacrandoque cum bonis capite eius qui regni occu-

pandi consilia inisset gratae in uolgus leges fuere.
3 Quas cum solus pertulisset, ut sua unius in his gratia
esset, tum deinde comitia collegae subrogando habuit.
4 Creatus Sp. Lucretius consul, qui magno natu, non 10
sufficientibus iam uiribus ad consularia munera
obeunda, intra paucos dies moritur. Suffectus in
5 Lucreti locum M. Horatius Puluillus. Apud quosdam
ueteres auctores non inuenio Lucretium consulem;
Bruto statim Horatium suggerunt; credo, quia nulla 15
gesta res insignem fecerit consulatum, memoria
intercidisse.
6 Nondum dedicata erat in Capitolio Iouis aedes;
Valerius Horatiusque consules sortiti uter dedicaret.
Horatio sorte euenit: Publicola ad Veientium bellum 20
7 profectus. Aegrius quam dignum erat tulere Valeri
necessarii dedicationem tam incliti templi Horatio
dari. Id omnibus modis impedire conati, postquam
alia frustra temptata erant, postem iam tenenti consuli foedum inter precationem deum nuntium in- 25
cutiunt, mortuum eius filium esse, funestaque familia
8 dedicare eum templum non posse. Non crediderit
factum an tantum animo roboris fuerit, nec traditur
certum nec interpretatio est facilis. Nihil aliud ad
eum nuntium a proposito auersus quam ut cadauer 30
efferri iuberet, tenens postem precationem peragit et
dedicat templum.
9 Haec post exactos reges domi militiaeque gesta
primo anno.

508 B.C. *Publius Valerius (second time) and T. Lucretius*
consuls. King Porsenna of Clusium supports the
Tarquins by invading Roman territory. The Senate
secure the loyalty of the Plebeians by granting them con-
cessions.

1 **9.** Inde P. Valerius iterum T. Lucretius consules
facti. Iam Tarquinii ad Lartem Porsennam, Clusinum
regem, perfugerant. Ibi miscendo consilium preces-
que nunc orabant, ne se, oriundos ex Etruscis, eiusdem sanguinis nominisque, egentes exsulare pateretur, 5
2 nunc monebant etiam ne orientem morem pellendi
reges inultum sineret. satis libertatem ipsam habere
3 dulcedinis. nisi quanta ui ciuitates eam expetant
tanta regna reges defendant, aequari summa infimis;
nihil excelsum, nihil quod supra cetera emineat, in 10
ciuitatibus fore adesse finem regnis, rei inter deos
4 hominesque pulcherrimae. Porsenna cum regem esse
Romae tutum, tum Etruscae gentis regem, amplum
5 Tuscis ratus, Romam infesto exercitu uenit. Non
unquam alias ante tantus terror senatum inuasit; 15
adeo ualida res tum Clusina erat magnumque Porsennae nomen. Nec hostes modo timebant sed suos-
met ipsi ciues, ne Romana plebs, metu perculsa,
receptis in urbem regibus uel cum seruitute pacem
6 acciperet. Multa igitur blandimenta plebi per id tem- 20
pus ab senatu data. Annonae in primis habita cura,
et ad frumentum comparandum missi alii in Volscos,
alii Cumas. Salis quoque uendendi arbitrium, quia
impenso pretio uenibat, in publicum omne sumptum,

ademptum priuatis; portoriisque et tributo plebes 25
liberata, ut diuites conferrent qui oneri ferendo
essent: pauperes satis stipendii pendere, si liberos
7 educent. Itaque haec indulgentia patrum asperis
postmodum rebus in obsidione ac fame adeo con-
cordem ciuitatem tenuit, ut regium nomen non 30
8 summi magis quam infimi horrerent, nec quisquam
unus malis artibus postea tam popularis esset quam
tum bene imperando uniuersus senatus fuit.

How Horatius kept the bridge.

1 **10.** Cum hostes adessent, pro se quisque in urbem
ex agris demigrant; urbem ipsam saepiunt praesidiis.
2 Alia muris, alia Tiberi obiecto uidebantur tuta: pons
sublicius iter paene hostibus dedit, ni unus uir fuisset,
Horatius Cocles; id munimentum illo die fortuna 5
3 urbis Romanae habuit. Qui positus forte in statione
pontis cum captum repentino impetu Ianiculum atque inde citatos decurrere hostes uidisset trepidamque
turbam suorum arma ordinesque relinquere, reprehensans singulos, obsistens obtestansque deum et 10
hominum fidem testabatur nequiquam deserto
4 praesidio eos fugere; si transitum [pontem] a tergo
reliquissent, iam plus hostium in Palatio Capitolioque
quam in Ianiculo fore. Itaque monere, praedicere ut
pontem ferro, igni, quacumque ui possint, interrum- 15
pant: se impetum hostium, quantum corpore uno pos-
5 set obsisti, excepturum. Vadit inde in primum aditum

pontis, insignisque inter conspecta cedentium pugna
terga obuersis comminus ad ineundum proelium
armis, ipso miraculo audaciae obstupefecit hostes. 20
6 Duos tamen cum eo pudor tenuit, Sp. Larcium ac T.
7 Herminium, ambos claros genere factisque. Cum his
primam periculi procellam et quod tumultuosissi-
mum pugnae erat parumper sustinuit; deinde eos
quoque ipsos exigua parte pontis relicta reuocantibus 25
8 qui rescindebant cedere in tutum coegit. Circumferens inde truces minaciter oculos ad proceres
Etruscorum nunc singulos prouocare, nunc increpare omnes: seruitia regum superborum, suae liberta-
9 tis immemores alienam oppugnatum uenire. Cunctati 30
aliquamdiu sunt, dum alius alium, ut proelium
incipiant, circumspectant; pudor deinde commouit
aciem, et clamore sublato undique in unum hostem
10 tela coniciunt. Quae cum in obiecto cuncta scuto
haesissent, neque ille minus obstinatus ingenti pon- 35
tem obtineret gradu, iam impetu conabantur de-
trudere uirum, cum simul fragor rupti pontis, simul
clamor Romanorum, alacritate perfecti operis sub-
11 latus, pauore subito impetum sustinuit   Tum Cocles
' Tiberine pater ' inquit, ' te sancte precor, haec 40
arma et hunc militem propitio flumine accipias.'
Ita sic armatus in Tiberim desiluit multisque super-
incidentibus telis incolumis ad suos tranauit, rem
ausus plus famae habituram ad posteros quam fidei.
12 Grata erga tantam uirtutem ciuitas fuit; statua in 45
comitio posita; agri quantum uno die circumarauit,

13 datum. Priuata quoque inter publicos honores studia
eminebant; nam in magna inopia pro domesticis
copiis unusquisque ei aliquid, fraudans se ipse uictu
suo, contulit.   50

*Porsenna besieges Rome closely. By a well-planned stratagem
Valerius destroys a marauding band of the enemy.*

1 **11.** Porsinna primo conatu repulsus, consiliis ab
oppugnanda urbe ad obsidendam uersis, praesidio in
Ianiculo locato, ipse in plano ripisque Tiberis castra
2 posuit, nauibus undique accitis et ad custodiam ne
quid Romam frumenti subuehi sineret, et ut prae- 5
datum milites trans flumen per occasiones aliis atque
3 aliis locis traiceret; breuique adeo infestum omnem
Romanum agrum reddidit ut non cetera solum ex
agris sed pecus quoque omne in urbem compelleretur,
neque quisquam extra portas propellere auderet. 10
4 Hoc tantum licentiae Etruscis non metu magis quam
consilio concessum. Namque Valerius consul intentus in occasionem multos simul et effusos improuiso
adoriundi, in paruis rebus neglegens ultor, grauem se
5 ad maiora uindicem seruabat. Itaque ut eliceret 15
praedatores, edicit suis postero die frequentes porta
Esquilina, quae auersissima ab hoste erat, expellerent
pecus, scituros id hostes ratus, quod in obsidione et
6 fame seruitia infida transfugerent. Et sciere perfugae
indicio; multoque plures, ut in spem uniuersae 20
praedae, flumen traiciunt.
7   P. Valerius inde T. Herminium cum modicis copiis

ad secundum lapidem Gabina uia occultum considere
iubet, Sp. Larcium cum expedita iuuentute ad
portam Collinam stare donec hostis praetereat; inde 25
8 se obicere ne sit ad flumen reditus. Consulum alter
T. Lucretius porta Naeuia cum aliquot manipulis
militum egressus; ipse Valerius Caelio monte cohortes
9 delectas educit, hique primi apparuere hosti. Herminius ubi tumultum sensit, concurrit ex insidiis, 30
uersisque in Lucretium Etruscis terga caedit; dextra
laeuaque, hinc a porta Collina, illinc ab Naeuia,
10 redditus clamor; ita caesi in medio praedatores,
neque ad pugnam uiribus pares et ad fugam saeptis
omnibus uiis. Finisque ille tam effuse euagandi Etrus- 35
cis fuit.

The story of Mucius Scaevola.

1   12. Obsidio erat nihilo minus et frumenti cum summa caritate inopia, sedendoque expugnaturum se
2 urbem spem Porsinna habebat, cum C. Mucius, adulescens nobilis, cui indignum uidebatur populum
Romanum seruientem cum sub regibus esset nullo 5
bello nec ab hostibus ullis obsessum esse, liberum
3 eundem populum ab iisdem Etruscis obsideri quorum
saepe exercitus fuderit,—itaque magno audacique
aliquo facinore eam indignitatem uindicandam
ratus, primo sua sponte penetrare in hostium castra 10
4 constituit; dein metuens ne si consulum iniussu et
ignaris omnibus iret, forte deprehensus a custodibus

Romanis retraheretur ut transfuga, fortuna tum urbis
5 crimen adfirmante, senatum adit. ' Transire Tiberim ' inquit, ' patres, et intrare, si possim, castra 15
hostium uolo, non praedo nec populationum in uicem
ultor; maius si di iuuant in animo est facinus.'
Adprobant patres; abdito intra uestem ferro pro-
6 ficiscitur. Vbi eo uenit, in confertissima turba prope
7 regium tribunal constitit. Ibi cum stipendium militi- 20
bus forte daretur et scriba cum rege sedens pari fere
ornatu multa ageret eumque milites uolgo adirent,
timens sciscitari uter Porsinna esset, ne ignorando
regem semet ipse aperiret quis esset, quo temere
traxit fortuna facinus, scribam pro rege obtruncat. 25
8 Vadentem inde qua per trepidam turbam cruento
mucrone sibi ipse fecerat uiam, cum concursu ad
clamorem facto conprehensum regii satellites retraxissent, ante tribunal regis destitutus, tum quoque inter
tantas fortunae minas metuendus magis quam metu- 30
9 ens, ' Romanus sum ' inquit ' ciuis; C. Mucium
uocant. Hostis hostem occidere uolui, nec ad mortem
minus animi est, quam fuit ad caedem; et facere et
10 pati fortia Romanum est. Nec unus in te ego hos
animos gessi; longus post me ordo est idem petentium 35
decus. Proinde in hoc discrimen, si iuuat, accingere
ut in singulas horas capite dimices tuo, ferrum hostem-
11 que in uestibulo habeas regiae. Hoc tibi iuuentus
Romana indicimus bellum. Nullam aciem, nullum
proelium timueris; uni tibi et cum singulis res erit.' 40
12 Cum rex simul ira infensus periculoque conterritus

circumdari ignes minitabundus iuberet nisi expro-
meret propere quas insidiarum sibi minas per ambages
13 iaceret, ' En tibi ' inquit, ' ut sentias quam uile corpus sit iis qui magnam gloriam uident;' dextramque 45
accenso ad sacrificium foculo inicit. Quam cum uelut
alienato ab sensu torreret animo, prope attonitus
miraculo rex cum ab sede sua prosiluisset amouerique
14 ab altaribus iuuenem iussisset, ' Tu uero abi ' inquit,
' in te magis quam in me hostilia ausus. Iuberem 50
macte uirtute esse, si pro mea patria ista uirtus staret;
nunc iure belli liberum te, intactum inuiolatumque
15 hinc dimitto. Tunc Mucius, quasi remunerans
meritum, ' Quando quidem ' inquit ' est apud te
uirtuti honos, ut beneficio tuleris a me quod minis 55
nequisti, trecenti coniurauimus principes iuuentutis
16 Romanae ut in te hac uia grassaremur. Mea prima
sors fuit; ceteri ut cuiusque ceciderit primi quoad te
opportunum fortuna dederit, suo quisque tempore
aderunt.' 60

Porsenna and the Romans agree on terms of peace. The
exploit of Cloelia wins the admiration both of Porsenna
and the Romans.

1　**13.** Mucium dimissum, cui postea Scaeuolae a
clade dextrae manus cognomen inditum, legati a
2 Porsinna Romam secuti sunt; adeo mouerat eum et
primi periculi casus, a quo nihil se praeter errorem
insidiatoris texisset, et subeunda dimicatio totiens 5
quot coniurati superessent, ut pacis condiciones ultro

3 ferret Romanis. Iactatum in condicionibus nequiquam de Tarquiniis in regnum restituendis, magis
quia id negare ipse nequiuerat Tarquiniis quam quod
4 negatum iri sibi ab Romanis ignoraret. De agro 10
Veientibus restituendo impetratum, expressaque
necessitas obsides dandi Romanis, si Ianiculo praesidium deduci uellent. His condicionibus composita
pace, exercitum ab Ianiculo deduxit Porsinna et agro
5 Romano excessit. Patres C. Mucio uirtutis causa 15
trans Tiberim agrum dono dedere, quae postea sunt
6 Mucia prata appellata. Ergo ita honorata uirtute,
feminae quoque ad publica decora excitatae, et Cloelia uirgo una ex obsidibus, cum castra Etruscorum
forte haud procul ripa Tiberis locata essent, frustrata 20
custodes, dux agminis uirginum inter tela hostium
Tiberim tranauit, sospitesque omnes Romam ad pro-
7 pinquos restituit. Quod ubi regi nuntiatum est,
primo incensus ira oratores Romam misit ad Cloeliam
obsidem deposcendam: alias haud magni facere. 25
8 Deinde in admirationem uersus, supra Coclites Mu-
ciosque dicere id facinus esse, et prae se ferre quem ad
modum si non dedatur obses, pro rupto foedus se
habiturum, sic deditam intactam inuiolatamque ad
9 suos remissurum. Vtrimque constitit fides; et 30
Romani pignus pacis ex foedere restituerunt, et apud
regem Etruscum non tuta solum sed honorata etiam
uirtus fuit, laudatamque uirginem parte obsidum se
10 donare dixit; ipsa quos uellet legeret. Productis
omnibus elegisse impubes dicitur; quod et uirginitati 35

decorum et consensu obsidum ipsorum probabile
erat eam aetatem potissimum liberari ab hoste quae
11 maxime opportuna iniuriae esset. Pace redintegrata
Romani nouam in femina uirtutem nouo genere hon-
oris, statua equestri, donauere: in summa Sacra uia 40
posita uirgo insidens equo.

The origin of the term ' of selling King Porsenna's goods '.
Defeat of the Etruscan forces under Arruns, Porsenna's
son, by combined forces of Cumae and the Latins. How
the Tuscan Quarter acquired its name.

1 **14.** Huic tam pacatae profectioni ab urbe regis
Etrusci abhorrens mos traditus ab antiquis usque ad
nostram aetatem inter cetera sollemnia manet, bona
2 Porsennae regis uendendi. Cuius originem moris
necesse est aut inter bellum natam esse neque omis- 5
sam in pace, aut a mitiore creuisse principio quam hic
prae se ferat titulus bona hostiliter uendendi.
3 Proximum uero est ex iis quae traduntur Porsennam
discedentem ab Ianiculo castra opulenta, conuecto
ex propinquis ac fertilibus Etruriae aruis commeatu, 10
Romanis dono dedisse, inopi tum urbe ab longinqua
4 obsidione; ea deinde, ne populo immisso diriperentur
hostiliter, uenisse, bonaque Porsennae appellata,
gratiam muneris magis significante titulo quam
auctionem fortunae regiae quae ne in potestate 15
quidem populi Romani esset.
5 Omisso Romano bello Porsenna, ne frustra in ea
loca exercitus adductus uideretur, cum parte copi-

arum filium Arruntem Ariciam oppugnatum mittit.
6 Primo Aricinos res necopinata perculerat; arcessita 20
deinde auxilia et a Latinis populis et a Cumis tantum
spei fecere, ut acie decernere auderent. Proelio inito,
adeo concitato impetu se intulerant Etrusci ut fun-
7 derent ipso incursu Aricinos: Cumanae cohortes arte
aduersus uim usae declinauere paululum, effuseque 25
praelatos hostes conuersis signis ab tergo adortae
sunt. Ita in medio prope iam uictores caesi Etrusci.
8 Pars perexigua, duce amisso, quia nullum propius
perfugium erat, Romam inermes et fortuna et specie
supplicum delati sunt. Ibi benigne excepti diuisique 30
9 in hospitia. Curatis uolneribus, alii profecti domos,
nuntii hospitalium beneficiorum: multos Romae
hospitum urbisque caritas tenuit. His locus ad
habitandum datus quem deinde Tuscum uicum appel-
larunt. 35

507, 506 B.C. *Porsenna is convinced by the firmness of the
Roman senate of the uselessness of supporting the Tarquins' claims. He restores to them territory near Veii and
returns to Tusculum.*

1 **15.** Sp. Larcius inde et T. Herminius, P. Lucretius
inde et P. Valerius Publicola consules facti. Eo anno
postremum legati a Porsenna de reducendo in regnum
Tarquinio uenerunt; quibus cum responsum esset
missurum ad regem senatum legatos, missi confestim 5
2 honoratissimus quisque ex patribus. non quin breuiter reddi responsum potuerit non recipi reges, ideo

potius delectos patrum ad eum missos quam legatis
eius Romae daretur responsum, sed ut in perpetuum
mentio eius rei finiretur, neu in tantis mutuis bene- 10
ficiis in uicem animi sollicitarentur, cum ille peteret
quod contra libertatem populi Romani esset, Romani,
nisi in perniciem suam faciles esse uellent, negarent
3 cui nihil negatum uellent.   non in regno populum
Romanum sed in libertate esse.   ita induxisse in 15
animum, hostibus portas potius quam regibus
patefacere; ea esse uota omnium ut qui libertati erit
4 in illa urbe finis, idem urbi sit.   proinde si saluam
esse uellet Romam, ut patiatur liberam esse orare.
5   Rex uerecundia uictus ' Quando id certum atque 20
obstinatum est ' inquit, ' neque ego obtundam saepius eadem nequiquam agendo, nec Tarquinios spe
auxilii, quod nullum in me est, frustrabor. Alium
hinc, seu bello opus est seu quiete, exsilio quaerant
locum, ne quid meam uobiscum pacem distineat.' 25
6 Dictis facta amiciora adiecit; obsidum quod reliquum
erat reddidit; agrum Veientem, foedere ad Ianiculum
7 icto ademptum restituit.   Tarquinius spe omni
reditus incisa exsulatum ad generum Mamilium
Octauium Tusculum abiit.   Romanis pax fida cum 30
Porsenna fuit.

505 B.C. *Successful war with the Sabines and in* 504 B.C. *the
migration of the Claudii and their clients to Rome.* 503
B.C., *Death of P. Valerius.   Two Latin colonies revolt
to the Aurunci, who are decisively defeated.*

1 **16.** Consules M. Valerius P. Postumius. Eo anno
bene pugnatum cum Sabinis; consules triumpharunt.
2 Maiore inde mole Sabini bellum parabant. Aduersus
eos et ne quid simul ab Tusculo, unde etsi non aper-
tum, suspectum tamen bellum erat, repentini peri- 5
culi oreretur, P. Valerius quartum T. Lucretius iterum
3 consules facti. Seditio inter belli pacisque auctores
orta in Sabinis aliquantum inde uirium transtulit ad
4 Romanos. Namque Attius Clausus, cui postea Appio Claudio fuit Romae nomen, cum pacis ipse auctor 10
a turbatoribus belli premeretur nec par factioni esset,
ab Inregillo, magna clientium comitatus manu, Ro-
5 mam transfugit. His ciuitas data agerque trans
Anienem; Vetus Claudia tribus—additis postea nouis
tribulibus—qui ex eo uenirent agro appellati. Appius 15
inter patres lectus, haud ita multo post in principum
6 dignationem peruenit. Consules infesto exercitu in
agrum Sabinum profecti cum ita uastatione, dein
proelio adflixissent opes hostium ut diu nihil inde
rebellionis timeri posset, triumphantes Romam 20
redierunt.
7 P. Valerius, omnium consensu princeps belli pacisque artibus, anno post Agrippa Menenio P. Postumio
consulibus moritur, gloria ingenti, copiis familiaribus
adeo exiguis, ut funeri sumptus deesset; de publico 25
8 est datus. Luxere matronae ut Brutum. Eodem
anno duae coloniae Latinae, Pometia et Cora, ad
Auruncos deficiunt. Cum Auruncis bellum initum;
fusoque ingenti exercitu, qui se ingredientibus fines

consulibus ferociter obtulerat, omne Auruncum 30
9 bellum Pometiam compulsum est. Nec magis post
proelium quam in proelio caedibus temperatum est;
et caesi aliquanto plures erant quam capti, et captos
passim trucidauerunt; ne ab obsidibus quidem, qui
trecenti accepti numero erant, ira belli abstinuit. Et 35
hoc anno Romae triumphatum.

502 B.C. *After an Auruncan victory over Roman forces, the
Romans execute a terrible vengeance on Pometia.*

1   **17.** Secuti consules Opiter Verginius Sp. Cassius
Pometiam primo ui, deinde uineis aliisque operibus
2 oppugnarunt. In quos Aurunci magis iam inexpiabili
odio quam spe aliqua aut occasione coorti, cum plures
igni quam ferro armati excucurrissent, caede incen- 5
3 dioque cuncta complent. Vineis incensis, multis
hostium uolneratis et occisis, consulum quoque
alterum—sed utrum auctores non adiciunt—graui
4 uolnere ex equo deiectum prope interfecerunt. Romam inde male gesta re reditum; inter multos saucios 10
consul spe incerta uitae relatus. Interiecto deinde
haud magno spatio, quod uolneribus curandis sup-
plendoque exercitui satis esset, cum ira maiore, tum
5 uiribus etiam auctis Pometiae arma inlata. Et cum
uineis refectis aliaque mole belli iam in eo esset ut in 15
6 muros euaderet miles, deditio est facta. Ceterum nihilo
minus foeda, dedita urbe, quam si capta foret, Aurunci passi; principes securi percussi, sub corona
uenierunt coloni alii, oppidum dirutum, ager ueniit.

7 Consules magis ob iras grauiter ultas quam ob mag- 20
nitudinem perfecti belli triumpharunt.

501 B.C. *In the general expectation of war, suggestions are
made that a dictator be appointed.*

1 **18.** Insequens annus Postumum Cominium et T.
2 Largium consules habuit. Eo anno Romae, cum per
ludos ab Sabinorum iuuentute per lasciuiam scorta
raperentur, concursu hominum rixa ac prope pro-
lium fuit, paruaque ex re ad rebellionem spectare 5
3 [res] uidebatur. Id quoque accesserat quod
triginta iam coniurasse populos concitante
4 Octauio Mamilio satis constabat. In hac tantarum
exspectatione rerum sollicita ciuitate, dictatoris
primum creandi mentio orta. Sed nec quibus 10
consulibus quia ex factione Tarquiniana essent
—id quoque enim traditur—parum creditum sit,
nec quis primum dictator creatus sit, satis constat.
5 Apud ueterrimos tamen auctores T. Largium dictatorem primum, Sp. Cassium magistrum equitum 15
creatos inuenio. Consulares legere; ita lex iubebat
6 de dictatore creando lata. Eo magis adducor ut
credam Largium, qui consularis erat, potius quam
M'. Valerium Marci filium Volesi nepotem, qui nondum consul fuerat, moderatorem et magistrum con- 20
7 sulibus appositum; quin si maxime ex ea familia legi
dictatorem uellent, patrem multo potius M. Valerium
spectatae uirtutis et consularem uirum legissent.
8 Creato dictatore primum Romae, postquam prae-

ferri secures uiderunt, magnus plebem metus incessit, 25
ut intentiores essent ad dicto parendum; neque
enim ut in consulibus qui pari potestate essent,
alterius auxilium neque prouocatio erat neque ullum
9 usquam nisi in cura parendi auxilium. Sabinis etiam
creatus Romae dictator, eo magis quod propter se 30
creatum crediderant, metum incussit. Itaque legatos
10 de pace mittunt. Quibus orantibus dictatorem sena-
tumque ut ueniam erroris hominibus adulescentibus
darent, responsum ignosci adulescentibus posse, seni-
11 bus non posse qui bella ex bellis sererent. Actum 35
tamen est de pace, impetrataque foret si, quod impen-
sae factum in bellum erat, praestare Sabini—id enim
postulatum erat—in animum induxissent. Bellum
indictum: tacitae indutiae quietum annum tenuere.

499 B.C. *The remarkable battle of Lake Regillus against the
Latins under Octavius Mamilius.*

1   **19.** Consules Ser. Sulpicius M'. Tullius; nihil
dignum memoria actum; T. Aebutius deinde et C.
2 Vetusius. His consulibus Fidenae obsessae, Crustumeria capta; Praeneste ab Latinis ad Romanos
desciuit, nec ultra bellum Latinum, gliscens iam per 5
3 aliquot annos, dilatum. A. Postumius dictator, T.
Aebutius magister equitum, magnis copiis peditum
equitumque profecti, ad lacum Regillum in agro
4 Tusculano agmini hostium occurrerunt, et quia Tarquinios esse in exercitu Latinorum auditum est, 10
sustineri ira non potuit quin extemplo confligerent.

5 Ergo etiam proelium aliquanto quam cetera grauius atque atrocius fuit. Non enim duces ad regendam modo consilio rem adfuere, sed suismet ipsi corpori- bus dimicantes miscuere certamina, nec quisquam 15 procerum ferme hac aut illa ex acie sine uolnere 6 praeter dictatorem Romanum excessit. In Post- umium prima in acie suos adhortantem instruentem- que Tarquinius Superbus, quamquam iam aetate et uiribus erat grauior, equum infestus admisit, ictusque 20 ab latere concursu suorum receptus in tutum est. 7 Et ad alterum cornu Aebutius magister equitum in Octauium Mamilium impetum dederat; nec fefellit ueniens Tusculanum ducem, contraque et ille concitat 8 equum. Tantaque uis infestis uenientium hastis fuit 25 ut brachium Aebutio traiectum sit, Mamilio pectus 9 percussum. Hunc quidem in secundam aciem Latini recepere; Aebutius cum saucio brachio tenere telum 10 non posset, pugna excessit. Latinus dux nihil deter- ritus uolnere proelium ciet et quia suos perculsos 30 uidebat, arcessit cohortem exsulum Romanorum, cui L. Tarquini filius praeerat. Ea quo maiore pugnabat ira ob erepta bona patriamque ademptam, pugnam parumper restituit.

In the fighting, M. Valerius, brother of P. Valerius, is slain: so too are Mamilius and Herminius on the Latin side. The battle is won by the Roman cavalry who rally the de- moralised infantry by fighting on foot in the front line.

1   **20.** Referentibus iam pedem ab ea parte Romanis,

M. Valerius Publicolae frater, conspicatus ferocem
iuuenem Tarquinium ostentantem se in prima exsulum
acie, domestica etiam gloria accensus ut cuius familiae
2 decus eiecti reges erant, eiusdem interfecti forent, 5
subdit calcaria equo et Tarquinium infesto spiculo
3 petit. Tarquinius retro in agmen suorum infenso
cessit hosti: Valerium temere inuectum in exsulum
aciem ex transuerso quidam adortus transfigit, nec
quicquam equitis uolnere equo retardato, moribun- 10
dus Romanus labentibus super corpus armis ad ter-
4 ram defluxit. Dictator Postumius postquam cecidisse talem uirum, exsules ferociter citato agmine
5 inuehi, suos perculsos cedere animaduertit, cohorti
suae, quam delectam manum praesidii causa circa se 15
habebat, dat signum ut quem suorum fugientem
uiderint, pro hoste habeant. Ita metu ancipiti uersi
6 a fuga Romani in hostem et restituta acies. Cohors
dictatoris tum primum proelium iniit; integris corporibus animisque fessos adorti exsules caedunt.   20
7   Ibi alia inter proceres coorta pugna. Imperator
Latinus, ubi cohortem exsulum a dictatore Romano
prope circumuentam uidit, ex subsidiariis manipulos
8 aliquot in primam aciem secum rapit. Hos agmine
uenientes T. Herminius legatus conspicatus, interque 25
eos insignem ueste armisque Mamilium noscitans,
tanto ui maiore quam paulo ante magister equitum
9 cum hostium duce proelium iniit, ut et uno ictu trans-
fixum per latus occiderit Mamilium et ipse inter spoliandum corpus hostis ueruto percussus, cum uictor in 30

castra esset relatus, inter primam curationem ex-
10 spirauerit. Tum ad equites dictator aduolat, obtes-
tans ut fesso iam pedite descendant ex equis et pugnam capessant. Dicto paruere; desiliunt ex equis,
prouolant in primum et pro antesignanis parmas 35
11 obiciunt. Recipit extemplo animum pedestris acies,
postquam iuuentutis proceres aequato genere pugnae
secum partem periculi sustinentes uidit. Tum demum impulsi Latini perculsaque inclinauit acies.
12 Equiti admoti equi, ut persequi hostem posset; secuta 40
et pedestris acies. Ibi nihil nec diuinae nec humanae
opis dictator praetermittens aedem Castori uouisse
fertur ac pronuntiasse militi praemia, qui primus, qui
13 secundus castra hostium intrasset; tantusque ardor
fuit ut eodem impetu quo fuderant hostem Romani 45
castra caperent. Hoc modo ad lacum Regillum pugnatum est. Dictator et magister equitum triumphantes in urbem rediere.

498-495 B.C. *Various events described: the dedication of a
Temple to Saturn, the institution of the Saturnalia, the
death of Tarquinius Superbus, and the recolonisation of
Signia.*

1   **21.** Triennio deinde nec certa pax nec bellum fuit.
Consules Q. Cloelius et T. Larcius, inde A. Sem-
2 pronius et M. Minucius. His consulibus aedis Saturno
dedicata, Saturnalia institutus festus dies. A. deinde
3 Postumius et T. Verginius consules facti. Hoc de- 5
mum anno ad Regillum lacum pugnatum apud quos-

dam inuenio; A. Postumium, quia collega dubiae
fidei fuerit, se consulatu abdicasse; dictatorem inde
4 factum. Tanti errores implicant temporum, aliter
apud alios ordinatis magistratibus, ut nec qui con- 10
sules secundum quos, nec quid quoque anno actum
sit, in tanta uetustate non rerum modo sed etiam
auctorum digerere possis.

5   Ap. Claudius deinde et P. Seruilius consules facti.
Insignis hic annus est nuntio Tarquini mortis. 15
Mortuus Cumis, quo se post fractas opes Latinorum
6 ad Aristodemum tyrannum contulerat. Eo nuntio
erecti patres, erecta plebes; sed patribus nimis luxur-
iosa ea fuit laetitia; plebi, cui ad eam diem summa
ope inseruitum erat, iniuriae a primoribus fieri 20
7 coepere. Eodem anno Signia colonia, quam rex
Tarquinius deduxerat, suppleto numero colonorum
iterum deducta est. Romae tribus una et uiginti
factae. Aedes Mercuri dedicata est idibus Maiis.

*Preparations for war on the part of the Volsci are reported by the
Latins to the Romans, who gratefully return 6,000 prisoners. Bonds of friendship are formed between many of the
prisoners and their hosts.*

1   **22.** Cum Volscorum gente Latino bello neque pax
neque bellum fuerat; nam et Volsci comparauerant
auxilia quae mitterent Latinis, ni maturatum ab
dictatore Romano esset, et maturauit Romanus ne
proelio uno cum Latino Volscoque contenderet. 5
2 Hac ira consules in Volscum agrum legiones duxere.

Volscos consilii poenam non metuentes necopinata
res perculit; armorum immemores obsides dant
trecentos principum a Cora atque Pometia liberos.
3 Ita sine certamine inde abductae legiones. Nec ita 10
multo post Volscis leuatis metu suum rediit ingenium.
Rursus occultum parant bellum, Hernicis in societa-
4 tem armorum adsumptis. Legatos quoque ad sol-
licitandum Latium passim dimittunt; sed recens ad
Regillum lacum accepta cladis Latinos ira odioque 15
eius, quicumque arma suaderet, ne ab legatis quidem
uiolandis abstinuit; comprehensos Volscos Romam
duxere. Ibi traditi consulibus indicatumque est
5 Volscos Hernicosque parare bellum Romanis. Relata
re ad senatum adeo fuit gratum patribus ut et 20
captiuorum sex milia Latinis remitterent et de
foedere, quod prope in perpetuum negatum fuerat,
6 rem ad nouos magistratus traicerent. Enimuero
tum Latini gaudere facto; pacis auctores in ingenti
gloria esse. ⸳ Coronam auream Ioui donum in 25
Capitolium mittunt. Cum legatis donoque qui captiuorum remissi ad suos fuerant, magna circumfusa
7 multitudo, uenit. Pergunt domos eorum apud quem
quisque seruierant; gratias agunt liberaliter habiti
cultique in calamitate sua; inde hospitia iungunt. 30
Nunquam alias ante publice priuatimque Latinum
nomen Romano imperio coniunctius fuit.

*The wretched plight of an ex-centurion under the harsh law
of debt leads to a serious riot, which is quelled by the prompt*

action of the consuls and a meeting of the senate. Appius
Claudius demands repressive action, Publius Servilius a
more temperate policy.

1   **23.** Sed et bellum Volscum imminebat et ciuitas
secum ipsa discors intestino inter patres plebemque
flagrabat odio, maxime propter nexos ob aes alienum.
2 Fremebant se, foris pro libertate et imperio dimicantes, domi a ciuibus captos et oppressos esse, tuti- 5
oremque in bello quam in pace et inter hostes quam
inter ciues libertatem plebis esse; inuidiamque eam
sua sponte gliscentem insignis unius calamitas accen-
3 dit. Magno natu quidam cum omnium malorum
suorum insignibus se in form proiecit. Obsita erat 10
squalore uestis, foedior corporis habitus pallore ac
4 macie perempti; ad hoc promissa barba et capilli
efferauerant speciem oris. Noscitabatur tamen in
tanta deformitate, et ordines duxisse aiebant, aliaque militiae decora uolgo miserantes eum iactabant; 15
ipse testes honestarum aliquot locis pugnarum cica-
5 trices aduerso pectore ostentabat. Sciscitantibus
unde ille habitus, unde deformitas, cum circumfusa
turba esset prope in contionis modum, Sabino bello
ait se militantem, quia propter populationes agri non 20
fructu modo caruerit, sed uilla incensa fuerit, direpta
omnia, pecora abacta, tributum iniquo suo tempore
6 imperatum, aes alienum fecisse. id cumulatum usuris
primo se agro paterno auitoque exuisse, deinde fortunis aliis; postremo uelut tabem peruenisse ad cor- 25
pus; ductum se ab creditore non in seruitium, sed in

7 ergastulum et carnificinam esse. Inde ostentare tergum foedum recentibus uestigiis uerberum. Ad haec
uisa auditaque clamor ingens oritur. Non iam foro
se tumultus tenet, sed passim totam urbem peruadit. 30
8 Nexi, uincti solutique, se undique in publicum pro-
ripiunt, implorant Quiritium fidem. Nullo loco deest
seditionis uoluntarius comes; multis passim agmini-
bus per omnes uias cum clamore in forum curritur.
9 Magno cum periculo suo qui forte patrum in foro 35
10 erant in eam turbam inciderunt; nec temperatum
manibus foret, ni propere consules, P. Seruilius et Ap.
Claudius, ad comprimendam seditionem interuenis-
sent. At in eos multitudo uersa ostentare uincula
11 sua deformitatemque aliam. Haec se meritos dicere, 40
exprobrantes suam quisque alius alibi militiam;
postulare multo minaciter magis quam suppliciter ut
senatum uocarent; curiamque ipsi futuri arbitri
12 moderatoresque publici consilii circumsistunt. Pauci
admodum patrum, quos casus obtulerat, contracti ab 45
consulibus; ceteros metus non curia modo sed etiam
foro arcebat, nec agi quicquam per infrequentiam
13 poterat senatus. Tum uero eludi atque extrahi se
multitudo putare, et patrum qui abessent, non casu,
non metu, sed impediendae rei causa abesse, et con- 50
sules ipsos tergiuersari, nec dubie ludibrio esse
14 miserias suas. Iam prope erat ut ne consulum quidem
maiestas coerceret iras hominum, cum incerti morando
an ueniendo plus periculi contraherent, tandem in
senatum ueniunt. Frequentique tandem curia non 55

modo inter patres sed ne inter consules quidem ipsos
15 satis conueniebat. Appius, uehementis ingenii uir,
imperio consulari rem agendam censebat; uno aut
altero arrepto, quieturos alios: Seruilius, lenibus
remediis aptior, concitatos animos flecti quam frangi 60
putabat cum tutius tum facilius esse.

*Threats of a Volscian attack induce the senate to follow the
lead of Servilius who makes concessions to the people's
demands. They agree to fight.*

1   **24.** Inter haec maior alius terror: Latini equites
cum tumultuoso aduolant nuntio Volscos infesto
exercitu ad urbem oppugnandam uenire. Quae
audita—adeo duas ex una ciuitate discordia fecerat—
2 longe aliter patres ac plebem adfecere. Exsultare 5
gaudio plebes; ultores superbiae patrum adesse dicere
deos; alius alium confirmare ne nomina darent; cum
omnibus potius quam solos perituros; patres militarent, patres arma caperent, ut penes eosdem
3 pericula belli, penes quos praemia, essent. At uero 10
curia, maesta ac trepida ancipiti metu et ab ciue et ab
hoste, Seruilium consulem, cui ingenium magis
populare erat, orare ut tantis circumuentam terrori-
4 bus expediret rem publicam. Tum consul misso
senatu in contionem prodit. Ibi curae esse patribus 15
ostendit ut consulatur plebi; ceterum deliberationi
de maxima quidem illa sed tamen parte ciuitatis
5 metum pro uniuersa re publica interuenisse; nec
posse, cum prope ad portas essent, bello praeuerti

quicquam, nec, si sit laxamenti aliquid, aut plebi 20
honestum esse, nisi mercede prius accepta, arma pro
patria non cepisse, neque patribus satis decorum per
metum potius quam postmodo uoluntate adflictis
6 ciuium suorum fortunis consuluisse. Contioni deinde
edicto addidit fidem quo edixit ne quis ciuem Ro- 25
manum uinctum aut clausum teneret, quo minus ei
nominis edendi apud consules potestas fieret, neu quis
militis, donec in castris esset, bona possideret aut
7 uenderet, liberos nepotesue eius moraretur. Hoc
proposito edicto, et qui aderant nexi profiteri extem- 30
plo nomina, et undique ex tota urbe proripientium se
ex priuato, cum retinendi ius creditori non esset, con-
8 cursus in forum ut sacramento dicerent fieri. Magna
ea manus fuit, neque aliorum magis in Volsco bello
uirtus atque opera enituit. Consul copias contra 35
hostem educit; paruo dirimente interuallo castra
ponit.

Defeat of the Volscians.

1 **25.** Proxima inde nocte Volsci, discordia Romana
freti, si qua nocturna transitio proditioue fieri posset,
temptant castra. Sensere uigiles; excitatus exer-
2 citus; signo dato concursum est ad arma; ita frustra
id inceptum Volscis fuit. Reliquum noctis utrimque 5
quieti datum. Postero die prima luce Volsci fossis
3 repletis uallum inuadunt. Iamque ab omni parte
munimenta uellebantur, cum consul, quamquam

cuncti undique et nexi ante omnes ut signum daret
clamabant, experiendi animos militum causa parum- 10
per moratus, postquam satis apparebat ingens ardor,
dato tandem ad erumpendum signo militem auidum
4 certaminis emittit.   Primo statim incursu pulsi
hostes; fugientibus, quoad insequi pedes potuit,
terga caesa; eques usque ad castra pauidos egit. 15
Mox ipsa castra legionibus circumdatis, cum Volscos
inde etiam pauor expulisset, capta direptaque.
5 Postero die ad Suessam Pometiam quo confugerant
hostes legionibus ductis, intra paucos dies oppidum
capitur; captum praedae datum.   Inde paulum 20
6 recreatus egens miles; consul cum maxima gloria sua
uictorem exercitum Romam reducit.   Decedentem
Romam Ecetranorum Volscorum legati, rebus suis
timentes post Pometiam captam, adeunt.   His ex
senatus consulto data pax, ager ademptus.   25

Defeat of the Sabines and Auruncans.

1   **26.** Confestim et Sabini Romanos territauere;
tumultus enim fuit uerius quam bellum.   Nocte in
urbem nuntiatum est exercitum Sabinum praedabun-
dum ad Anienem amnem peruenisse; ibi passim diripi
2 atque incendi uillas.   Missus extemplo eo cum omni- 5
bus copiis equitum A. Postumius, qui dictator bello
Latino fuerat; secutus consul Seruilius cum delecta
3 peditum manu.   Plerosque palantes eques circum-
uenit, nec aduenienti peditum agmini restitit Sabina

legio. Fessi cum itinere tum populatione nocturna, 10
magna pars in uillis repleti cibo uinoque, uix fugae
quod satis esset uirium habuere.

4 Nocte una audito perfectoque bello Sabino, postero
die in magna iam spe undique partae pacis, legati
Aurunci senatum adeunt, ni decedatur Volsco agro 15
5 bellum indicentes. Cum legatis simul exercitus
Auruncorum domo profectus erat; cuius fama haud
procul iam ab Aricia uisi tanto tumultu conciuit
Romanos ut nec consuli ordine patres nec pacatum
responsum arma inferentibus arma ipsi capientes 20
6 dare possent. Ariciam infesto agmine itur; nec
procul inde cum Auruncis signa conlata, proelioque
uno debellatum est.

*Appius Claudius ignores the concessions promised by his
colleague Servilius, and the latter, when appealed to by the
people, fails to help. The unrest continues into the next
year (494) and the people refuse to enlist for the campaign
against the Sabines. They show their temper by allocating
the dedication of the temple of Mercury to a senior centurion
and violently resisting arrest for debt.*

1 **27.** Fusis Auruncis, uictor tot intra paucos dies
bellis Romanus promissa consulis fidemque senatus
exspectabat, cum Appius et insita superbia animo et
ut collegae uanam faceret fidem, quam asperrime
poterat ius de creditis pecuniis dicere. Deinceps et 5
qui ante nexi fuerant creditoribus tradebantur et
2 nectebantur alii. Quod ubi cui militi inciderat, col-

legam appellabat. Concursus ad Seruilium fiebat;
illius promissa iactabant; illi exprobrabant sua
quisque belli merita cicatricesque acceptas. Pos- 10
tulabant ut aut referret ad senatum, aut ut auxilio
3 esset consul ciuibus suis, imperator militibus. Mouebant consulem haec, sed tergiuersari res cogebat;
adeo in alteram causam non collega solum praeceps
erat sed omnis factio nobilium. Ita medium se 15
gerendo nec plebis uitauit odium nec apud patres
4 gratiam iniit. Patres mollem consulem et ambitiosum
rati, plebes fallacem, breuique apparuit aequasse
5 eum Appi odium. Certamen consulibus inciderat,
uter dedicaret Mercuri aedem. Senatus a se rem ad 20
populum reiecit: utri eorum dedicatio iussu populi
data esset, eum praeesse annonae, mercatorum collegium instituere, sollemnia pro pontifice iussit sus-
6 cipere. Populus dedicationem aedis dat M. Laetorio,
primi pili centurioni, quod facile appareret non tam 25
ad honorem eius cui curatio altior fastigio suo data
7 esset factum quam ad consulum ignominiam. Saeuire
inde utique consulum alter patresque; sed plebi
creuerant animi et longe alia quam primo insti-
8 tuerant uia grassabantur. Desperato enim consulum 30
senatusque auxilio, cum in ius duci debitorem uidissent, undique conuolabant. Neque decretum exaudiri consulis prae strepitu et clamore poterat, neque
9 cum decresset quisquam obtemperabat. Vi agebatur, metusque omnis et periculum, cum in con- 35
spectu consulis singuli a pluribus uiolarentur, in

10 creditores a debitoribus uerterant. Super haec timor
incessit Sabini belli; dilectuque decreto nemo nomen
dedit, furente Appio et insectante ambitionem collegae, qui populari silentio rem publicam proderet et 40
ad id quod de credita pecunia ius non dixisset, adiceret
ut ne dilectum quidem ex senatus consulto haberet;
11 non esse tamen desertam omnino rem publicam neque
proiectum consulare imperium; se unum et suae et
12 patrum maiestatis uindicem fore. Cum circumstaret 45
cotidiana multitudo licentia accensa, arripi unum
insignem ducem seditionum iussit. Ille cum a lictoribus iam traheretur prouocauit; nec cessisset pro-
uocationi consul, quia non dubium erat populi iudicium, nisi aegre uicta pertinacia foret consilio magis 50
et auctoritate principum quam populi clamore; adeo
13 supererant animi ad sustinendam inuidiam. Crescere
inde malum in dies, non clamoribus modo apertis sed,
quod multo perniciosius erat, secessione occultisque
conloquiis. Tandem inuisi plebi consules magistratu 55
abeunt, Seruilius neutris, Appius patribus mire
gratus.

494 B.C. *Secret meetings of the people alarm the consuls and the
senate. The former, stung by the senate's reproaches,
attempt to hold the levy, but without success.*

1 **28.** A. Verginius inde et T. Vetusius consulatum
ineunt. Tum uero plebs incerta quales habitura
consules esset, coetus nocturnos, pars Esquiliis, pars

in Auentino facere, ne in foro subitis trepidaret con-
2 siliis et omnia temere ac fortuito ageret. Eam rem 5
consules rati, ut erat, perniciosam ad patres deferunt,
sed delatum consulere ordine non licuit; adeo
tumultuose excepta est clamoribus undique et indignatione patrum, si quod imperio consulari exsequen-
dum esset, inuidiam eius consules ad senatum 10
3 reicerent: profecto si essent in re publica magistratus,
nullum futurum fuisse Romae nisi publicum con-
4 cilium; nunc in mille curias contionesque [cum alia
in Esquiliis, alia in Auentino fiant concilia] dispersam
et dissipatam esse rem publicam. unum hercule 15
uirum—id enim plus esse quam consulem—qualis
Ap. Claudius fuerit, momento temporis discussurum
5 illos coetus fuisse. Correpti consules cum, quid ergo
se facere uellent—nihil enim segnius molliusue quam
patribus placeat acturos—percontarentur, decernunt 20
ut dilectum quam acerrimum habeant: otio lasciuire
6 plebem. Dimisso senatu consules in tribunal escen-
dunt; citant nominatim iuniores. Cum ad nomen
nemo responderet, circumfusa multitudo in contionis
7 modum negare ultra decipi plebem posse; nunquam 25
unum militem habituros ni praestaretur fides publica;
libertatem unicuique prius reddendam esse quam
arma danda, ut pro patria ciuibusque, non pro
8 dominis pugnent. Consules quid mandatum esset a
senatu uidebant, sed eorum, qui intra parietes curiae 30
ferociter loquerentur, neminem adesse inuidiae suae
participem; et apparebat atrox cum plebe certamen.

9 Prius itaque quam ultima experirentur senatum
iterum consulere placuit. Tum uero ad sellas consulum prope conuolare minimus quisque natu 35
patrum, abdicare consulatum iubentes et deponere
imperium, ad quod tuendum animus deesset.

The consuls ask for the moral support of the senate. As another
attempt to hold the levy almost ends in mob violence, the
senate is alarmed and hears three proposals, including
the demand of A. Claudius that a dictator be appointed,
for from that magistrate there could be no appeal.

1 **29.** Vtraque re satis experta tum demum consules:
' Ne praedictum negetis, patres conscripti, adest ingens seditio. Postulamus ut hi qui maxime ignauiam
increpant adsint nobis habentibus dilectum. Acerrimi cuiusque arbitrio, quando ita placet, rem age- 5
2 mus.' Redeunt in tribunal; citari nominatim unum
ex iis qui in conspectu erant dedita opera iubent.
Cum staret tacitus et circa eum aliquot hominum, ne
forte uiolaretur, constitisset globus, lictorem ad eum
3 consules mittunt. Quo repulso, tum uero indignum 10
facinus esse clamitantes qui patrum consulibus
aderant, deuolant de tribunali ut lictori auxilio essent.
4 Sed ab lictore nihil aliud quam prendere prohibito
cum conuersus in patres impetus esset, consulum
intercursu rixa sedata est, in qua tamen sine lapide, 15
sine telo plus clamoris atque irarum quam iniuriae
5 fuerat. Senatus tumultuose uocatus tumultuosius
consulitur, quaestionem postulantibus iis qui pulsati

fuerant, decernente ferocissimo quoque non sententiis
6 magis quam clamore et strepitu. Tandem cum 20
irae resedissent, exprobrantibus consulibus nihilo
plus sanitatis in curia quam in foro esse,
7 ordine consuli coepit. Tres fuere sententiae. P.
Verginius rem non uolgabat; de iis tantum qui fidem
secuti P. Seruili consulis Volsco Aurunco Sabinoque 25
8 militassent bello, agendum censebat. T. Largius,
non id tempus esse ut merita tantummodo exsoluerentur; totam plebem aere alieno demersam esse, nec
sisti posse ni omnibus consulatur; quin si alia aliorum
sit condicio, accendi magis discordiam quam sedari. 30
9 Ap. Claudius, et natura immitis et efferatus hinc
plebis odio, illinc patrum laudibus, non miseriis ait
sed licentia tantum concitum turbarum et lasciuire
10 magis plebem quam saeuire. Id adeo malum ex
prouocatione natum; quippe minas esse consulum, 35
non imperium, ubi ad eos qui una peccauerint pro-
11 uocare liceat. ' Agedum ' inquit, ' dictatorem, a quo
prouocatio non est, creemus; iam hic quo nunc
12 omnia ardent conticescet furor. Pulset tum mihi
lictorem qui sciet ius de tergo uitaque sua penes 40
unum illum esse cuius maiestatem uiolarit.'

*M'. Valerius is appointed dictator and, by promising to help the
nexi, holds the levy. Hostilities with the Aequi and Volsci.
The latter, in spite of their superior numbers, are out-
manoeuvred and decisively defeated by Verginius.*

1   **30.** Multis, ut erat, horrida et atrox uidebatur

Appi sententia; rursus Vergini Largique exemplo
haud salubres, utique Largi quae totam fidem
tolleret. Medium maxime et moderatum utroque
2 consilium Vergini habebatur; sed factione 5
respectuque rerum priuatarum, quae semper
offecere officientque publicis consiliis, Appius uicit,
ac prope fuit ut dictator ille idem crearetur;
3 quae res utique alienasset plebem periculosissimo
tempore, cum Volsci Aequique et Sabini forte una 10
4 omnes in armis essent. Sed curae fuit consulibus et
senioribus patrum, ut imperium sua ui uehemens man-
5 sueto permitteretur ingenio: M'. Valerium dictatorem
Volesi filium creant. Plebes etsi aduersus se creatum
dictatorem uidebat, tamen cum prouocationem fratris 15
lege haberet, nihil ex ea familia triste nec superbum
6 timebat; edictum deinde a dictatore propositum con-
firmauit animos, Seruili fere consulis edicto conueniens; sed et homini et potestati melius rati credi,
7 omisso certamine nomina dedere. Quantus nunquam 20
ante exercitus, legiones decem effectae; ternae inde
datae consulibus, quattuor dictator usus.
8   Nec iam poterat bellum differri. Aequi Latinum
agrum inuaserant. Oratores Latinorum ab senatu
petebant ut aut mitterent subsidium aut se ipsos 25
tuendorum finium causa capere arma sinerent.
9 Tutius uisum est defendi inermes Latinos quam pati
retractare arma. Vetusius consul missus est; is finis
populationibus fuit. Cessere Aequi campis, locoque
magis quam armis freti summis se iugis montium 30

10 tutabantur. Alter consul in Volscos profectus, ne et
ipse tereret tempus, uastandis maxime agris hostem
ad conferenda propius castra dimicandumque acie
11 exciuit. Medio inter castra campo ante suum quis-
12 que uallum infestis signis constitere. Multitudine 35
aliquantum Volsci superabant; itaque effusi et contemptim pugnam iniere. Consul Romanus nec pro-
mouit aciem, nec clamorem reddi passus defixis pilis
stare suos iussit: ubi ad manum uenisset hostis, tum
13 coortos tota ui gladiis rem gerere. Volsci cursu et 40
clamore fessi cum se uelut stupentibus metu intulis-
sent Romanis, postquam impressionem sensere ex
aduerso factam et ante oculos micare gladios, haud
secus quam si in insidias incidissent, turbati uertunt
terga; et ne ad fugam quidem satis uirium fuit, quia 45
14 cursu in proelium ierant. Romani contra, quia principio pugnae quieti steterant, uigentes corporibus,
facile adepti fessos, et castra impetu ceperunt et castris exutum hostem Velitras persecuti uno agmine
15 uictores cum uictis in urbem inrupere; plusque ibi 50
sanguinis promiscua omnium generum caede quam in
ipsa dimicatione factum. Paucis data uenia, qui
inermes in deditionem uenerunt.

The Sabines are defeated by the dictator, the Aequi by the consul.
At the refusal of the Senate to fulfil his promises, Valerius
resigns the dictatorship.

1   **31.** Dum haec in Volscis geruntur, dictator Sabinos,
ubi longe plurimum belli fuerat, fundit exuitque

2 castris. Equitatu immisso mediam turbauerat hostium
aciem, quam, dum se cornua latius pandunt, parum
apte introrsum ordinibus [aciem] firmauerant; tur- 5
batos pedes inuasit. Eodem impetu castra capta
3 debellatumque est. Post pugnam ad Regillum lacum
non alia illis annis pugna clarior fuit. Dictator trium-
phans urbem inuehitur. Super solitos honores locus
in circo ipsi posterisque ad spectaculum datus; sella 10
4 in eo loco curulis posita. Volscis deuictis Veliternus
ager ademptus; Velitras coloni ab urbe missi et colonia deducta. Cum Aequis post aliquanto pugnatum
est, inuito quidem consule quia loco iniquo subeun-
5 dum erat ad hostes; sed milites extrahi rem crimin- 15
antes ut dictator priusquam ipsi redirent in urbem
magistratu abiret inritaque, sicut ante consulis,
promissa eius caderent, perpulere ut forte temere in
6 aduersos montes agmen erigeret. Id male commissum ignauia hostium in bonum uertit, qui prius- 20
quam ad coniectum teli ueniretur, obstupefacti
audacia Romanorum, relictis castris quae munitis-
simis tenuerant locis, in auersas ualles desiluere.
Ibi satis praedae et uictoria incruenta fuit.
7 Ita trifariam re bello bene gesta, de domesticarum 25
rerum euentu nec patribus nec plebi cura decesserat:
tanta cum gratia tum arte praeparauerant fenera-
tores quae non modo plebem, sed ipsum etiam
8 dictatorem frustrarentur. Namque Valerius post
Vetusi consulis reditum omnium actionum in senatu 30
primam habuit pro uictore populo, rettulitque quid

9 de nexis fieri placeret. Quae cum reiecta relatio esset, 'Non placeo' inquit, 'concordiae auctor. Optabitis, mediusfidius, propediem, ut mei similes Romana plebis patronos habeat. Quod ad me at- 35 tinet, neque frustrabor ultra ciues meos neque ipse 10 frustra dictator ero. Discordiae intestinae, bellum externum fecere ut hoc magistratu egeret res publica: pax foris parta est, domi impeditur; priuatus potius quam dictator seditioni interero.' Ita curia egressus 40 11 dictatura se abdicauit. Apparuit causa plebi, suam uicem indignantem magistratu abisse; itaque uelut persoluta fide, quoniam per eum non stetisset quin praestaretur, decedentem domum cum fauore ac laudibus prosecuti sunt. 45

494 B.C. *The people secede to the 'Mount of Curses'. By means of a parable, Menenius Agrippa persuades them to return.*

1 **32.** Timor inde patres incessit ne, si dimissus exercitus foret, rursus coetus occulti coniurationesque fierent. Itaque quamquam per dictatorem dilectus habitus esset, tamen quoniam in consulum uerba iurassent sacramento teneri militem rati, per causam 5 renouati ab Aequis belli educi ex urbe legiones iussere. 2 Quo facto maturata est seditio. Et primo agitatum dicitur de consulum caede, ut soluerentur sacramento; doctos deinde nullam scelere religionem exsolui, Sicinio quodam auctore iniussu consulum in 10 Sacrum montem secessisse. Trans Anienem amnem

3 est, tria ab urbe milia passuum. Ea frequentior fama
  est quam cuius Piso auctor est, in Auentinum seces-
4 sionem factam esse. Ibi sine ullo duce uallo fossaque
  communitis castris quieti, rem nullam nisi neces- 15
  sariam ad uictum sumendo, per aliquot dies neque
5 lacessiti neque lacessentes sese tenuere. Pauor
  ingens in urbe, metuque mutuo suspensa erant omnia. Timere relicta ab suis plebis uiolentiam patrum;
  timere patres residem in urbe plebem, incerti manere 20
6 eam an abire mallent: quamdiu autem tranquillam
  quae secesserit multitudinem fore? quid futurum
  deinde si quod externum interim bellum exsistat?
7 Nullam profecto nisi in concordia ciuium spem
  reliquam ducere; eam per aequa, per iniqua recon- 25
  ciliandam ciuitati esse.
8   Placuit igitur oratorem ad plebem mitti Menenium
  Agrippam, facundum uirum et quod inde oriundus
  erat plebi carum. Is intromissus in castra prisco illo
  dicendi et horrido modo nihil aliud quam hoc nar- 30
9 rasse fertur: tempore quo in homine non ut nunc
  omnia in unum consentiant, sed singulis membris
  suum cuique consilium, suus sermo fuerit, indignatas
  reliquas partes sua cura, suo labore ac ministerio
  uentri omnia quaeri, uentrem in medio quietum nihil 35
10 aliud quam datis uoluptatibus frui; conspirasse inde
  ne manus ad os cibum ferrent, nec os acciperet datum,
  nec dentes quae acciperent conficerent. Hac ira,
  dum uentrem fame domare uellent, ipsa una membra
11 totumque corpus ad extremam tabem uenisse. inde ap- 40

paruisse uentris quoque haud segne ministerium esse,
nec magis ali quam alere eum, reddentem in omnes
corporis partes hunc quo uiuimus uigemusque, diui-
sum pariter in uenas maturum confecto cibo san-
12 guinem. Comparando hinc quam intestina corporis 45
seditio similis esset irae plebis in patres, flexisse
mentes hominum.

493 B.C. *Terms of the reconciliation: the appointment of
Tribunes of the Plebs and their persons made sacrosanct. An
important treaty with the Latins; the exploits of Cn. Marcius
(Coriolanus) at Corioli; death of Menenius Agrippa.*

1 **33.** Agi deinde de concordia coeptum, concessum-
que in condiciones ut plebi sui magistratus essent
sacrosancti quibus auxilii latio aduersus consules
esset, neue cui patrum capere eum magistratum
2 liceret. Ita tribuni plebei creati duo, C. Licinius et 5
L. Albinus; ii tres collegas sibi creauerunt. In his
Sicinium fuisse, seditionis auctorem: de duobus, qui
3 fuerint minus conuenit. Sunt qui duos tantum in
Sacro monte creatos tribunos esse dicant, ibique
sacratam legem latam. 10
Per secessionem plebis Sp. Cassius et Postumius
4 Cominius consulatum inierant. Iis consulibus cum
Latinis populis ictum foedus. Ad id feriendum consul alter Romae mansit: alter ad Volscum bellum
missus Antiates Volscos fundit fugatque; compulsos 15
in oppidum Longulam persecutus moenibus potitur.
5 Inde protinus Poluscam, item Volscorum, cepit; tum

magna ui adortus est Coriolos. Erat tum in castris
inter primores iuuenum Cn. Marcius, adulescens et
consilio et manu promptus, cui cognomen postea 20
6 Coriolano fuit. Cum subito exercitum Romanum
Coriolos obsidentem atque in oppidanos quos intus
clausos habebat intentum, sine ullo metu extrinsecus
imminentis belli, Volscae legiones profectae ab
Antio inuasissent, eodemque tempore ex oppido 25
7 erupissent hostes, forte in statione Marcius fuit. Is
cum delecta militum manu non modo impetum
erumpentium rettudit, sed per patentem portam
ferox inrupit in proxima urbis, caedeque facta ignem
temere arreptum imminentibus muro aedificiis iniecit. 30
8 Clamor inde oppidanorum mixtus muliebri puerilique
ploratu ad terrorem, ut solet, primum orto et Romanis auxit animum et turbauit Volscos utpote
9 capta urbe cui ad ferendam opem uenerant. Ita fusi
Volsci Antiates, Corioli oppidum captum; tantum- 35
que sua laude obstitit famae consulis Marcius ut, nisi
foedus cum Latinis in columna aenea insculptum
monumento esset ab Sp. Cassio uno, quia collega
afuerat, ictum, Postumium Cominium bellum gessisse
cum Volscis memoria cessisset. 40
10 Eodem anno Agrippa Menenius moritur, uir omni
in uita pariter patribus ac plebi carus, post secessionem
11 carior plebi factus. Huic interpreti arbitroque concordiae ciuium, legato patrum ad plebem, reductori
plebis Romanae in urbem sumptus funeri defuit; 45
extulit eum plebs sextantibus conlatis in capita.

492 B.C. *Famine in Rome is averted by purchase of corn from
Etruria and Sicily.   Coriolanus leads a movement to
cancel the concessions recently won by the people.*

1   **34.** Consules deinde T. Geganius P. Minucius facti.
Eo anno cum et foris quieta omnia a bello essent et
2 domi sanata discordia, aliud multo grauius malum
ciuitatem inuasit, caritas primum annonae ex incultis
per secessionem plebis agris, fames deinde, qualis 5
3 clausis solet.   Ventumque ad interitum seruitiorum
utique et plebis esset, ni consules prouidissent dimissis passim ad frumentum coemendum, non in
Etruriam modo dextris ab Ostia litoribus laeuoque
per Volscos mari usque ad Cumas, sed quaesitum in 10
Sicilia quoque; adeo finitimorum odia longinquis
4 coegerant indigere auxiliis.   Frumentum Cumis cum
coemptum esset, naues pro bonis Tarquiniorum ab
Aristodemo tyranno, qui heres erat, retentae sunt; in
Volscis Pomptinoque ne emi quidem potuit; peri- 15
culum quoque ab impetu hominum ipsis frumenta-
toribus fuit; ex Tuscis frumentum Tiberi uenit; eo
5 sustentata est plebs.   Incommodo bello in tam artis
commeatibus uexati forent, ni Volscos iam mouentes
6 arma pestilentia ingens inuasisset.   Ea clade conter- 20
ritis hostium animis, ut etiam ubi ea remisisset ter-
rore aliquo tenerentur, et Velitris auxere numerum
colonorum Romani, et Norbam in montes nouam
coloniam, quae arx in Pomptino esset, miserunt.
7   M. Minucio deinde et A. Sempronio consulibus 25
magna uis frumenti ex Sicilia aduecta, agitatumque

8 in senatu quanti plebi daretur. Multi uenisse tempus
premendae plebis putabant reciperandique iura quae
9 extorta secessione ac ui patribus essent. In primis
Marcius Coriolanus, hostis tribuniciae potestatis, 30
' Si annonam ' inquit, ' ueterem uolunt, ius pristinum
reddant patribus. Cur ego plebeios magistratus, cur
Sicinium potentem uideo, sub iugum missus, tam-
10 quam ab latronibus redemptus? Egone has indig-
nitates diutius patiar quam necesse est? Tarquinium 35
regem qui non tulerim, Sicinium feram? Secedat
nunc; auocet plebem; patet uia in Sacrum montem
aliosque colles; rapiant frumenta ex agris nostris
quemadmodum tertio anno rapuere. Fruantur
11 annona quam furore suo fecere. Audeo dicere hoc 40
malo domitos ipsos potius cultores agrorum fore
quam ut armati per secessionem coli prohibeant.'
12 Haud tam facile dictu est faciendumne fuerit quam
potuisse arbitror fieri ut condicionibus laxandi annonam et tribuniciam potestatem et omnia inuitis 45
iura imposita patres demerent sibi.

When called to account by the tribunes, Coriolanus goes into
exile and plans to revenge himself on his fellow-country-
men. He joins the Volsci.

1   **35.** Et senatui nimis atrox uisa sententia est et
plebem ira prope armauit. Fame se iam sicut hostes
peti, cibo uictuque fraudari; peregrinum frumentum,
quae sola alimenta ex insperato fortuna dederit, ab
ore rapi nisi Cn. Marcio uincti dedantur tribuni, nisi 5

de tergo plebis Romanae satisfiat; eum sibi carnificem nouum exortum, qui aut mori aut seruire iubeat.
2 In exeuntem e curia impetus factus esset, ni peropportune tribuni diem dixissent. Ibi ira est sup-
pressa; se iudicem quisque, se dominum uitae 10
3 necisque inimici factum uidebat. Contemptim
primo Marcius audiebat minas tribunicias: auxilii,
non poenae ius datum illi potestati, plebisque, non
patrum tribunos esse. Sed adeo infensa erat coorta
plebs ut unius poena defungendum esset patribus. 15
4 Restiterunt tamen aduersa inuidia, usique sunt qua
suis quisque, qua totius ordinis uiribus. Ac primo
temptata res est si dispositis clientibus absterrendo
singulos a coitionibus conciliisque disicere rem pos-
5 sent. Vniuersi deinde processere—quidquid erat 20
patrum, reos diceres—precibus plebem exposcentes,
unum sibi ciuem, unum senatorem, si innocentem ab-
6 soluere nollent, pro nocente donarent. Ipse cum die
dicta non adesset, perseueratum in ira est. Damnatus
absens in Volscos exsulatum abiit, minitans patriae 25
hostilesque iam tum spiritus gerens.
     Venientem Volsci benigne excepere, benigniusque
in dies colebant, quo maior ira in suos eminebat
crebraeque nunc querellae, nunc minae percipieban-
7 tur. Hospitio utebatur Atti Tulli. Longe is tum 30
princeps Volsci nominis erat Romanisque semper
infestus. Ita cum alterum uetus odium, alterum ira
recens stimularet, consilia conferunt de Romano
8 bello. Haud facile credebant plebem suam impelli

posse, ut totiens infeliciter temptata arma caperent: 35
multis saepe bellis, pestilentia postremo amissa iuuentute fractos spiritus esse; arte agendum in exoleto
iam uetustate odio, ut recenti aliqua ira exacerbaren-
tur animi.

*The celebration of the Great Games has to be repeated. A
plebeian, Titus Latinius, warned by a dream, a warning
confirmed by the loss of his son and his own severe illness,
tells the senate how the scourging of a slave has vitiated the
opening of the Games.*

1   **36.** Ludi forte ex instauratione magni Romae
parabantur. Instaurandi haec causa fuerat. Ludis
mane seruum quidam pater familiae, nondum com-
misso spectaculo, sub furca caesum medio egerat
circo; coepti inde ludi, uelut ea res nihil ad re- 5
2 ligionem pertinuisset. Haud ita multo post Tito
Latinio, de plebe homini, somnium fuit; uisus Iuppiter dicere sibi ludis praesultatorem displicuisse;
nisi magnifice instaurarentur ii ludi, periculum urbi
3 fore; iret, ea consulibus nuntiaret. Quamquam haud 10
sane liber erat religione animus, uerecundia tamen
maiestatis magistratuum timorem uicit, ne in ora
4 hominum pro ludibrio abiret. Magno illi ea cunctatio
stetit; filium namque intra paucos dies amisit.
Cuius repentinae cladis ne causa ei dubia esset, 15
aegro animi eadem illa in somnis obuersata species
uisa est rogitare, satin' magnam spreti numinis haberet
mercedem; maiorem instare ni eat propere ac nun-

5 tiet consulibus. Iam praesentior res erat. Cunctantem tamen ac prolatantem ingens uis morbi adorta est 20
6 debilitate subita. Tunc enimuero deorum cura ea
admonuit. Fessus igitur malis praeteritis instanti-
busque, consilio propinquorum adhibito, cum uisa
atque audita et obuersatum totiens somno Iouem,
minas irasque caelestes repraesentatas casibus suis 25
exposuisset, consensu inde haud dubio omnium qui
7 aderant in forum ad consules lectica defertur. Inde
in curiam iussu consulum delatus eadem illa cum
patribus ingenti omnium admiratione enarrasset,
8 ecce aliud miraculum: qui captus omnibus membris 30
delatus in curiam esset, eum functum officio pedibus
suis domum redisse traditum memoriae est.

Attius Tullius, a Volscian leader, deliberately arranges for
the large number of Volscian visitors to be insulted and
expelled from Rome.

1   **37.** Ludi quam amplissimi ut fierent senatus
decreuit. Ad eos ludos auctore Attio Tullio uis
2 magna Volscorum uenit. Priusquam committerentur
ludi, Tullius, ut domi compositum cum Marcio fuerat,
ad consules uenit; dicit esse quae secreto agere de re 5
3 publica uelit. Arbitris remotis, ' Inuitus ' inquit,
' quod sequius sit, de meis ciuibus loquor. Non
tamen admissum quicquam ab iis criminatum uenio,
4 sed cautum ne admittant. Nimio plus quam uelim,
5 nostrorum ingenia sunt mobilia. Multis id cladibus 10
sensimus, quippe qui non nostro merito sed vestra

patientia incolumes simus. Magna hic nunc Volscorum multitudo est; ludi sunt; spectaculo intenta
6 ciuitas erit. Memini quid per eandem occasionem ab
Sabinorum iuuentute in hac urbe commissum sit; hor- 15
ret animus, ne quid inconsulte ac temere fiat. Haec
nostra uestraque causa prius dicenda uobis, consules,
7 ratus sum. Quod ad me attinet, extemplo hinc
domum abire in animo est, ne cuius facti dictiue con-
8 tagione praesens uioler.' Haec locutus abiit. Con- 20
sules cum ad patres rem dubiam sub auctore certo
detulissent, auctor magis, ut fit, quam res ad prae-
cauendum uel ex superuacuo mouit, factoque senatus
consulto ut urbe excederent Volsci, praecones dimit-
tuntur qui omnes eos proficisci ante noctem iuberent. 25
9 Ingens pauor primo discurrentes ad suas res tollendas
in hospitia perculit; proficiscentibus deinde indignatio oborta, se ut consceleratos contaminatosque ab
ludis, festis diebus, coetu quodam modo hominum
deorumque abactos esse. 30

*Attius Tullius excites the Volscians' resentment by an im-
passioned speech, and they make war upon Rome.*

1 **38.** Cum prope continuato agmine irent, praegres-
sus Tullius ad caput Ferentinum, ut quisque ueniret,
primores eorum excipiens querendo indignandoque,
et eos ipsos, sedulo audientes secunda irae uerba, et
per eos multitudinem aliam in subiectum uiae cam- 5
2 pum deduxit. Ibi in contionis modum orationem
exorsus. ' Vt omnia ' inquit, ' obliuiscamini alia,

ueteres populi Romani iniurias cladesque gentis
Volscorum, hodiernam hanc contumeliam quo tandem animo fertis, qua per nostram ignominiam ludos 10
3 commisere?   An non sensistis triumphatum hodie
de uobis esse?   uos omnibus, ciuibus, peregrinis, tot
finitimis populis, spectaculo abeuntes fuisse? uestras
coniuges, uestros liberos traductos per ora hominum?
4 Quid eos qui audiuere uocem praeconis, quid, qui nos 15
uidere abeuntes, quid eos qui huic ignominioso agmini fuere obuii, existimasse putatis nisi aliquod
profecto nefas esse quo, si intersimus spectaculo,
uiolaturi simus ludos piaculumque merituri; ideo
5 nos ab sede piorum, coetu concilioque abigi?   Quid 20
deinde? illud non succurrit, uiuere nos quod matur-
arimus proficisci? si hoc profectio et non fuga est.   Et
hanc urbem uos non hostium ducitis, ubi si unum
diem morati essetis, moriendum omnibus fuit?
Bellum uobis indictum est, magno eorum malo qui 25
6 indixere si uiri estis.' Ita et sua sponte irarum pleni
et incitati domos inde digressi sunt, instigandoque
suos quisque populos effecere ut omne Volscum
nomen deficeret.

Tullius and Coriolanus lead the Volscian forces into Roman
territory and demand the return of ' Volscian' territory
as the price of peace. The people are unwilling to fight.

1   **39.** Imperatores ad id bellum de omnium populorum sententia lecti Attius Tullius et Cn. Marcius,
exsul Romanus, in quo aliquanto plus spei repositum.

2 Quam spem nequaquam fefellit, ut facile appareret
ducibus ualidiorem quam exercitu rem Romanam 5
esse. Circeios profectus primum colonos inde
Romanos expulit liberamque eam urbem Volscis
3 tradidit; Satricum, Longulam, Poluscam, Coriolos,
nouella haec Romanis oppida ademit; inde Lauinium
recepit; inde in Latinam uiam transuersis tramitibus 10
4 transgressus, tunc deinceps Corbionem, Vetelliam,
5 Trebium, Labicos, Pedum cepit. Postremum ad
urbem a Pedo ducit, et ad fossas Cluilias quinque ab
urbe milia passuum castris positis, populatur inde
agrum Romanum, custodibus inter populatores missis 15
6 qui patriciorum agros intactos seruarent, siue infensus
plebi magis, siue ut discordia inde inter patres pleb-
7 emque oreretur. Quae profecto orta esset—adeo
tribuni iam ferocem per se plebem criminando in
primores ciuitatis instigabant—; sed externus timor, 20
maximum concordiae uinculum, quamuis suspectos
8 infensosque inter se iungebat animos. Id modo non
conueniebat quod senatus consulesque nusquam alibi
spem quam in armis ponebant, plebes omnia quam
9 bellum malebat. Sp. Nautius iam et Sex. Furius 25
consules erant. Eos recensentes legiones, praesidia
per muros aliaque in quibus stationes uigiliasque esse
placuerat loca distribuentes, multitudo ingens pacem
poscentium primum seditioso clamore conterruit,
deinde uocare senatum, referre de legatis ad Cn. 30
10 Marcium mittendis coegit. Acceperunt relationem
patres, postquam apparuit labare plebis animos;

11 missique de pace ad Marcium oratores atrox responsum rettulerunt: si Volscis ager redderetur, posse
agi de pace: si praeda belli per otium frui uelint, 35
memorem se et ciuium iniuriae et hospitum beneficii
adnisurum, ut appareat exsilio sibi inritatos, non
12 fractos animos esse. Iterum deinde iidem missi non
recipiuntur in castra. Sacerdotes quoque suis insignibus uelatos isse supplices ad castra hostium 40
traditum est; nihilo magis quam legatos flexisse
animum.

*Coriolanus' mother, wife, and children visit him in his camp as
suppliants and prevail upon him to withdraw.*

1   **40.** Tum matronae ad Veturiam matrem Coriolani
Volumniamque uxorem frequentes coeunt. Id publicum consilium an muliebris timor fuerit, parum
2 inuenio: peruicere certe, ut et Veturia, magno natu
mulier, et Volumnia duos paruos ex Marcio ferens 5
filios secum in castra hostium irent et, quoniam armis
uiri defendere urbem non possent, mulieres precibus
3 lacrimisque defenderent. Vbi ad castra uentum est
nuntiatumque Coriolano est adesse ingens mulierum
agmen, ut qui nec publica maiestate in legatis nec in 10
sacerdotibus tanta offusa oculis animoque religione
motus esset, multo obstinatior aduersus lacrimas
4 muliebres erat; dein familiarium quidam qui insignem maestitia inter ceteras cognouerat Veturiam,
inter nurum nepotesque stantem, ' Nisi me frustran- 15
tur ' inquit, ' oculi, mater tibi coniunxque et liberi

5 adsunt.' Coriolanus prope ut amens consternatus ab
sede sua cum ferret matri obuiae complexum mulier,
in iram ex precibus uersa 'Sine, priusquam complexum accipio, sciam ' inquit, ' ad hostem an ad 20
filium uenerim, captiua materne in castris tuis sim.
6 In hoc me longa uita et infelix senecta traxit ut
exsulem te deinde hostem uiderem? Potuisti populari
7 hanc terram quae te genuit atque aluit? Non tibi,
quamuis infesto animo et minaci perueneras, ingredi- 25
enti fines ira cecidit? Non, cum in conspectu Roma
fuit, succurrit: Intra illa moenia domus ac penates
8 mei sunt, mater coniunx liberique? Ergo ego nisi peperissem, Roma non oppugnaretur; nisi filium haberem,
libera in libera patria mortua essem. Sed ego mihi mis- 30
erius nihil iam pati nec tibi turpius usquam possum,
9 nec ut sum miserrima, diu futura sum: de his uideris,
quos, si pergis, aut immatura mors aut longa seruitus
manet.' Vxor deinde ac liberi amplexi, fletusque ab
omni turba mulierum ortus et comploratio sui patri- 35
10 aeque fregere tandem uirum. Complexus inde suos
dimittit: ipse retro ab urbe castra mouit. Abductis
deinde legionibus ex agro Romano, inuidia rei oppressum perisse tradunt, alii alio leto. Apud Fabium,
longe antiquissimum auctorem, usque ad senectutem 40
11 uixisse eundem inuenio; refert certe hanc saepe eum
exacta aetate usurpasse uocem multo miserius seni
exsilium esse. Non inuiderunt laude sua mulieribus
uiri Romani—adeo sine obtrectatione gloriae alienae
12 uiuebatur—; monumento quoque quod esset, tem- 45

plum Fortunae muliebri aedificatum dedicatumque
est.

Rediere deinde Volsci adiunctis Aequis in agrum
Romanum; sed Aequi Attium Tullium haud ultra
13 tulere ducem. Hinc ex certamine Volsci Aequine 50
imperatorem coniuncto exercitui darent, seditio,
deinde atrox proelium ortum. Ibi fortuna populi
Romani duos hostium exercitus haud minus pernici-
oso quam pertinaci certamine confecit.

14 Consules T. Sicinius et C. Aquilius. Sicinio Volsci, 55
Aquilio Hernici—nam ii quoque in armis erant—
prouincia euenit. Eo anno Hernici deuicti: cum
Volscis aequo Marte discessum est.

488 (486) B.C. *Spurius Cassius, consul, proposes an agrarian
law, and is opposed by his colleague. He is accused of
aiming at royal power, tried, and put to death.*

1 **41.** Sp. Cassius deinde et Proculus Verginius consules facti. Cum Hernicis foedus ictum; agri partes
duae ademptae. Inde dimidium Latinis, dimidium
2 plebi diuisurus consul Cassius erat. Adiciebat huic
muneri agri aliquantum, quem publicum possideri a 5
priuatis criminabatur. Id multos quidem patrum,
ipsos possessores, periculo rerum suarum terrebat;
sed et publica patribus sollicitudo inerat largitione
3 consulem periculosas libertati opes struere. Tum
primum lex agraria promulgata est, nunquam deinde 10
usque ad hanc memoriam sine maximis motibus
4 rerum agitata. Consul alter largitioni resistebat

auctoribus patribus nec omni plebe aduersante, quae
primo coeperat fastidire munus uolgatum a ciuibus
5 isse in socios; saepe deinde et Verginium consulem 15
in contionibus uelut uaticinantem audiebat pestilens
collegae munus esse; agros illos seruitutem iis qui
6 acceperint laturos; regno uiam fieri. quid ita enim
adsumi socios et nomen Latinum, quid attinuisset
Hernicis, paulo ante hostibus, capti agri partem 20
tertiam reddi, nisi ut hae gentes pro Coriolano duce
7 Cassium habeant? Popularis iam esse dissuasor et
intercessor legis agrariae coeperat. Vterque deinde
consul ut certatim, plebi indulgere. Verginius dicere
passurum se adsignari agros, dum ne cui nisi ciui 25
8 Romano adsignentur: Cassius, quia in agraria largitione ambitiosus in socios eoque ciuibus uilior erat, ut
alio munere sibi reconciliaret ciuium animos, iubere
pro Siculo frumento pecuniam acceptam retribui
9 populo. Id uero haud secus quam praesentem mer- 30
cedem regni aspernata plebes; adeo propter suspicionem insitam regni, uelut abundarent omnia, munera
10 eius [in animis hominum] respuebantur. Quem ubi
primum magistratu abiit damnatum necatumque
constat. Sunt qui patrem auctorem eius supplicii 35
ferant: eum cognita domi causa uerberasse ac necasse
peculiumque filii Cereri consecrauisse; signum inde
factum esse et inscriptum: ' Ex Cassia familia datum.'
11 Inuenio apud quosdam, idque propius fidem est, a
quaestoribus Caesone Fabio et L. Valerio diem dictam 40
perduellionis, damnatumque populi iudicio, dirutas

publice aedes. Ea est area ante Telluris aedem.
12 Ceterum siue illud domesticum siue publicum fuit
iudicium, damnatur Seruio Cornelio Q. Fabio consulibus.   45

*485–483 B.C. The unpopularity of the Fabii as consuls. More
agitation; campaigns against the Volsci and Aequi, and
the condemnation of a Vestal Virgin.*

1   **42.** Haud diuturna ira populi in Cassium fuit.
Dulcedo agrariae legis ipsa per se, dempto auctore,
subibat animos, accensaque ea cupiditas est maligni-
tate patrum, qui deuictis eo anno Volscis Aequisque,
2 militem praeda fraudauere. Quidquid captum ex hosti- 5
bus est, uendidit Fabius consul ac redegit in publicum.
   Inuisum erat Fabium nomen plebi propter nouis-
simum consulem; tenuere tamen patres ut cum L.
3 Aemilio Caeso Fabius consul crearetur. Eo infestior 10
facta plebes seditione domestica bellum externum
exciuit. Bello deinde ciuiles discordiae intermissae;
uno animo patres ac plebs rebellantes Volscos et
4 Aequos duce Aemilio prospera pugna uicere. Plus
tamen hostium fuga quam proelium absumpsit; 15
5 adeo pertinaciter fusos insecuti sunt equites. Castoris
aedis eodem anno idibus Quintilibus dedicata est;
uota erat Latino bello a Postumio dictatore; filius
6 eius duumuir ad id ipsum creatus dedicauit. Sol-
licitati et eo anno sunt dulcedine agrariae legis animi 20
plebis. Tribuni plebi popularem potestatem lege
populari celebrabant: patres, satis superque gratuiti

furoris in multitudine credentes esse, largitiones
7 temeritatisque inuitamenta horrebant. Acerrimi
patribus duces ad resistendum consules fuere. Ea 25
igitur pars rei publicae uicit, nec in praesens modo
sed in uenientem etiam annum M. Fabium, Caesonis
fratrem, et magis inuisum alterum plebi accusatione
Sp. Cassi, L. Valerium, consules dedit.
8 Certatum eo quoque anno cum tribunis est. Vana 30
lex uanique legis auctores iactando inritum munus
facti. Fabium inde nomen ingens post tres continuos
consulatus unoque uelut tenore omnes expertos tribuniciis certaminibus habitum; itaque, ut bene
locatus, mansit in ea familia aliquamdiu honos. Bel- 35
9 lum inde Veiens initum, et Volsci rebellarunt; sed
ad bella externa prope supererant uires, abutebantur-
10 que iis inter semet ipsos certando. Accessere ad
aegras iam omnium mentes prodigia caelestia, prope
cotidianas in urbe agrisque ostentantia minas; 40
motique ita numinis causam nullam aliam uates
canebant publice priuatimque nunc extis, nunc per
11 aues consulti, quam haud rite sacra fieri; qui terrores
tamen eo euasere ut Oppia uirgo Vestalis damnata
incesti poenas dederit. 45

481–480 B.C. *Campaigns against the Aequi and Veii. Failure
of a tribune Spurius Licinius to force a land-law on the
patricians, owing to his fellow-tribunes' lack of support
and their aid to the consuls in holding the levies. Victory
over the Aequi, in spite of the infantry's failure to follow up
the cavalry's successful charge.*

1 **43.** Q. Fabius inde et C. Iulius consules facti. Eo
anno non segnior discordia domi et bellum foris atrocius fuit. Ab Aequis arma sumpta; Veientes agrum
quoque Romanorum populantes inierunt. Quorum
bellorum crescente cura, Caeso Fabius et Sp. Furius 5
2 consules fiunt. Ortonam, Latinam urbem, Aequi
oppugnabant: Veientes, pleni iam populationum,
3 Romam ipsam se oppugnaturos minabantur. Qui
terrores cum compescere deberent, auxere insuper
animos plebis, redibatque non sua sponte plebi mos 10
detractandi militiam, sed Sp. Licinius tribunus plebis, uenisse tempus ratus per ultimam necessitatem
legis agrariae patribus iniungendae, susceperat rem
4 militarem impediendam. Ceterum tota inuidia tribuniciae potestatis uersa in auctorem est, nec in eum 15
consules acrius quam ipsius collegae coorti sunt,
auxilioque eorum dilectum consules habent.
5 Ad duo simul bella exercitus scribitur; ducendus
Fabio in Aequos, Furio datur in Veientes. In
6 Veientes nihil dignum memoria gestum; et in 20
Aequis quidem Fabio aliquanto plus negotii cum
ciuibus quam cum hostibus fuit. Vnus ille uir, ipse
consul, rem publicam sustinuit, quam exercitus odio
7 consulis, quantum in se fuit, prodebat. Nam cum
consul praeter ceteras imperatorias artes, quas par- 25
ando gerendoque bello edidit plurimas, ita instruxis-
set aciem ut solo equitatu emisso exercitum hostium
8 funderet, insequi fusos pedes noluit; nec illos, et si
non adhortatio inuisi ducis, suum saltem flagitium et

publicum in praesentia dedecus, postmodo periculum, 30
si animus hosti redisset, cogere potuit gradum adceler-
9 are aut si aliud nihil, stare instructos. Iniussu signa
referunt, maestique—crederes uictos—exsecrantes
nunc imperatorem, nunc nauatam ab equite operam,
10 redeunt in castra. Nec huic tam pestilenti exemplo 35
remedia ulla ab imperatore quaesita sunt; adeo
excellentibus ingeniis citius defuerit ars qua ciuem
11 regant quam qua hostem superent. Consul Romam
rediit non tam belli gloria aucta quam inritato exacer-
batoque in se militum odio. Obtinuere tamen patres 46
ut in Fabia gente consulatus maneret: M. Fabium
consulem creant; Fabio collega Cn. Manlius datur.

480 B.C. *More discord is aroused by an agrarian law, proposed*
by the tribune T. Pontificius, and by his attempt to hinder
the levy, which, however, is held with the help of the other
tribunes. Appius Claudius gives his views on the need
to curb the tribunes' power. Party strife in Rome and lack
of discipline in the army encourage the Etruscan cities to
support Veii against Rome.

1 **44.** Et hic annus tribunum auctorem legis agrariae
habuit. Tib. Pontificius fuit. Is eandem uiam, uelut
processisset Sp. Licinio, ingressus dilectum paulisper
2 impediit. Perturbatis iterum patribus Ap. Claudius
uictam tribuniciam potestatem dicere priore anno, in 5
praesentia re, exemplo in perpetuum, quando inuen-
3 tum sit suis ipsam uiribus dissolui. neque enim
unquam defuturum qui et ex collega uictoriam sibi
et gratiam melioris partis bono publico uelit quaesi-

tam; et plures, si pluribus opus sit, tribunos ad 10
auxilium consulum paratos fore, et unum uel aduer-
4 sus omnes satis esse. darent modo et consules et
primores patrum operam ut, si minus omnes, aliquos
tamen ex tribunis rei publicae ac senatui conciliarent.
5 Praeceptis Appi moniti patres et uniuersi comiter ac 15
benigne tribunos appellare, et consulares ut cuique
eorum priuatim aliquid iuris aduersus singulos erat,
partim gratia, partim auctoritate obtinuere ut tribuniciae potestatis uires salubres uellent rei publicae
6 esse, quattuorque tribunorum aduersus unum mora- 20
torem publici commodi auxilio dilectum consules
habent.
7   Inde ad Veiens bellum profecti, quo undique ex
Etruria auxilia conuenerant, non tam Veientium
gratia concitata quam quod in spem uentum erat 25
discordia intestina dissolui rem Romanam posse.
8 Principesque in omnium Etruriae populorum con-
ciliis fremebant aeternas opes esse Romanas nisi
inter semet ipsi seditionibus saeuiant; id unum
uenenum, eam labem ciuitatibus opulentis repertam 30
9 ut magna imperia mortalia essent. diu sustentatum
id malum, partim patrum consiliis, partim patientia
plebis, iam ad extrema uenisse. duas ciuitates ex
una factas; suos cuique parti magistratus, suas leges
10 esse. primum in dilectibus saeuire solitos, eosdem in 35
bello tamen paruisse ducibus. qualicumque urbis
statu, manente disciplina militari sisti potuisse; iam
non parendi magistratibus morem in castra quoque

11 Romanum militem sequi. proximo bello in ipsa acie,
in ipso certamine, consensu exercitus traditam ultro 40
uictoriam uictis Aequis, signa deserta, imperatorem
in acie relictum, iniussu in castra reditum. profecto
12 si instetur, suo milite uinci Romam posse. nihil
aliud opus esse quam indici ostendique bellum;
cetera sua sponte fata et deos gesturos. Hae spes 45
Etruscos armauerant, multis in uicem casibus uictos
uictoresque.

*In the campaign, the consuls, uncertain of the temper of the
troops, refuse to engage, in spite of the taunts of the enemy
—a policy which succeeds in goading their men to demand
battle. Finally the men swear to win certain victory for
their consuls, and they give the signal.*

1   **45.** Consules quoque Romani nihil praeterea aliud
quam suas uires, sua arma horrebant; memoria pessimi proximo bello exempli terrebat ne rem commit-
2 terent eo ubi duae simul acies timendae essent. Itaque castris se tenebant, tam ancipiti periculo auersi: 5
diem tempusque forsitan ipsum leniturum iras sani-
3 tatemque animis allaturum. Veiens hostis Etrus-
cique eo magis praepropere agere; lacessere ad
pugnam primo obequitando castris prouocandoque,
postremo ut nihil mouebant, qua consules ipsos, qua 10
4 exercitum increpando: simulationem intestinae discordiae remedium timoris inuentum, et consules magis
non confidere quam non credere suis militibus;
nouum seditionis genus, silentium otiumque inter

armatos. Ad haec in nouitatem generis originisque 15
5 qua falsa, qua uera iacere. Haec cum sub ipso uallo
portisque streperent, haud aegre consules pati; at
imperitae multitudini nunc indignatio, nunc pudor
pectora uersare et ab intestinis auertere malis; nolle
inultos hostes, nolle successum non patribus, non 20
consulibus; externa et domestica odia certare in
6 animis. Tandem superant externa; adeo superbe
insolenterque hostis eludebat. Frequentes in praetorium conueniunt; poscunt pugnam, postulant ut
7 signum detur. Consules uelut deliberabundi capita 25
conferunt, diu conloquuntur. Pugnare cupiebant, sed
retro reuocanda et abdenda cupiditas erat, ut aduer-
sando remorandoque incitato semel militi adderent
8 impetum. Redditur responsum immaturam rem agi;
nondum tempus pugnae esse; castris se tenerent. 30
Edicunt inde ut abstineant pugna: si quis iniussu
9 pugnauerit, ut in hostem animaduersuros. Ita dimissis, quo minus consules uelle credunt, crescit ardor
pugnandi. Accendunt insuper hostes ferocius multo,
ut statuisse non pugnare consules cognitum est: 35
10 quippe impune se insultaturos; non credi militi arma;
rem ad ultimum seditionis erupturam, finemque
uenisse Romano imperio. His freti occursant portis,
ingerunt probra; aegre abstinent quin castra oppug-
11 nent. Enimuero non ultra contumeliam pati Ro- 40
manus posse; totis castris undique ad consules curritur; non iam sensim, ut ante, per centurionum
principes postulant, sed passim omnes clamoribus

agunt. Matura res erat; tergiuersantur tamen.
12 Fabius deinde ad crescentem tumultum iam metu 45
seditionis collega concedente, cum silentium classico
fecisset: ' Ego istos, Cn. Manli, posse uincere scio:
13 uelle ne scirem, ipsi fecerunt. Itaque certum est non
dare signum nisi uictores se redituros ex hac pugna
iurant. Consulem Romanum miles semel in acie 50
fefellit: deos nunquam fallet.' Centurio erat M.
14 Flauoleius, inter primores pugnae flagitator. ' Victor ' inquit, ' M. Fabi, reuertar ex acie '; si fallat,
Iouem patrem Gradiuumque Martem aliosque iratos
inuocat deos. Idem deinceps omnis exercitus in se 55
quisque iurat. Iuratis datur signum; arma capiunt;
15 eunt in pugnam irarum speique pleni. Nunc iubent
Etruscos probra iacere, nunc armati sibi quisque
16 lingua promptum hostem offerri. Omnium illo die,
qua plebis, qua patrum, eximia uirtus fuit; Fabium 60
nomen maxime enituit; multis ciuilibus certaminibus
infensos plebis animos illa pugna sibi reconciliare
statuunt.

*In the fighting, which is long and fierce, the Fabii distinguish
themselves. Quintus Fabius is slain.*

1 **46.** Instruitur acies, nec Veiens hostis Etruscaeque
legiones detractant. Prope certa spes erat non magis
secum pugnaturos quam cum Aequis; maius quoque
aliquod in tam inritatis animis et occasione ancipiti
2 haud desperandum esse facinus. Res aliter longe 5

euenit; nam non alio ante bello infestior Romanus—
adeo hinc contumeliis hostes, hinc consules mora
3 exacerbauerant—proelium iniit.   Vix explicandi
ordinis spatium Etruscis fuit, cum pilis inter primam
trepidationem abiectis temere magis quam emissis, 10
pugna iam in manus, iam ad gladios, ubi Mars est
4 atrocissimus, uenerat.   Inter primores genus Fabium
insigne spectaculo exemploque ciuibus erat.   Ex his
Q. Fabium—tertio hic anno ante consul fuerat—
principem in confertos Veientes euntem ferox uiribus 15
et armorum arte Tuscus, incautum inter multas
uersantem hostium manus, gladio per pectus transfigit; telo extracto praeceps Fabius in uolnus abiit.
5   Sensit utraque acies unius uiri casum, cedebatque
inde Romanus cum M. Fabius consul transiluit iacen- 20
tis corpus obiectaque parma, ' Hoc iurastis ' inquit,
6 ' milites, fugientes uos in castra redituros?   Adeo
ignauissimos hostes magis timetis quam Iouem
Martemque per quos iurastis?   At ego iniuratus aut
uictor reuertar aut prope te hic, Q. Fabi, dimicans 25
cadam.'   Consuli tum Caeso Fabius, prioris anni
consul: ' Verbisne istis, frater, ut pugnent, te im-
7 petraturum credis?   Di impetrabunt per quos iura-
uere; et nos, ut decet proceres, ut Fabio nomine est
dignum, pugnando potius quam adhortando accenda- 30
mus militum animos.'   Sic in primum infestis hastis
prouolant duo Fabii, totamque mouerunt secum
aciem.

The consul Gnaeus Manlius is also slain and the Etruscans are routed. The surviving consul, M. Fabius, refuses to celebrate a triumph.

1 **47.** Proelio ex parte una restituto, nihilo segnius in cornu altero Cn. Manlius consul pugnam ciebat,
2 ubi prope similis fortuna est uersata. Nam ut altero in cornu Q. Fabium, sic in hoc ipsum consulem Manlium iam uelut fusos agentem hostes et impigre milites 5 secuti sunt et, ut ille graui uolnere ictus ex acie cessit,
3 interfectum rati gradum rettulere; cessissentque loco, ni consul alter cum aliquot turmis equitum in eam partem citato equo aduectus, uiuere clamitans collegam, se uictorem fuso altero cornu adesse, rem 10
4 inclinatam sustinuisset. Manlius quoque ad restituendam aciem se ipse coram offert. Duorum consulum cognita ora accendunt militum animos. Simul et uanior iam erat hostium acies, dum abundante multitudine freti, subtracta subsidia mittunt ad cas- 15
5 tra oppugnanda. In quae haud magno certamine impetu facto cum praedae magis quam pugnae memores tererent tempus, triarii Romani qui primam inruptionem sustinere non potuerant, missis ad consules nuntiis quo loco res essent, conglobati ad 20 praetorium redeunt et sua sponte ipsi proelium reno-
6 uant. Et Manlius consul reuectus in castra, ad omnes portas milite opposito hostibus uiam clauserat. Ea desperatio Tuscis rabiem magis quam audaciam accendit. Nam cum incursantes quacumque exitum 25 ostenderet spes uano aliquotiens impetu issent,

globus iuuenum unus in ipsum consulem insignem
7 armis inuadit. Prima excepta a circumstantibus
tela; sustineri deinde uis nequit; consul mortifero
8 uolnere ictus cadit, fusique circa omnes. Tuscis 30
crescit audacia; Romanos terror per tota castra
trepidos agit, et ad extrema uentum foret ni legati
rapto consulis corpore patefecissent una porta hosti-
9 bus uiam. Ea erumpunt; consternatoque agmine
abeuntes in uictorem alterum incidunt consulem; 35
ibi iterum caesi fusique passim.

Victoria egregia parta, tristis tamen duobus tam
10 claris funeribus. Itaque consul decernente senatu
triumphum, si exercitus sine imperatore triumphare
possit, pro eximia eo bello opera facile passurum 40
respondit; se familia funesta Q. Fabi fratris morte,
re publica ex parte orba consule altero amisso
publico priuatoque deformem luctu lauream non
11 accepturum. Omni acto triumpho depositus triumphus clarior fuit; adeo spreta in tempore gloria 45
interdum cumulatior rediit. Funera deinde duo
deinceps collegae fratrisque ducit, idem in utroque
laudator, cum concedendo illis suas laudes ipse maxi-
mam partem earum ferret. Neque immemor eius quod
initio consulatus imbiberat, reconciliandi animos 50
12 plebis, saucios milites curandos diuidit patribus.
Fabiis plurimi dati, nec alibi maiore cura habiti.
Inde populares iam esse Fabii, nec hoc ulla nisi
salubri rei publicae arte.

497 B.C. *The consul K. Fabius' suggestion that public land be distributed among the people is rejected by the senate. Raids of the Aequi on Latin territory. Fighting is continued with the Veientines after their defeat of a Roman force. Fabius and his clan offer to undertake the campaign against Veii.*

1 **48.** Igitur non patrum magis quam plebis studiis K. Fabius cum T. Verginio consul factus neque belli neque dilectus neque ullam aliam priorem curam agere quam ut iam aliqua ex parte inchoata concordiae spe, primo quoque tempore cum patribus coalescerent 5
2 animi plebis. Itaque principio anni censuit priusquam quisquam agrariae legis auctor tribunus exsisteret, occuparent patres ipsi suum munus facere; captiuum agrum plebi quam maxime aequaliter darent; uerum esse habere eos quorum sanguine ac 10
3 sudore partus sit. Aspernati patres sunt; questi quoque quidam nimia gloria luxuriare et euanescere uiuidum quondam illud Caesonis ingenium.
4 Nullae deinde urbanae factiones fuere; uexabantur incursionibus Aequorum Latini. Eo cum exercitu 15 Caeso missus in ipsorum Aequorum agrum depopulandum transit. Aequi se in oppida receperunt murisque se tenebant; eo nulla pugna memorabilis
5 fuit. At a Veiente hoste clades accepta temeritate alterius consulis, actumque de exercitu foret, ni K. 20 Fabius in tempore subsidio uenisset. Ex eo tempore neque pax neque bellum cum Veientibus fuit; res
6 proxime formam latrocinii uenerat. Legionibus

Romanis cedebant in urbem; ubi abductas senserant
legiones, agros incursabant, bellum quiete, quietem 25
bello in uicem eludentes. Ita neque omitti tota res
nec perfici poterat; et alia bella aut praesentia
instabant, ut ab Aequis Volscisque, non diutius quam
recens dolor proximae cladis transiret quiescentibus,
aut mox moturos apparebat Sabinos semper 30
7 infestos Etruriamque omnem. Sed Veiens hostis,
adsiduus magis quam grauis, contumeliis saepius
quam periculo animos agitabat, quod nullo tempore
8 neglegi poterat aut auerti alio sinebat. Tum Fabia
gens senatum adiit. Consul pro gente loquitur: 35
' Adsiduo magis quam magno praesidio, ut scitis,
patres conscripti, bellum Veiens eget. Vos alia bella
curate, Fabios hostes Veientibus date. Auctores
sumus tutam ibi maiestatem Romani nominis fore.
9 Nostrum id nobis uelut familiare bellum priuato 40
sumptu gerere in animo est; res publica et milite illic
10 et pecunia uacet.' Gratiae ingentes actae. Consul e
curia egressus comitante Fabiorum agmine, qui in
uestibulo curiae senatus consultum exspectantes
steterant, domum redit. Iussi armati postero die ad 45
limen consulis adesse; domos inde discedunt.

*306 members of the Fabian clan leave Rome amid the prayers
and blessings of their fellow-citizens. Occupying a fort in
the Cremera, they bring peace and security to the surrounding districts. A Veientine force which had attacked the fort
is defeated by the Roman army.*

1 **49.** Manat tota urbe rumor; Fabios ad caelum
laudibus ferunt: familiam unam subisse ciuitatis
onus; Veiens bellum in priuatam curam, in priuata
2 arma uersum. si sint duae roboris eiusdem in urbe
gentes, deposcant haec Volscos sibi, illa Aequos: 5
populo Romano tranquillam pacem agente omnes
finitimos subigi populos posse. Fabii postera die
3 arma capiunt; quo iussi erant conueniunt. Consul
paludatus egrediens in uestibulo gentem omnem
suam instructo agmine uidet; acceptus in medium 10
signa ferri iubet. Nunquam exercitus neque minor
numero neque clarior fama et admiratione hominum
4 per urbem incessit. Sex et trecenti milites, omnes
patricii, omnes unius gentis, quorum neminem
ducem sperneres, egregius quibuslibet temporibus 15
senatus, ibant, unius familiae uiribus Veienti populo
5 pestem minitantes. Sequebatur turba propria alia
cognatorum sodaliumque, nihil medium, nec spem
nec curam, sed immensa omnia uoluentium animo,
alia publica sollicitudine excitata, fauore et admira- 20
6 tione stupens. Ire fortes, ire felices iubent, inceptis
euentus pares reddere; consulatus inde ac triumphos,
7 omnia praemia ab se, omnes honores sperare. Praetereuntibus Capitolium arcemque et alia templa,
quidquid deorum oculis, quidquid animo occurrit, 25
precantur ut illud agmen faustum atque felix mittant,
8 sospites breui in patriam ad parentes restituant. In
cassum missae preces. Infelici uia, dextro iano portae
Carmentalis, profecti ad Cremeram flumen perueni-

unt.   Is opportunus uisus locus communiendo 30
praesidio.

9 L. Aemilius inde et C. Seruilius consules facti.   Et
donec nihil aliud quam in populationibus res fuit, non
ad praesidium modo tutandum Fabii satis erant, sed
tota regione qua Tuscus ager Romano adiacet, sua 35
tuta omnia, infesta hostium, uagantes per utrumque
10 finem, fecere.   Interuallum deinde haud magnum
populationibus fuit, dum et Veientes accito ex Etruria exercitu praesidium Cremerae oppugnant, et
Romanae legiones ab L. Aemilio consule adductae 40
cominus cum Etruscis dimicant acie;   quamquam
11 uix dirigendi aciem spatium Veientibus fuit;   adeo
inter primam trepidationem, dum post signa ordines
introeunt subsidiaque locant, inuecta subito ab
latere Romana equitum ala non pugnae modo incipi- 45
12 endae sed consistendi ademit locum.   Ita fusi retro
ad saxa Rubra—ibi castra habebant,—pacem supplices petunt.   Cuius impetratae, ab insita animis
leuitate, ante deductum Cremera Romanum praesidium paenituit.   50

477 B.C. *The Fabii, emboldened by their successful raids, are
drawn into an ambush and annihilated.*

1 **50.** Rursus cum Fabiis erat Veienti populo, sine
ullo maioris belli apparatu, certamen;   nec erant
incursiones modo in agros aut subiti impetus in incursantes, sed aliquotiens aequo campo conlatisque
2 signis certatum, gensque una populi Romani saepe 5

ex opulentissima, ut tum res erant, Etrusca ciuitate
3 uictoriam tulit. Id primo acerbum indignumque
Veientibus est uisum; inde consilium ex re natum
insidiis ferocem hostem captandi; gaudere etiam
4 multo successu Fabiis audaciam crescere. Itaque et 10
pecora praedantibus aliquotiens, uelut casu incidissent, obuiam acta, et agrestium fuga uasti relicti agri,
et subsidia armatorum ad arcendas populationes
missa saepius simulato quam uero pauore refugerunt.
5 Iamque Fabii adeo contempserant hostem ut sua 15
inuicta arma neque loco neque tempore ullo creder-
ent sustineri posse. Haec spes prouexit ut ad conspecta procul a Cremera magno campi interuallo
pecora, quamquam rara hostium apparebant arma,
6 decurrerent. Et cum improuidi effuso cursu insidias 20
circa ipsum iter locatas superassent palatique passim
uaga, ut fit pauore iniecto, raperent pecora, subito ex
insidiis consurgitur; et aduersi et undique hostes
7 erant. Primo clamor circumlatus exterruit, dein tela
ab omni parte accidebant; coeuntibusque Etruscis, 25
iam continenti agmine armatorum saepti, quo magis
se hostis inferebat, cogebantur breuiore spatio et ipsi
8 orbem colligere, quae res et paucitatem eorum insignem et multitudinem Etruscorum, multiplicatis in
9 arto ordinibus, faciebat. Tum omissa pugna, quam in 30
omnes partes parem intenderant, in unum locum se
omnes inclinant; eo nisi corporibus armisque rupere
10 cuneo uiam. Duxit uia in editum leniter collem.
Inde primo restitere; mox, ut respirandi superior

locus spatium dedit recipiendique a pauore tanto 35
animum, pepulere etiam subeuntes, uincebatque
auxilio loci paucitas, ni iugo circummissus Veiens in
11 uerticem collis euasisset. Ita superior rursus hostis
factus. Fabii caesi ad unum omnes praesidiumque
expugnatum. Trecentos sex perisse satis conuenit, 40
unum prope puberem aetate relictum, stirpem genti
Fabiae dubiisque rebus populi Romani saepe domi
bellique uel maximum futurum auxilium.

477–476 B.C. *An Etruscan force in the Janiculum is ambushed
and severely defeated. On their withdrawal to their fort,
the rashness of the Roman consul Seruilius leads to a
Roman victory.*

1   **51.** Cum haec accepta clades est, iam C. Horatius
et T. Menenius consules erant. Menenius aduersus
2 Tuscos uictoria elatos confestim missus. Tum
quoque male pugnatum est, et Ianiculum hostes occu-
pauere; obsessaque urbs foret, super bellum annona 5
premente—transierant enim Etrusci Tiberim—, ni
Horatius consul ex Volscis esset reuocatus. Adeoque id bellum ipsis institit moenibus, ut primo
pugnatum ad Spei sit aequo Marte, iterum ad portam
3 Collinam. Ibi quamquam paruo momento superior 10
Romana res fuit, meliorem tamen militem, recepto
pristino animo, in futura proelia id certamen fecit.
4   A. Verginius et Sp. Seruilius consules fiunt. Post
acceptam proxima pugna cladem Veientes abstinuere
acie; populationes erant, et uelut ab arce Ianiculo 15

passim in Romanum agrum impetus dabant; non
5 usquam pecora tuta, non agrestes erant. Capti
deinde eadem arte sunt qua ceperant Fabios.
Secuti dedita opera passim ad inlecebras propulsa
pecora praecipitauere in insidias; quo plures erant, 20
6 maior caedes fuit. Ex hac clade atrox ira maioris
cladis causa atque initium fuit.   Traiecto enim
nocte Tiberi, castra Seruili consulis adorti sunt
oppugnare. Inde fusi magna caede in Ianiculum se
7 aegre recepere.   Confestim consul et ipse transit 25
Tiberim, castra sub Ianiculo communit. Postero die
luce orta nonnihil et hesterna felicitate pugnae ferox,
magis tamen quod inopia frumenti quamuis in prae-
8 cipitia, dum celeriora essent, agebat consilia, temere
aduerso Ianiculo ad castra hostium aciem erexit, 30
foediusque inde pulsus quam pridie pepulerat, inter-
9 uentu collegae ipse exercitusque est seruatus. Inter
duas acies Etrusci, cum in uicem his atque illis terga
darent, occidione occisi. Ita oppressum temeritate
felici Veiens bellum.   35

476–475 B.C. *Peace abroad and an easier corn-market at home*
     encourage party-strife. There is another agrarian pro-
     posal and the indictment of another patrician, Titus
     Menenius.

1   **52.** Vrbi cum pace laxior etiam annona rediit, et
aduecto ex Campania frumento, et postquam timor
sibi cuique futurae inopiae abiit, eo quod abditum
2 fuerat prolato. Ex copia deinde otioque lasciuire

rursus animi et pristina mala, postquam foris deerant, 5
domi quaerere. Tribuni plebem agitare suo ueneno,
agraria lege; in resistentes incitare patres, nec in
3 uniuersos modo sed in singulos. Q. Considius et
T. Genucius, auctores agrariae legis, T. Menenio
diem dicunt. Inuidiae erat amissum Cremerae prae- 10
sidium, cum haud procul inde statiua consul habuis-
4 set; ea oppressit, cum et patres haud minus quam pro
Coriolano adnisi essent et patris Agrippae fauor
5 hauddum exoleuisset. In multa temperarunt tribuni;
cum capitis anquisissent, duorum milium aeris dam- 15
nato multam dixerunt. Ea in caput uertit; negant
tulisse ignominiam aegritudinemque; inde morbo
absumptum.
6   Alius deinde reus, Sp. Seruilius, ut consulatu abiit,
C. Nautio et P. Valerio consulibus, initio statim anni 20
ab L. Caedicio et T. Statio tribunis die dicta, non ut
Menenius, precibus suis aut patrum sed cum multa
fiducia innocentiae gratiaeque tribunicios impetus
7 tulit. Et huic proelium cum Tuscis ad Ianiculum erat
crimini. Sed feruidi animi uir ut in publico periculo 25
ante, sic tum in suo, non tribunos modo sed plebem
oratione feroci refutando exprobrandoque T. Meneni
damnationem mortemque, cuius patris munere restituta quondam plebs eos ipsos quibus tum saeuiret
magistratus, eas leges haberet, periculum audacia 30
8 discussit. Iuuit et Verginius collega testis productus,
participando laudes; magis tamen Menenianum—
adeo mutauerant animum—profuit iudicium.

*The Romans are successful in campaigns with the Veientines
and the Sabines. Invasion by Volscian and Aequian
forces is repelled by the Latins and Hernicans without
Roman aid.*

1   **53.** Certamina domi finita: Veiens bellum exortum, quibus Sabini arma coniunxerant. P. Valerius
consul accitis Latinorum Hernicorumque auxiliis
cum exercitu Veios missus castra Sabina, quae pro
moenibus sociorum locata erant, confestim adgredi-   5
tur; tantamque trepidationem iniecit ut dum dis-
persi alii alia manipulatim excurrunt ad arcendam
hostium uim, ea porta cui signa primum intulerat
2 caperetur.   Intra uallum deinde caedes magis quam
proelium esse.   Tumultus e castris et in urbem 10
penetrat; tamquam Veiis captis, ita pauidi Veientes
ad arma currunt.   Pars Sabinis eunt subsidio, pars
Romanos toto impetu intentos in castra adoriuntur.
3 Paulisper auersi turbatique sunt; deinde et ipsi utroque uersis signis resistunt, et eques ab consule immis- 15
sus Tuscos fundit fugatque, eademque hora duo
exercitus, duae potentissimae et maxime finitimae
4 gentes superatae sunt.   Dum haec ad Veios geruntur,
Volsci Aequique in Latino agro posuerant castra
populatique fines erant.   Eos per se ipsi Latini 20
adsumptis Hernicis, sine Romano aut duce aut
5 auxilio castris exuerunt; ingenti praeda praeter
suas reciperatas res potiti sunt.   Missus tamen
ab Roma consul in Volscos C. Nautius; mos,
credo, non placebat, sine Romano duce exercituque 25

socios propriis uiribus consiliisque bella gerere.
6 Nullum genus calamitatis contumeliaeque non editum
in Volscos est, nec tamen perpelli potuere ut acie
dimicarent.

473 B.C. *A truce for 40 years with Veii is followed by party-*
strife and another land-law. The retiring consuls, im-
peached by the tribune Gnaeus Genucius, canvass
support and vividly picture the perils of holding office.
Excitement fades on the sudden death of the prosecuting
tribune.

1 **54.** L. Furius inde et C. Manlius consules. Manlio
Veientes prouincia euenit; non tamen bellatum;
indutiae in annos quadraginta petentibus datae fru-
2 mento stipendioque imperato. Paci externae confestim continuatur discordia domi. Agrariae legis 5
tribuniciis stimulis plebs furebat. Consules, nihil
Meneni damnatione, nihil periculo deterriti Seruili
summa ui resistunt. Abeuntes magistratu Cn. Genucius tribunus plebis arripuit.
3 L. Aemilius et Opiter Verginius consulatum ineunt; 10
Vopiscum Iulium pro Verginio in quibusdam annali-
bus consulem inuenio. Hoc anno, quoscumque consules
habuit, rei ad populum Furius et Manlius circumeunt
sordidati non plebem magis quam iuniores patrum.
4 Suadent monent honoribus et administratione rei 15
publicae abstineant; consulares uero fasces, praetex-
tam, curulemque sellam nihil aliud quam pompam
funeris putent; claris insignibus uelut infulis uelatos

5 ad mortem destinari. quod si consulatus tanta dulcedo sit, iam nunc ita in animum inducant consulatum 20
captum et oppressum ab tribunicia potestate esse;
consuli, uelut apparitori tribunicio, omnia ad nutum
6 imperiumque tribuni agenda esse; si se commouerit,
si respexerit patres, si aliud quam plebem esse in re
publica crediderit, exsilium Cn. Marci, Meneni 25
damnationem et mortem sibi proponat ante oculos.
7 His accensi uocibus patres consilia inde non publica
sed in priuato seductaque a plurium conscientia habuere, ubi cum id modo constaret, iure an iniuria,
eripiendos esse reos, atrocissima quaeque maxime 30
placebat sententia, nec auctor quamuis audaci facin-
8 ori deerat. Igitur iudicii die, cum plebs in foro
erecta exspectatione staret, mirari primo quod non
descenderet tribunus; dein cum iam mora suspectior
fieret, deterritum a primoribus credere et desertam 35
9 ac proditam causam publicam queri; tandem qui
obuersati uestibulo tribuni fuerant nuntiant domi
mortuum esse inuentum. Quod ubi in totam contionem pertulit rumor, sicut acies funditur duce
occiso, ita dilapsi passim alii alio. Praecipuus pauor 40
tribunos inuaserat, quam nihil auxilii sacratae leges
10 haberent morte collegae monitos. Nec patres satis
moderate ferre laetitiam, adeoque neminem noxiae
paenitebat, ut etiam insontes fecisse uideri uellent,
palamque ferretur malo domandam tribuniciam 45
potestatem.

473 B.C.   *The plebeians are depressed by the loss of their tribune*
and the successful holding of a levy, but are aroused by the
refusal of a Volero Publilius to enlist and his successful
resistance to arrest. In the uproar the lictors are man-
handled and the consul driven from the Forum. An open
clash between the two parties is only just averted.

1 **55.** Sub hac pessimi exempli uictoria dilectus
edicitur, pauentibusque tribunis sine intercessione
2 ulla consules rem peragunt. Tum uero irasci plebs
tribunorum magis silentio quam consulum imperio,
et dicere actum esse de libertate sua; rursus ad an- 5
tiqua reditum; cum Genucio una mortuam ac
sepultam tribuniciam potestatem. aliud agendum
3 ac cogitandum quo modo resistatur patribus; id
autem unum consilium esse ut se ipsa plebs, quando
aliud nihil auxilii habeat, defendat. quattuor et 10
uiginti lictores apparere consulibus et eos ipsos plebis
homines; nihil contemptius neque infirmius, si sint
qui contemnant; sibi quemque ea magna atque
4 horrenda facere. His uocibus alii alios cum incitas-
sent, ad Voleronem Publilium de plebe hominem 15
quia, quod ordines duxisset, negaret se militem fieri
debere, lictor missus est a consulibus. Volero appellat
5 tribunos. Cum auxilio nemo esset, consules spoliari
hominem et uirgas expediri iubent. ' Prouoco '
inquit, ' ad populum ' Volero, ' quoniam tribuni 20
ciuem Romanum in conspectu suo uirgis caedi malunt
quam ipsi in lecto suo a uobis trucidari.' Quo ferocius
clamitabat, eo infestius circumscindere et spoliare

6 lictor. Tum Volero et praeualens ipse et adiuuantibus aduocatis repulso lictore, ubi indignantium pro 25
se acerrimus erat clamor, eo se in turbam confertis-
7 simam recipit clamitans: ' Prouoco et fidem plebis
imploro. Adeste ciues, adeste, commilitones; nihil
est quod exspectetis tribunos quibus ipsis uestro
8 auxilio opus est.' Concitati homines ueluti ad proe- 30
lium se expediunt, apparebatque omne discrimen
adesse; nihil cuiquam sanctum, non publici fore, non
9 priuati iuris. Huic tantae tempestati cum se consules
obtulissent, facile experti sunt parum tutam maiestatem sine uiribus esse. Violatis lictoribus, fascibus 35
fractis, e foro in curiam conpelluntur, incerti quatenus
10 Volero exerceret uictoriam. Conticescente deinde
tumultu cum in senatum uocari iussissent, queruntur
11 iniurias suas, uim plebis, Voleronis audaciam. Multis
ferociter dictis sententiis, uicere seniores quibus ira 40
patrum aduersus temeritatem plebis certari non
placuit.

472–471 B.C. *Volero, now a tribune, proposes that the tribunes*
be elected at a plebeian assembly by tribes. The senate
fail to get it vetoed by his fellow tribunes. Discussions of
the new law continue into the new year while both sides
muster their forces, the senate being reinforced by Appius
Claudius who is bitterly attacked by Volero's colleague
Laetorius. Open fighting is prevented by the other consul,
Quinctius.

1   **56.** Voleronem amplexa fauore plebs proximis

comitiis tribunum plebi creat in eum annum qui
2 L. Pinarium P. Furium consules habuit. Contraque omnium opinionem, qui eum uexandis prioris
anni consulibus permissurum tribunatum credebant, 5
post publicam causam priuato dolore habito, ne
uerbo quidem uiolatis consulibus, rogationem tulit
ad populum ut plebeii magistratus tributis comitiis
3 fierent. Haud parua res sub titulo prima specie
minime atroci ferebatur, sed quae patriciis omnem 10
potestatem per clientium suffragia creandi quos
4 uellent tribunos auferret. Huic actioni gratissimae
plebi cum summa ui resisterent patres, nec quae una
uis ad resistendum erat, ut intercederet aliquis ex
collegio, auctoritate aut consulum aut principum 15
adduci posset, res tamen suo ipsa molimine grauis
5 certaminibus in annum extrahitur. Plebs Voleronem
tribunum reficit: patres, ad ultimum dimicationis
rati rem uenturam, Ap. Claudium Appi filium, iam
inde a paternis certaminibus inuisum infestumque 20
plebi, consulem faciunt. Collega ei T. Quinctius
datur.
6　Principio statim anni nihil prius quam de lege
agebatur. Sed ut inuentor legis Volero, sic Laetorius,
collega eius, auctor cum recentior tum acrior erat. 25
7 Ferocem faciebat belli gloria ingens, quod aetatis eius
haud quisquam manu promptior erat. Is, cum Volero
nihil praeterquam de lege loqueretur, insectatione
abstinens consulum, ipse accusationem Appi
familiaeque superbissimae ac crudelissimae in plebem 30

8 Romanam exorsus, cum a patribus non consulem, sed
carnificem ad uexandam et lacerandam plebem creatum esse contenderet, rudis in militari homine lingua
9 non suppetebat libertati animoque. Itaque deficiente
oratione, 'Quando quidem non facile loquor' inquit, 35
'Quirites, quam quod locutus sum praesto, crastino
die adeste; ego hic aut in conspectu uestro moriar aut
10 perferam legem.' Occupant tribuni templum postero
die; consules nobilitasque ad impediendam legem in
contione consistunt. Submoueri Laetorius iubet, 40
11 praeterquam qui suffragium ineant. Adulescentes
nobiles stabant nihil cedentes uiatori. Tum ex his
prendi quosdam Laetorius iubet. Consul Appius
negare ius esse tribuno in quemquam nisi in plebeium;
12 non enim populi sed plebis eum magistratum esse; nec 45
illam ipsam submouere pro imperio posse more maior-
um, quia ita dicatur: 'Si uobis uidetur, discedite,
Quirites'. Facile contemptim de iure disserendo
13 perturbare Laetorium poterat. Ardens igitur ira
tribunus uiatorem mittit ad consulem, consul lictorem 50
ad tribunum, priuatum esse clamitans, sine imperio,
14 sine magistratu; uiolatusque esset tribunus, ni et
contio omnis atrox coorta pro tribuno in consulem
esset, et concursus hominum in forum ex tota urbe
concitatae multitudinis fieret. Sustinebat tamen 55
15 Appius pertinacia tantam tempestatem, certatum-
que haud incruento proelio foret, ni Quinctius, consul
alter, consularibus negotio dato ut collegam ui, si
aliter non possent, de foro abducerent, ipse nunc

plebem saeuientem precibus lenisset, nunc orasset 60
tribunos ut concilium dimitterent; darent irae
16 spatium; non uim suam illis tempus adempturum,
sed consilium uiribus additurum; et patres in populi
et consulem in patrum fore potestate.

471 B.C. *The senators support the conciliatory action of
Quinctius and try to restrain Appius who rails at them for
their cowardice. The proposal is passed.*

1   **57.** Aegre sedata ab Quinctio plebs, multo aegrius
consul alter a patribus. Dimisso tandem concilio
2 plebis senatum consules habent. Vbi cum timor
atque ira in uicem sententias uariassent, quo magis
spatio interposito ab impetu ad consultandum 5
auocabantur, eo plus abhorrebant a certatione animi,
adeo ut Quinctio gratias agerent quod eius opera
3 mitigata discordia esset. Ab Appio petitur ut tantam
consularem maiestatem esse uellet quanta esse in
concordi ciuitate posset; dum tribuni et consules ad 10
se quisque omnia trahant, nihil relictum esse uirium
in medio; distractam laceratamque rem publicam;
magis quorum in manu sit quam ut incolumis sit
4 quaeri. Appius contra testari deos atque homines
rem publicam prodi per metum ac deseri; non con- 15
sulem senatui sed senatum consuli deesse; grauiores
accipi leges quam in Sacro monte acceptae sint. Victus tamen patrum consensu quieuit; lex silentio
perfertur.

471 B.C. *War with the Volsci and the Aequi. In the campaign against the former, Appius tries to exercise a harsh discipline in his army, but fails, owing to their united refusal to co-operate.*

1 **58.** Tum primum tributis comitiis creati tribuni sunt. Numero etiam additos tres, perinde ac duo 2 antea fuerint, Piso auctor est. Nominat quoque tribunos, Cn. Siccium, L. Numitorium, M. Duillium, Sp. Icilium, L. Maecilium. 5
3 Volscum Aequicumque inter seditionem Romanam est bellum coortum. Vastauerant agros ut si qua secessio plebis fieret ad se receptum haberet; com- 4 positis deinde rebus castra retro mouere. Ap. Claudius in Volscos missus, Quinctio Aequi prouincia 10 euenit. Eadem in militia saeuitia Appi quae domi esse, liberior, quod sine tribuniciis uinculis erat. 5 Odisse plebem plus quam paterno odio: se uictum ab ea; se unico consule electo aduersus tribuniciam potestatem perlatam legem esse, quam minore con- 15 atu, nequaquam tanta patrum spe, priores impedie- 6 rint consules. Haec ira indignatioque ferocem animum ad uexandum saeuo imperio exercitum stimulabat. Nec ulla ui domari poterat; tantum certa- 7 men animis imbiberant. Segniter, otiose, negle- 20 genter, contumaciter omnia agere; nec pudor nec metus coercebat. Si citius agi uellet agmen, tardius sedulo incedere; si adhortator operis adesset, omnes 8 sua sponte motam remittere industriam; praesenti uoltus demittere, tacite praetereuntem exsecrari, ut 25

inuictus ille odio plebeio animus interdum moueretur.
9 Omni nequiquam acerbitate prompta, nihil iam cum
militibus agere; a centurionibus corruptum exercitum dicere; tribunos plebei cauillans interdum et
Volerones uocare.   30

As part of their disobedience campaign, the Roman forces
suffer every humiliation at the hands of the enemy except
the capture of their camp. Appius, anxious for a head-on
clash, is restrained by his fellow-officers. When a Roman
withdrawal from enemy territory becomes a rout, Appius
seizes his chance to execute a terrible punishment.

1   **59.** Nihil eorum Volsci nesciebant, instabantque
eo magis, sperantes idem certamen animorum aduersus Appium habiturum exercitum Romanum quod
2 aduersus Fabium consulem habuisset. Ceterum multo Appio quam Fabio uiolentior fuit; non enim uin- 5
cere tantum noluit, ut Fabianus exercitus, sed uinci
uoluit. Productus in aciem turpi fuga petit castra,
nec ante restitit quam signa inferentem Volscum
munimentis uidit foedamque extremi agminis cae-
3 dem. Tum expressa uis ad pugnandum, ut uictor 10
iam a uallo submoueretur hostis, satis tamen appareret capi tantum castra militem Romanum
noluisse, alioqui gaudere sua clade atque ignominia.
4 Quibus nihil infractus ferox Appi animus cum insuper
saeuire uellet contionemque aduocaret, concurrunt 15
ad eum legati tribunique, monentes ne utique experiri
uellet imperium, cuius uis omnis in consensu oboe-

5 dientium esset; negare uolgo milites se ad contionem
ituros passimque exaudiri uoces postulantium ut
castra ex Volsco agro moueantur; hostem uictorem 20
paulo ante prope in portis ac uallo fuisse, ingentisque
mali non suspicionem modo sed apertam speciem
6 obuersari ante oculos. Victus tandem, quando
quidem nihil praeter tempus noxae lucrarentur,
remissa contione iter in insequentem diem pronun- 25
tiari cum iussisset, prima luce classico signum pro-
7 fectionis dedit. Cum maxime agmen e castris ex-
plicaretur, Volsci, ut eodem signo excitati, nouissimos adoriuntur. A quibus perlatus ad primos tumultus eo pauore signaque et ordines turbauit ut neque 30
8 imperia exaudiri neque instrui acies posset. Nemo
ullius nisi fugae memor. Ita effuso agmine per stra-
gem corporum armorumque euasere ut prius hostis
9 desisteret sequi quam Romanus fugere. Tandem
conlectis ex dissipato cursu militibus consul, cum 35
reuocando nequiquam suos persecutus esset, in pacato
agro castra posuit; aduocataque contione inuectus
haud falso in proditorem exercitum militaris dis-
10 ciplinae, desertorem signorum, ubi signa, ubi arma
essent singulos rogitans, inermes milites, signo amisso 40
11 signiferos, ad hoc centuriones duplicariosque qui
reliquerant ordines, uirgis caesos securi percussit:
cetera multitudo sorte decimus quisque ad supplicium
lecti.

*Quinctius, on the other hand, has good relations with his men
in his campaign against the Aequi, in which, as a result,
he collects a vast amount of booty.*

1   **60.** Contra ea in Aequis inter consulem ac milites
comitate ac beneficiis certatum est. Et natura
Quinctius erat lenior, et saeuitia infelix collegae quo
2 is magis gauderet ingenio suo effecerat. Huic tantae
concordiae ducis exercitusque non ausi offerre se Aequi, 5
uagari populabundum hostem per agros passi; nec
ullo ante bello latius inde acta est praeda. Ea omnis
3 militi data est. Addebantur et laudes, quibus haud
minus quam praemio gaudent militum animi. Cum
duci, tum propter ducem patribus quoque placatior 10
exercitus rediit, sibi parentem, alteri exercitui
dominum datum ab senatu memorans.
4   Varia fortuna belli, atroci discordia domi forisque
annum exactum insignem maxime comitia tributa
efficiunt, res maior uictoria suscepti certaminis 15
5 quam usu. Plus enim dignitatis comitiis ipsis de-
tractum est patres ex concilio submouendo, quam
uirium aut plebi additum est aut demptum patribus.

470 B.C. *In a dispute about a land-bill, Appius Claudius is
indicted, but shows such equanimity that the trial is allowed
to lapse. His sickness is followed by his death and funeral
at which his qualities are praised as much as his pride
and arrogance had previously been hated.*

1   **61.** Turbulentior inde annus excepit L. Valerio
T. Aemilio consulibus, cum propter certamina

ordinum de lege agraria tum propter iudicium Ap.
2 Claudi, cui acerrimo aduersario legis causamque pos-
sessorum publici agri tamquam tertio consuli sus- 5
tinenti M. Duillius et Cn. Siccius diem dixere.
3 Nunquam ante tam inuisus plebi reus ad iudicium
uocatus populi est, plenus suarum, plenus pater-
4 narum irarum. Patres quoque non temere pro ullo
aeque adnisi sunt: propugnatorem senatus maies- 10
tatisque uindicem suae, ad omnes tribunicios plebeios-
que oppositum tumultus, modum dumtaxat in cer-
5 tamine egressum, iratae obici plebi. Vnus e patribus
ipse Ap. Claudius et tribunos et plebem et suum
iudicium pro nihilo habebat. Illum non minae plebis, 15
non senatus preces perpellere unquam potuere, non
modo ut uestem mutaret aut supplex prensaret
homines, sed ne ut ex consueta quidem asperitate
orationis, cum ad populum agenda causa esset, ali-
6 quid leniret atque submitteret. Idem habitus oris, 20
eadem contumacia in uoltu, idem in oratione spiritus
erat, adeo ut magna pars plebis Appium non minus
7 reum timeret quam consulem timuerat. Semel
causam dixit, quo semper agere omnia solitus erat,
accusatorio spiritu, adeoque constantia sua et tri- 25
bunos obstupefecit et plebem ut diem ipsi sua uolun-
8 tate prodicerent, trahi deinde rem sinerent. Haud
ita multum interim temporis fuit; ante tamen quam
9 prodicta dies ueniret, morbo moritur. Cuius laudationem cum tribunus plebis impedire conaretur, plebs 30
fraudari sollemni honore supremum diem tanti uiri

noluit, et laudationem tam aequis auribus mortui
audiuit quam uiui accusationem audierat et exsequias
frequens celebrauit.

*In campaigns against the Aequi and Sabini, there is a remark-
able change in the weather.*

1 **62.** Eodem anno Valerius consul cum exercitu in
Aequos profectus, cum hostem ad proelium elicere
non posset, castra oppugnare est adortus. Prohibuit
foeda tempestas cum grandine ac tonitribus caelo
2 deiecta. Admirationem deinde auxit signo receptui 5
dato adeo tranquilla serenitas reddita ut uelut numine
aliquo defensa castra oppugnare iterum religio fuerit.
3 Omnis ira belli ad populationem agri uertit. Alter
consul Aemilius in Sabinis bellum gessit. Et ibi, quia
hostis moenibus se tenebat, uastati agri sunt. 10
4 Incendiis deinde non uillarum modo sed etiam
uicorum quibus frequenter habitabatur Sabini exciti
cum praedatoribus occurrissent, ancipiti proelio
digressi postero die rettulere castra in tutiora loca.
5 Id satis consuli uisum cur pro uicto relinqueret hos- 15
tem, integro inde decedens bello.

*469 B.C. Further friction about the land-law is interrupted by
the news that the Volsci are on the march. Successes are
gained against them and the Sabini who make a raid upon
Rome.*

1 **63.** Inter haec bella manente discordia domi,
consules T. Numicius Priscus A. Verginius facti.

2 Non ultra uidebatur latura plebes dilationem agrariae
legis, ultimaque uis parabatur, cum Volscos adesse
fumo ex incendiis uillarum fugaque agrestium cog- 5
nitum est. Ea res maturam iam seditionem ac
3 prope erumpentem repressit. Consules coacti extemplo ab senatu ad bellum educta ex urbe iuuentute
4 tranquilliorem ceteram plebem fecerunt. Et hostes
quidem nihil aliud quam perfusis uano timore Ro- 10
5 manis citato agmine abeunt: Numicius Antium
aduersus Volscos, Verginius contra Aequos profectus.
Ibi ex insidiis prope magna accepta clade uirtus
militum rem prolapsam neglegentia consulis restituit.
6 Melius in Volscis imperatum est; fusi primo proelio 15
hostes fugaque in urbem Antium, ut tum res erant
opulentissimam, acti. Quam consul oppugnare non
ausus Caenonem, aliud oppidum nequaquam tam
7 opulentum, ab Antiatibus cepit. Dum Aequi Volsci-
que Romanos exercitus tenent, Sabini usque ad por- 20
tas urbis populantes incessere. Deinde ipsi paucis
post diebus ab duobus exercitibus, utroque per iram
consule ingresso in fines, plus cladium quam intulerant
acceperunt.

469–468 B.C. *The year follows the usual pattern: political*
dissension at Rome, war abroad, and then peace. More
fighting with the Sabini, and the Volsci, which results in
heavy losses on both sides. Quinctius the consul keeps the
Volsci guessing.

1   **64.** Extremo anno pacis aliquid fuit, sed, ut semper

alias, sollicitae certamine patrum et plebis.
2 Irata plebs interesse consularibus comitiis noluit;
per patres clientesque patrum consules creati T.
Quinctius Q. Seruilius. Similem annum priori 5
habent, seditiosa initia, bello deinde externo
3 tranquilla. Sabini Crustuminos campos citato agmine transgressi cum caedes et incendia circum
Anienem flumen fecissent, a porta prope Collina
moenibusque pulsi ingentes tamen praedas hominum 10
4 pecorumque egere. Quos Seruilius consul infesto
exercitu insecutus ipsum quidem agmen adipisci
aequis locis non potuit, populationem adeo effuse
fecit, ut nihil bello intactum relinquerent multiplici-
que capta praeda rediret. 15
5   Et in Volscis res publica egregie gesta cum ducis
tum militum opera. Primum aequo campo signis
conlatis pugnatum, ingenti caede utrimque, plurimo
6 sanguine; et Romani, quia paucitas damno sentiendo
propior erat, gradum rettulissent, ni salubri mendacio 20
consul fugere hostes ab cornu altero clamitans con-
citasset aciem. Impetu facto dum se putant uincere
7 uicere. Consul metuens ne nimis instando renouaret
8 certamen, signum receptui dedit. Intercessere pauci
dies, uelut tacitis indutiis utrimque quiete sumpta, 25
per quos ingens uis hominum ex omnibus Volscis
Aequisque populis in castra uenit, haud dubitans si
9 senserint Romanos nocte abituros. Itaque tertia
10 fere uigilia ad castra oppugnanda ueniunt. Quinctius
sedato tumultu quem terror subitus exciuerat, cum 30

manere in tentoriis quietum militem iussisset, Hernicorum cohortem in stationem educit, cornicines tubicinesque in equos impositos canere ante uallum
11 iubet sollicitumque hostem ad lucem tenere. Reliquum noctis adeo tranquilla omnia in castris fuere ut 35 somni quoque Romanis copia esset. Volscos species armatorum peditum, quos et plures esse et Romanos putabant, fremitus hinnitusque equorum, qui et insueto sedente equite et insuper aures agitante sonitu saeuiebant, intentos uelut ad impetum hostium 40 tenuit.

The Romans defeat the Volsci and capture their camp after a spirited charge uphill.

1 **65.** Vbi inluxit, Romanus integer satiatusque somno productus in aciem fessum stando et uigiliis
2 Volscum primo impetu perculit; quamquam cessere magis quam pulsi hostes sunt, quia ab tergo erant cliui in quos post principia integris ordinibus tutus 5 receptus fuit. Consul ubi ad iniquum locum uentum est, sistit aciem. Miles aegre teneri, clamare et
3 poscere ut perculsis instare liceat. Ferocius agunt equites; circumfusi duci uociferantur se ante signa ituros. Dum cunctatur consul uirtute militum fretus, 10 loco parum fidens, conclamant se ituros clamoremque res est secuta. Fixis in terram pilis quo leuiores
4 ardua euaderent, cursu subeunt. Volscus effusis ad primum impetum missilibus telis, saxa obiacentia

pedibus ingerit in subeuntes, turbatosque ictibus 15
crebris urget ex superiore loco. Sic prope oneratum
est sinistrum Romanis cornu, ni referentibus iam
gradum consul increpando simul temeritatem, simul
5 ignauiam, pudore metum excussisset. Restitere
primo obstinatis animis; deinde ut obtinentes locum 20
uim pro ui referebant, audent ultro gradum inferre
et clamore renouato commouent aciem; tum rursus
impetu capto enituntur atque exsuperant iniquitatem
6 loci. Iam prope erat ut ui summum cliui iugum
euadarent cum terga hostes dedere, effusoque cursu 25
paene agmine uno fugientes sequentesque castris
incidere. In eo pauore castra capiuntur: qui Vol-
7 scorum effugere potuerunt, Antium petunt. Antium
et Romanus exercitus ductus. Paucos circumsessum
dies deditur, nulla oppugnantium noua ui, sed quod 30
iam inde ab infelici pugna castrisque amissis ceci-
derant animi.

NOTES

Chapter i

Line 1. **iam hinc,** *lit.,* 'now from here' = 'henceforth', 'from this point on ', is translated with **peragam,** the verb on which all the previous words depend. The order of the Latin may be almost retained, if we take first the accusatives **res . . . gestas** on which **liberi populi Romani** depend, **annuos magistratus,** etc. e.g. ' the achievements in peace and war of a free Rome, their annual magistracies . . . I shall henceforth deal with '.

ll. 2–3. **imperia . . . hominum,** ' and the authority of law superior to (that) of men '.

At this date Rome was by no means a democracy, as political power belonged only to the patrician families. But the expulsion of the kings was the first step, and the election of two *annual* consuls who took over the functions of the king the next one. See the introduction p. xvi.

l. 3. **Quae,** co-ordinating relative = ' this '. **proximi regis,** i.e. Tarquinius Superbus (' the Proud '), 535–510 B.C. **quae . . . fecerat,** *lit.,* ' the tyranny of the last king had brought it about that this liberty should be the more acceptable '.

l. 5. **regnarunt.** Verb forms containing the letter **u** often drop that and the following vowel.

ll. 5–7. **ut . . . numerentur.** Begin with this order: **ut haud immerito omnes numerentur deinceps conditores** (' [as] successive founders ') **partium certe** (' at least ') **urbis, quas ipsi addiderunt nouas sedes** (' [as] new homes ') **multitudinis auctae ab se.**

l. 8. **neque ambigitur quin,** ' and there is no doubt that '.

l. 9. **superbo . . . rege,** ' by driving out the haughty king '.

ll. 9–10. **pessimo . . . facturus fuerit,** ' would have acted with the greatest harm to his country '. Note that the future participle and the appropriate part of the auxiliary **sum** is the regular way of rendering in a subordinate clause a verb which would also be subjunctive in a main clause.

l. 10. **cupidine,** 'through a desire for'. **libertatis immaturae;** objective genitive depends upon **cupidine.**

l. 11. **priorum regum alicui** ' from any of the earlier kings '. **alicui,** dative of the person interested,[1] the case found after many compound verbs.

ll. 11–12. **Quid enim futurum fuit,** ' for what was likely to happen ', is effectively used instead of **quid fuisset,** ' what would have happened '.

ll. 12–19. **si illa** .... Break this long sentence up by translating **adepta** = adepta esset, ' had obtained ', and inserting ' and ' before **soluta regio metu,** ' freed from the fear of their kings'. **regio metu** = metu regum, the latter being objective genitive.

coepta esset = coepisset ' had begun '. When this verb has a *passive* infinitive dependent upon it, as here **agitari,** it is often put in the passive too. **serere certamina:** *sc.* ' (had begun) to engage in conflicts '.

priusquam . . . consociasset, ' before the pledges of wives and children and love of the soil itself to which men grow accustomed with the lapse of time had united their feelings '. **adsuescitur** is impersonal passive.

consociasset agrees with the nearest subject and illustrates the note of l. 5 above.

ll. 19–20. **dissipatae . . . forent,** ' the state not yet matured (i.e. before it had matured) would have broken up through dissension.'

ll. 20–22. **quas . . . possent,** '(but) the mild control of authority favoured it (**quas**) and by nurturing (it) brought it to-such-a-point (**eo**) that it could produce the good fruit of liberty when-its-powers-were-ripened (**maturis iam viribus,** abl. absol.).

ll. 23–25. **Libertatis . . . numeres. Libertatis originem** is the object of **numeres** (potential subj.) with which you should begin: ' you may count the beginning of liberty '. **inde magis quia,** ' rather from-the-fact (**inde**) that '. **annuum** is predicative.

[1] This includes the dat. of advantage and disadvantage (so-called).

deminutum sit, the subj. is used because the reason is a false one; *lit.,* ' anything was diminished ' =' there was any diminution '.

ll. 25–26. **omnia . . . insignia,** i.e. ' of the kings '. See the introductio⹁ p. xvii.

ll. 26–27. ꜣ . . . **ne,** '(but) only that (one thing) was provided against lest '. Note: (i) asyndeton, cf. note on Chap 12. l. 6, (ii) the prohibition is implied in the reason given for it.

ll. 28–29. **Brutus prior habuit,** the regular Latin for 'Brutus was the first to have . **collega** = T. Tarquinius Collatinus.

ll. 29–30. **qui . . . fuit,** *lit.,* ' he had not been a fiercer champion of liberty as he was later a guardian '. =' he was later as fierce in guarding liberty as he had been in championing it '.

l. 30. **Omnium primum,** ' first of all '.

l. 31. **auidum . . . populum,** ' (while the) people (were) eager for their newly-won liberty '; the phrase is object of **adegit.**

l. 33. **(eos) passuros (esse),** ' that they would allow '.

l. 34. **quo** replaces **ut** in a purpose clause containing a comparative. **plus uirium** is the object of **faceret.**

l. 34. **frequentia ordinis,** ' by (increasing) the numbers of the order '.

l. 35. **patrum** ' of the senators '.

ll. 35–36. **primoribus . . . lectis,** ' by choosing leading men of the equestrian rank '. At this time only wealthy men could serve as cavalry, for they alone could provide the horse and equipment. Later on in Roman History, ' equestrian rank ' was second in social status and position to the senatorial order.

l. 37. **traditumque inde fertur,** *lit.,* ' from that time it is said to have been handed down '. **ut . . . uocarentur,** ' that (there) be summoned into the Senate '.

l. 38. **qui patres . . . essent,** ' those who were the Fathers and those who were the Enrolled '. Livy assumes that the former were the old members, the latter the newly elected members. Senators were later addressed as **patres conscripti,** and Livy may have been tempted to explain the appellation in the way above. The origin of the term is, however, obscure.

ll. 39–40. conscriptos . . . lectos, 'they called the appointed (ones) (i.e. the new members of the Senate) the Enrolled '.

l. 40. id mirum . . . profuit ad, ' (it is) wonderful how much (this) was useful for '. mirum quantum has no influence on the mood of profuit. As it is probable that no plebeian became a member of the senate until after 400 B.C., Livy is wrong in supposing, as he seems to here, that these new members of the senate were plebeians.

CHAPTER 2

l. 1. habita cura, supply est, ' attention was paid to '.

l. 3. necubi . . . esset, lit., ' lest anywhere there should be regret for the kings ', i.e. ' that the people should not have feelings of regret for the kings '.

ll. 3–4. regem sacrificolum. In appointing a ' king of sacrifices ', the senate felt that they would avoid giving offence to the gods.

l. 4. pontifici, i.e. the pontifex maximus. To take over the king's priestly office and duties, the senate appointed a pontifex maximus with general control of the state religion and a rex sacrificolus to perform the sacrifices and ritual.

l. 5. ne additus nomini honos aliquid libertati officeret, ' lest the office added to the title might in-any-way do-hurt-to their liberty '. aliquid, adverbial acc. of extent of action.

l. 6. Ac nescio an, ' I do not know whether ', is often translated by ' perhaps '.

l. 6. nimium goes with muniendo and is amplified by undique minimisque rebus ' on every side and in the smallest details '.

l. 8. consulis alterius, ' of one of the consuls ', i.e. L. Tarquinius Collatinus who was a nephew of the Tarquinius Priscus in l. 10 the latter was the father of Tarquinius Superbus.

l. 8. nihil aliud, ' in no other way ', adverbial acc. of extent.

l. 9. fuit: the colon is often a useful signal that a passage of in-direct speech (oratio obliqua) is about to begin. Here Livy gives us the reasons the Romans had for the unpopularity of Collatinus.

l. 10. **adsuesse** = **adsueuisse**. Cf. **regnasse** = **regnauisse** and the note in Chap. I l. 5. The syncopated form, as it is called, will be commented upon only occasionally.

l. 10. **factum**, supply as often **esse**.

ll. 11-13. **ne . . . repetisse**, *lit.*, ' S. Tarquinius, not even after an interval, having forgotten the throne as though (it belonged) to another, had sought it with violence and crime as if (it were) the heritage of his family '.

The interval is the rule of Servius Tullius who did not belong to the Tarquinii, and **tamquam alieni** tells us why we might have expected Tarquinius to forget the throne.

l. 15. **nescire Tarquinios**, ' the Tarquins did not know (how)'.

ll. 16-17. **Hinc . . . sermo**, *lit.*, ' the talk of (men) gently-sounding in this way (**hinc**) at first the temper (of the citizens) '. Perhaps we might begin: ' as men talked . . . , gossip spread (**datus est**)'.

ll. 18-19. **ad contionem** ' to a public meeting '.

l. 20. **passuros**, ' that (they) would allow '.

ll. 20-21. **nec . . . unde . . . foret;** the antecedent to **unde** has to be supplied, ' nor (anyone) to be at Rome whence (= from whom) there could be danger to liberty '.

ll. 21-23. **id . . . contemnendam.** Note: (i) the indirect speech until l. 28 and (ii) the gerundives which, *passive* in Latin, are often better translated as active in English: *lit.*, ' that was to-be-defended . . . and nothing (**neque ullam rem**) . . . to be thought lightly of,' i.e. ' they were to defend . . . and not think lightly of anything . . .'.

l. 24. **nec dicturum fuisse**, ' nor would he have spoken '. In acc. and infin., the imperfect and pluperfect subj. active in the apodosis of conditional clauses becomes future participle + **fuisse.** cf. Chap. I, ll. 9-10.

l. 25. **non . . . Romanum**, ' the Roman people did not believe '.

l. 32. **auctore me**, abl. absol., ' at my instigation '.

l. 32. **sed** = **sed etiam**.

l. 32. **si quid deest**, *lit.*, ' if anything is lacking ', obj. of **augebunt**. Translate: ' whatever you are short of '.

l. 33. **amicus,** ' (as) a friend '. **forsitan** with **vano.**

l. 34. **ita persuasum est animis.** Note that **persuadeo**, an intransitive verb (takes the dat.) is used in the pass. *only* impersonally. ' Their minds are so persuaded ' = ' the people are so convinced '. **hinc,** ' from here ', = ' from us ' *or* ' from Rome '.   **abiturum.** Supply **esse** to give fut. infin. active. This omission, so common in Latin, will be noted only where such help is really necessary to the student.

ll. 35–37. **consuli . . . uocem. Consuli,** dat.,[1] where we would use the genitive, dependent upon **uocem:** ' astonishment at so strange and sudden a change (obj. gen.) at first had choked the consul's voice '.

l. 37. **dicere . . . incipientem.**   Retain the order by saying ' then (as he was) beginning to speak '.

ll. 38–39. **et ceteri quidem . . . minus,** *lit.,* ' and *the others* moved (him) less ', = ' the others failed to influence him '.   **quidem** emphasises the preceding word: here it also points a contrast between this statement and the following one without a word like 'but'.

ll. 41–42. **agere . . . coepit,** ' began to plead (with him) by entreating in-various-ways and alternately advising '. Note: (i) Livy is very fond of using the abl. of the gerund or noun with the gerundive almost with the force of a present participle active. It is really an abl. of manner. (ii) **alternis:** *sc.* **uicibus.** We might render: ' with varied alternation of entreaty and advice '.

l. 42. **se,** i.e. Collatinus.

l. 43. **postmodum priuato sibi,** ' to him afterwards as a private citizen ', i.e. ' to him after his year of office '.

l. 43. **eadem illa,** neut. pl., subject of **acciderent:** ' those same things ' = ' the same fate' i.e. banishment.

ll. 43–44. **cum . . . ignominia.** The **cum** phrase is balanced not by another similar one, but by an abl. absol. **addita . . . ignominia,** ' together with confiscation of his property and the addition of other ignominy besides '.

_____
[1] Known as ' the dative of the person interested *or* concerned'.

The greatest ignominy that could happen to a citizen was the loss of citizenship and exile.

l. 47. **ex,** 'in accordance with'. **senatus consulto.** See the introduction p. xvii for a comment on the senate and the **comitia centuriata** l. xviii.

l. 49. **quo adiutore,** abl. absol., 'with whose help'.

CHAPTER 3

l. 1. **cum,** concessive 'although': hence the subjunctive **esset.**

ll. 2–3. **id . . . fuit,** *lit.,* '*that* was later than the expectation of all', i.e. 'it happened later than all expected'.

l. 3. **id** is in apposition to the clause **per . . . amissa est.**

ll. 5–6. **nec ii . . . orti,** 'and they were not of undistinguished family'. **tenui loco,** abl. of origin. **orti,** perfect participle from **orior.**

l. 6. **in regno,** 'under the monarchy'.

l. 8. **more regio,** *lit.,* 'in princely fashion', i.e. 'like princes'.

l. 8. **eam** goes with **licentiam. tum** = 'now'. **quaerentes,** 'missing'.

l. 10. **inter se,** 'to each other'. The colon after **querebantur** (note the conative force of the imperfect: 'began to complain'), introduces indirect speech to l. 18.

In this oratio obliqua, note that Livy retains primary tenses of the subjunctive (present and perfect) where strict usage would demand historic tenses (imperfect and pluperfect) in subordinate clauses after a past main verb. For a fuller discussion, see the introduction, p. xv.

l. 11. **a quo . . . sit,** 'from whom one could obtain (a request) whether right or wrong was needful'; note: **impetres** indefinite subj., (consecutive) and **opus,** 'need', followed by nominative (apposition) whereas it usually has ablative. E.g. 'I need a horse': **opus est mihi equo.**

l. 13. **posse,** '(a king) could': similarly with **nosse.**

l. 16. habere, ' (the law) had '.

ll. 16–17. si modum excesseris, *lit.*, ' if you exceeded the measure ', i.e. ' if you (i.e. one) went too far '.

ll. 17–18. in . . . erroribus, ' in so many human mistakes ', i.e. ' when men were so inclined to err '. Note this use of **in** (='in view of', 'considering') in phrases of this type, common in Livy. **sola innocentia,** ' on innocence alone ': the abl. is instrumental.

ll. 18–19. iam . . . animis; animis could be abl. in abl. absol., or dat. after **superueniunt:** ' when their feelings were now . . . disaffected '. **sua sponte,** *lit.*, ' on their own ' =here ' in themselves '.

l. 20. tantum, adv., ' merely '.

l. 21. postquam, ' when ' is nearly always a more fitting translation than ' after '.

l. 22. ea consultatio, ' deliberation about that (question)'; **tenuit** ' kept (the senators)'. Note **ea** =**de ea re.**

ll. 22–23. ne non . . . essent, *lit.*, ' lest if it- (the property, *neut. pl., in Latin*) were-not-restored it might prove the pretext for war, (while) if-it-were-restored it might prove the means and assistance of it '.

ll. 24–25. moliri, struere, historic infinitives to be rendered by past tenses.

ll. 25–26. et tamquam . . . ambientes, ' and canvassing as though (to attain) that which seemed to be done ', i.e. ' to attain their apparent object '.

l. 27. a quibus. . . . The antecedent is **iis** which, following the usual Latin practice, is placed after the relative clause, ' to those by whom . . .'.

CHAPTER 4

l. 1. Vitellius . . . fratribus. There are two groups of brothers. **res,** ' the plan '.

l. 5. auunculi, will be, of course, the Vitellii brothers.

ll. 6–7. conscii . . . abiit, ' were admitted (as) accomplices whose memory (i.e. names) has departed (i.e. have been lost) owing-to-lapse-of-time '. **uetustate,** abl. of cause.

l. 7. **uicisset,** ' had prevailed '.

l. 8. **quae ... bona,** ' which supported the return of the property ' **reddenda bona,** *lit.,* ' the property to-be-returned '.

l. 8. **eam** is attracted into the gender of the predicate, **causam.**

l. 9. **quod,** ' because ', **spatium,** ' time '. **sumpsissent:** subj., because it gives the reason alleged by the envoys.

l. 11. **quibus ... asportarent,** ' in which to carry away ...'. Note the relative introducing a purpose clause.

l. 14. **qui** here means ' how '. **credituros** (esse) ..., ' how would they (the princes) believe that not idle (tales) on matters of such importance were being brought by the envoys '. Perhaps better in the active, ' that their envoys were not bringing ...'.

Note that rhetorical[1] questions in the 1st and 3rd person become acc. + infin. in indirect speech.

l. 16. **cum,** ' when ': its verb is **cenatum esset,** ' there was a dinner party ', impersonal passive: cf. **pugnatum est,** ' there was fighting '.

l. 17. **pridie quam,** ' on the night before ' is here followed by the subj., although it seems to be strictly temporal. See introduction, p. xv.

l. 19. **ut fit,** *lit.,* ' as it happens ', i.e. ' as is natural '.

ll. 20–21. **qui ... agi,** ' who had already previously sensed something afoot ' (*lit.,* ' it to be done ').

ll. 21–22. **ut ... darentur;** the ut clause is explanatory of **eam occasionem,** itself the object of **exspectabat.**

l. 22. **quae deprehensae,** ' which seized ', i.e. ' the seizure of which '.

l. 26. **litterarum,** objective gen., dependent upon **cura. habita** (est), ' care was especially (in primis) taken of the letters '. As ' letters ' is also the subject of **interciderent,** we might say, ' they took special care (to see) that the letters ...'.

[1] In this type of question the speaker asks, not a genuine question (i.e. for information), but a question for effect.

ll. 28–29. **addubitatum est,** impersonal passive again: ' there was uncertainty ' or ' they were uncertain '.

ll. 29–30. **et ... ualuit,** 'and although they seemed to have brought it about (= acted in such a way) that they should be treated as enemies (**hostium loco**), yet the law of nations prevailed '.

Included in the latter was the personal inviolability of heralds and ambassadors.

CHAPTER 5

l. 2. **integra,** ' afresh ', i.e. ' for fresh consideration '.

l. 3. **diripienda,** *lit.,* ' to be plundered ', i.e. ' as plunder '.

l. 4. **contacta** is nom., in agreement with **plebs,** subject (understood) of **amitteret,** and **regia praeda** is abl.

l. 5. **cum iis,** i.e. with the Tarquin princes.

l. 5. **ager,** ' the lands '. The **bona** so far mentioned referred to the moveable property.

l. 6. **consecratus Marti,** '(was) consecrated to Mars (and)'.

l. 7. **Martius campus,** ' the field of Mars ' was the place where the army mustered and exercised and where the **comitia centuriata** met. As Rome grew in size, it became also a popular recreation ground.

ll. 7–8. **seges ... messi,** 'a crop of spelt is said to have been ripe for the harvest '. Note that Latin prefers the personal construction with the passive of **dico** and **video.** We prefer *impersonal*: ' it is said that ...'.

l. 8. **Quem,** coordinating relative with **fructum.** ' this '. **religiosum erat,** *lit.,* ' it was a matter of religious scruple '. Translate ' religious scruple forbade (them) '.

ll. 9–11. **desectam ... in Tiberim.** Note the use of participles in Latin where English would prefer coordinate main verbs: *lit.,* ' a large body of men having been sent together poured the having been cut crop straw all and (lit., with the straw) into the Tiber, from their baskets '.

Translate ' a large . . . was sent in . . . cut the crop . . ., and threw it . . .'. Cf. **nuntium captum interfecerunt**, ' they captured and killed the messenger '. **fudere =fuderunt.**

l. 12. **mediis caloribus,** ' in mid-summer '.

l. 13. **aceruos sedisse . . . ,** acc. + infin., ' they say ' to be supplied.

l. 13. **inde,** *lit.,* ' thence ', =' from these (heaps) '. It is coordinate with **aliis . . . invectis,** *lit.,* ' other (things) which . . . having been carried to-the-same-spot (**eodem**)', i.e. ' from the accumulation at the same spot of all the stuff which a river by chance brings down '.

ll. 13-15. **insulam factam (esse)**; ' an island was formed '.

ll. 15-16. **manuque adiutum (esse),** *lit.,* ' and it was helped by hand '. Note the impersonal use again. Say: ' it was strengthened further '.

l. 16. **ut . . . ,** ' so that the site was high and solid enough for supporting . . .'.
The island was called Tiberina and had on it later a temple to the god of healing, Aesculapius.

ll. 18-19. **sumptum que. . . . sumere supplicium** is the usual Latin for ' to inflict capital punishment '.

l. 19. **conspectius eo quod,** ' the more conspicuous because '. **eo,** abl. of cause, emphasing **quod;** ' for this reason that '.

l. 20. **consulatus** is nominative.

ll. 21-22. **qui . . . dedit.** Note again the relative clause precedes and is picked up by the antecedent **eum.** English uses the reverse order: ' fate appointed the very man (as) . . . who ought to have been removed (as) an onlooker '.

l. 24. **consulis liberi** is the subject.

ll. 24-25. **oculos** has **omnium** dependent upon it: ' the gaze of all '.

l. 25. **miserebat. . . . homines** (acc.) becomes the subject in English of the verb (impersonal in Latin): ' men pitied . . .'.

l. 26. **meriti essent.** The subjunctive is due to the clause being in virtual indirect speech. In other words it gives the thoughts of the spectators.

ll. 26–31. **illos ... proderent.** Note: (i) indirect speech. (ii) **patriam ... esset,** are all the objects of **proderent.** (iii) **quidquid ... esset,** ' whatever there was of Roman gods and men ' = ' all the gods and men of Rome '.

Begin: ' (to think) that those (young men) in that year in particular, had brought themselves to betray their freed country ... to one (who had) formerly (been) a proud tyrant (and was) then a dangerous exile '.

ll. 31–32. **in sedem suam,** ' to their tribunal '.

l. 33. **nudatos ... caedunt.** Note again the use of the participle where English prefers a main verb: ' they stripped and flogged them '.

ll. 34–36. **cum ... ministerium,** *lit.,* ' while, between all the time, the father, his countenance and face were for a spectacle, a father's feelings being prominent amid the administration of the nation's punishment, i.e. ' while all the time men watched the father's countenance and looks, as his feelings were ...'. **spectaculo,** predicative dative.

l. 37. **in utramque partem,** ' in both respects ', i.e. by reward as well as by punishment. **exemplum nobile,** ' a notable example '.

l. 38. **praemium,** '(as) a reward '. **indici** is the dative of **index.**

ll. 39–40. **ille dicitur liberatus,** personal construction: cf. the note on Chap. 5, l. 7–8.

l. 40. **uindicta** is the staff with which a master touched a slave in the act of giving him his freedom. It appears from this passage that Livy may have believed that the name **uindicta** arose from the slave's name. This is an instance of the invention of a name or incident to explain a custom or practice the origin of which has long been forgotten.

l. 42. **obseruatum,** *sc.,* **est:** impersonal passive, ' it became the practice '. **qui,** '(those) who '.

l. 43. **accepti uiderentur,** ' seemed to have been received ', i.e. ' were regarded as having been received '.

CHAPTER 6

l. 2. **dolore,** 'by resentment'. **tantae . . . spei,** obj. gen., 'at such great hopes falling to no effect ' = ' at the failure of such great hopes '.

l. 3. **postquam,** ' when ' may be dropped in translation, to make **uidit** a main verb, linked with **ratus,** ' thinking ' by ' and '.

ll. 3–4. **dolo uiam obsaeptam,** ' the road (was) closed against treachery '. **dolo** is dat., dependent upon **obsaeptam.**

l. 5. **circumire, orare,** historic infins.: **supplex,** '(as) a suppliant '.

ll. 6–9. **ne ex se ortum . . . sinerent,** ' not to allow (a man) sprung from themselves . . . to perish . . .'.

ll. 6–7. **eiusdem sanguinis,** the genitive of quality is usually dependent upon a noun. The Tarquins were Etruscans, like the people of Veii and Tarquinii.

l. 7. **ex tanto . . . regno,** ' from a royal power just now so great ', i.e. ' after enjoying just before so great a royal power '.

l. 9. **alios . . . ,** accusative and infin. **alios** is a natural exaggeration, for of the seven Roman kings, only one had been called from abroad to rule at Rome (**in regnum Romam**), the second, Numa Pompilius (715–673 B.C.).

l. 10. **se regem,** ' (whereas) he himself (while) king '.

ll. 10–11. **a proximis**—a reference to the consuls, Brutus and Collatinus, who were related to him.

ll. 11–13. **eos inter se partes regni rapuisse,** ' they had seized amongst themselves part of the kingdom ', obviously means ' they had shared with one another the kingdom they had seized '.

l. 12. **uisus sit.** Note primary sequence: the strict usage would demand **uisus esset.**

l. 14. **se** is the subject of **repetere, patriam regnumque** the object.

l. 16. **ferrent, adiuuarent,** indirect command ' let them bring ', ' let them help '. Similarly **irent,** l. 17.

l. 17. **ueteres,** ' long-standing '.

l. 17. **ultum,** acc. of the supine, expressing purpose.

l. 18. **agrum ademptum,** ' their estates taken away ' = ' the loss of their estates '. Cf. **urbs condita,** ' the city founded ' = ' the foundation of the city '.

ll. 18–20. **ac . . . fremunt,** ' and all threateningly cried out that at any rate with a Roman as their leader wrongs (were) to be wiped out and the things lost in war to be recovered ', i.e. ' that . . . they ought to wipe out . . . and recover their losses in war '.

pro se quisque, *lit.,* ' each for himself ' = ' all '.

l. 22. **suos,** ' their fellow-countrymen '.

ll. 25–26. **uentum est,** the impersonal passive, in Latin = ' they came ', i.e. personal and active in English.

ll. 26–27. **quadrato agmine,** ' marching in battle-order '.

ll. 28–29. **primus agminis,** ' at the head of the column '.

l. 31. **procul** goes with **cognouit: consulem esse,** ' that it was a consul '.

l. 32. **Brutum,** ' that it was Brutus '.

ll. 33–34. **nos extorres,** ' us into exile '. **ultores,** ' to avenge '. See introduction p. xvi.

l. 37. **sensit in se iri Brutus,** ' Brutus realised that the attack was directed against him '. **iri** is the infinitive of **itur,** impersonal passive; cf. **uentum est** above.

l. 38. **tum,** ' in those days ': **ipsis,** ' in person '.

ll. 40–41. **neuter . . . memor,** i.e. **neuter memor protegendi sui corporis dum** (' provided that '). . . .

l. 41. **contrario ictu,** ' by a thrust from-opposite-direction ', i.e. ' by each other's thrust '.

ll. 42–43. **haerentes, moribundi, lapsi sint,** plural to agree with the logical subject ' they ' implied in the grammatical one, **uterque,** ' each (of two) '. **lapsi sint,** perfect subj. as often in consecutive clauses to express the immediate result.

ll. 45–46. **ibi . . . est,** ' there (i.e. in this encounter) success was varied (i.e. now with one, now with the other side), and it was fought almost with equal Mars ', i.e. ' both sides had almost an equal success in the fighting '.

l. 48. **Tarquiniensis,** collective sing., ' the men of Tarquinii '.

l. 49. **ab sua parte,** ' on their side of the field '.

CHAPTER 7

l. 2. **omissa inrita re,** ' giving up the enterprise (as) lost '.

ll. 3–4. **suas . . . domos.** Livy uses **quisqve** =**uterque,** ' each of the two ', because of its constant use with **suus.**

l. 4. **adiciunt,** *sc.,* ' the annalists '. **huic pugnae** ' to (the story of) this battle '. The semicolon after **pugnae** introduces indirect speech.

l. 5. **ex silua Arsia;** the Arsian forest is north west of Rome in Etruria. **editam (esse),** ' came forth '.

l. 6. **Siluani.** Silvanus was a Roman god associated with land uncleared of forest.

l. 7. **uno plus Tuscorum cecidisse,** ' more of the Tuscans by one fell ', i.e. ' the losses of the Tuscans were greater by one '. **uno,** abl. of the measure of difference.

l. 8. **inde,** ' from there ', i.e. ' from the battle-field '. **ut uictores,** ' as victors '. **pro uictis,** ' like (men) defeated '.

ll. 12–13. **quanto . . . apparatu,** i.e. (**tanto**) **apparatu quanto potuit,** ' with as much pomp as he could for-those-days (**tum**) '.

l. 13. **multo,** abl. of the measure of difference. **morti,** abstract, ' to death ' for the concrete **mortuo,** ' to the dead man '.

l. 14. **eo . . . insignis,** *lit.,* ' for-the-reason before all conspicuous ' =' all the more conspicuous '. For, **eo,** cf. Chap. 5, l. 19.

l. 15. **annum,** ' for a year ', acc. of duration of time.

ll. 15–16. **quod . . . fuisset.** The subjunctive is used because the **quod** clause gives the reasons in the minds of the matrons (virtual indirect speech). **violatae pudicitiae.** The violation of the chaste Lucretia, wife of Collatinus, by Sextus, the son of Tarquinius Superbus, was, according to the story, the direct cause of the uprising which, under the leadership of Brutus, led to the expulsion of the Tarquin family; *see* Livy, Bk. I, 57–60.

ll. 17–19. **consuli . . . orta,** *lit.*, ' for the consul who . . . , as the feelings of the populace are fickle, from his (previous) popularity, not only unpopularity but suspicion along with a cruel accusation arose ', i.e. 'then the surviving consul (so fickle are the feelings of the people) lost his popularity: not only did he become disliked but also suspected on a cruel accusation '.

l. 20. **fama ferebat,** ' rumour reported ', = ' it was reported '.

l. 20. **nec** = et non, ' both not ' but the ' both ', as often in Latin, can be ignored.

l. 21. **aedificabat in summa Velia,** Supply ' house 'as the object. The Velia is a ridge which overlooks the forum. Valerius' house would seem to dominate it like a fortress (**arx**).

ll. 21–22. **alto . . . loco,** abl. of place without a preposition; common in Livy (cf. introduction, p. xvi.).

ll. 22–25. **haec . . . escendit.** Note the construction of the Latin period: (i) **cum** clause (ii) abl. absol. (iii) main verb. English would probably prefer *three* coordinate main verbs.

l. 23. **indignitate,** abl. of cause, ' because of their unworthiness *or* injustice '.

ll. 24–25. **submissis fascibus,** ' with lowered fasces ', i.e. in a courtesy salute to the people. For the fasces, see the introduction p. xvii.

l. 25. **in contionem,** ' the tribunal (to speak) '.

ll. 27–28. **populi . . . esse,** ' that the people's majesty and power were superior to the consul's '.

l. 29. **laudare,** historic infinitive.

ll. 31–32. **matura . . . inuidiam,** abl. absol., ' when his fame was at its greatest (**matura**) and was not yet changed into unpopularity.'

l. 32. **occubuisset.** The subjunctive mood shows that the clause is in virtual indirect speech and gives the thoughts in the mind of Valerius.

ll. 33–34. **ex liberatore patriae,** ' after having been the liberator of his country '. **recidisse,** ' had sunk to (the level of) the Aquilii and Vitellii.'

ll. 35–36. **nunquamne ulla uirtus erit**, *lit.*, ' will any merit never be ': perhaps more natural in English as ' will no merit ever be '.

l. 35. **uobis**, ' in your eyes '.

ll. 36–38. **ego timerem**, deliberative subj., ' was *I* to suspect '. Note: (i) the acc. + infin., a rare construction (for the common **ut** or **ne** clause) after **timeo**. (ii) **cupiditatis** depends upon **crimen** and **regni** (obj. gen.) on **cupiditatis**.

l. 39. **arce. . . .** The Capitoline Hill consists of two peaks, the arx and the Capitolium. The latter name is, however, often applied to the whole Hill.

l. 39. **metui**, pres. infin. pass.

l. 40. **tam leui momento**, abl., ' on so trivial a circumstance.'

l. 42. **ut . . . referat**, order for translation: **ut referat magis ubi. . . . qui = qualis.**

l. 43. **aedes** in the meaning ' house ' is plural.

l. 45. **suspectum.** As **suspicio** means ' look up to ', ' admire ', and it is chiefly in the perf. part. pass. **suspectus**, we have the meaning ' suspected ', there is an obvious play on words here, ' above me whom you (looked up to[1] and) suspected '.

l. 46. **aedificent quibus.** The subject of **aedificent** is the un-expressed antecedent of **quibus**, ' let (those) build to whom . . .'.

ll. 48–49. **uicae . . . aedes.** Note **aedes**, sg. means ' temple ', **Vica Pota** is a goddess either of victory (**uinco, potior**) or of food and drink (**uictus, potus**).

CHAPTER 8

l. 1. **latae.** Supply **sunt** and **a consule. quae** introduces a consecutive clause: hence **absoluerent**, ' such as to release '. Similarly, **quae . . . uerterent**, ' as to reverse (the situation) '.

ll. 3–4. **inde . . . est**, ' as-a-result (**inde**) arose his surname, (that) of the People's Friend '.

ll. 4–7. **ante . . . fuere.** Begin with **ante omnes** (especially)

[1] i.e. when he was on the summit of the Velia.

gratae in uolgus fuere leges de prouocatione ... (de) sacrandoque. . . .

For the Lex Valeria de provocatione, see the introduction, p. xvii.

sacrandoque, 'and (about) declaring accursed the life with the property (i.e. and the property) of anyone who formed plans . . .'. A man declared 'accursed' (sacer) was denied all political, social, and religious rights, and so could be slain with impunity.

inisset = iniuisset; the pluperfect subj., representing an original fut. perf. indic., shows that the relative clause is in *virtual* indirect speech.

ll. 8–9. ut . . . esset, 'that the popularity arising-from-them (in his) might be his alone'; sua unius = sui unius, ' of himself alone '.

l. 9. collegae subrogando, dat. of work contemplated (dat. of purpose) dependent upon comitia, ' elections for . . .'.

l. 14. auctores. For Livy's authorities, see the introduction, p. xiii.

l. 15. Bruto . . . suggerunt, ' they put the name of Horatius immediately after (that of) Brutus.'

ll. 16–17. memoria intercidisse, 'that he was lost from recollection' (=' was forgotten ').

l. 18. Iouis aedes. A temple to Jupiter in the Capitolium had been begun by the fifth Roman king, L. Tarquinius Priscus (616–579 B.C.) and completed by the seventh and last king, Tarquinius Superbus, (535–509 B.C.). It was then dedicated to a group of three deities, Jupiter Optimus Maximus, Minerva, and Juno. The temple (with additions) lasted until 83 B.C., when it was burned down, but the original platform is said still to exist.

l. 19. sortiti. Supply sunt: uter dedicaret, ' as to which should dedicate it '. dedicaret, subj. in indirect question, was also subj. (deliberative) in the direct one: ' which of us two is to dedicate it '.

ll. 21–22. aegrius. . . . Valeri necessarii is the subject. Note aegre ferre, ' to be annoyed at '. aegrius is the comparative of aegre.

l. 23. **conati.** Translate as **conati sunt** and insert ' and ' before **postquam.**

ll. 24–25. **postem. . . . tenenti consuli** is dat. (of disadvantage) dependent upon **incutiunt,** but it would be easier to translate as though it were abl. absol., ' just as the consul was holding the door-post in the midst of his prayers to the gods, they interrupted him with the evil news that . . .'; *lit.,* ' they threw in the evil news . . .'.

l. 26. **funestaque familia,** abl. absol., ' and while his family was in mourning '. A corpse polluted a household.

l. 27. **non crediderit.** It is often necessary to supply **utrum** ' whether ' before double indirect questions.

ll. 28–29. **nec traditur certum,** ' is not handed down for certain ', i.e. ' there is no certain tradition '.

l. 29. **nihil aliud,** adverbial acc. of extent, ' in no other way ', goes closely with **quam ut.**

l. 33. **post exactos reges,** ' after the expelled kings ' = ' after the expulsion of the kings '.

CHAPTER 9

l. 2. **Porsennam.** This spelling occurs here and up to Chap. 10 inclusive. From Chaps. 11–13, we have the spelling **Porsinna.** One explanation (that of the editors, O. T.) is that Livy may have written **Porsenna** at first, and then found **Porsinna** in the authority he was following in the later chapters.

l. 3. **miscendo,** modal use of the abl. of the gerund. See note on Chapter 2, ll. 41–42.

l. 6. **orientem,** *lit.,* ' rising ', i.e. ' growing '.

ll. 7–12. **satis . . . ,** acc. + infin., with subjunctive, in subordinate clauses, as often in Livy, in primary sequence.

l. 7. **satis,** with **dulcedinis** dependent upon it, is the object of **habere.**

ll. 8–9. **nisi. . . .** Note: (i) the necessity to supply **tanta** to the correlative **quanta,** (ii) the relative clause precedes and contains the antecedent **ui** with which the understood **tanta** agrees; ' unless the kings defended their royal power with as much energy as . . . '.

Becoming familiar with this typical Latin order is essential for the student and it should be mastered as quickly as possible.

l. 9. **aequari ... infimis,** 'the highest was (=would be) made equal to the lowest '.

l. 11. **rei,** 'an office ' is dative in apposition to **regnis.**

ll. 12–14. **Porsenna cum ... ratus,** ' Porsenna, thinking that it (would be) not only safe for the Etruscans that there should be a king at Rome but also an honour (that he should be) a king of Etruscan race '.

l. 15. **alias** is an adverb, ' at any other time '.

l. 17. **hostes** is acc. pl.

l. 19. **receptis ... regibus,** ' by admitting the princes into the city '.

l. 24. **uenibat,** from **uēneo -ire,** ' I go for sale ' = ' I am sold'.

ll. 24–25. **in publicum ... priuatis,** ' (was) entirely taken into the (power of the) state (and) taken away from individuals '. Thus the price could be controlled.

ll. 25–26. **portoriis ... liberata,** ' the plebs were freed from dues and the property tax '. The former were indirect taxes, the latter was direct, originally imposed to defray the cost of war, later regarded as a loan (to be repaid from the spoils of war), and finally abolished in 167 B.C.

ll. 26–27. **qui ... essent,** ' inasmuch as (**qui,** causal) they were for (i.e. capable of) bearing the burden '. **oneri ferendo,** dat. of work contemplated.

ll. 27–28. **pauperes ... educent,** acc. +infin.; **pauperes** are the same as the **plebs** above. If the military organisation by wealth can be attributed to Servius Tullius, the sixth Roman king (and this is doubtful), the **pauperes** would be those who had no property qualification, whereas the **diuites** would be the top classes (whether patricians or wealthy plebeians).

l. 28. **patrum,** subj. gen., ' on the part of the Fathers '.

ll. 28–29. **asperis ... fame,** abl. absol., ' when (later) the situation was difficult in the siege and famine '.

l. 31. **horrerent,** ' shuddered at ': this verb, normally intrans., is used sometimes, as here, transitively by a natural extension of its meaning.

l. 32. **malis artibus,** ' by unscrupulous practices '.

l. 33. **bene imperando,** ' by its wise rule '.

l. 33. **uniuersus,** ' as a whole '.

CHAPTER 10

l. 2. **praesidiis,** ' with strong points '.

l. 3. **alia . . . alia,** *n. pl.,* ' some parts . . . others '.

l. 3. **Tiberi obiecto,** *lit.,* ' by the Tiber thrown in the way (to the enemy) ', i.e. ' by the barrier of the Tiber '.

ll. 3–4. **pons sublicius.** The ' bridge of piles ', which until the 2nd century B.C. was the only bridge over the Tiber, gave access to the city from the Janiculan hill.

l. 4. **iter . . . dedit, ni . . . fuisset,** ' almost gave a passage (and would have done so), had not there been one man '. The translation shows what is the real grammatical apodosis to **si . . . fuisset.** For greater vividness, Livy states as a fact, what would have been a fact, if the protasis had been fulfilled.

l. 5. **Cocles** means ' one-eyed ' (co- ' one ', **oculus,** ' eye '), but the name does not necessarily mean that Horatius had only one eye.

l. 5. **id munimentum,** object of **habuit,** ' that protection ', = ' him as a protection '. **id** (for **eum**) is attracted into the gender of the predicate.

ll. 6–12. **Qui. . . . qui,** coordinating relative = ' he '. Drop the **cum,** ' when ' and make **uidisset** the main verb. Start a fresh sentence at **reprehensans.**

The Janiculum is a hill on the right bank of the Tiber.

l. 10. **deum,** gen. pl. **fidem,** ' the conscience '.

ll. 10–11. **deserto praesidio,** abl. absol., best translated by conditional clause, ' if they deserted their post '.

l. 12. **si transitum . . . reliquissent,** ' if they crossed and left the bridge in their rear'. For the translation, cf., Chap. 5, ll. 9–11.

l. 14. **monere, praedicere,** historic infinitives to be translated as perfect indicatives. This infinitive is usually followed by historic sequence, but Livy, like other historians, has both historic and primary sequence, sometimes, as here in the same passage: so we have **possint** and **interrumpant,** (primary), and **possent** (historic).

ll. 16–17. **quantum . . . obsisti.** Note again: (i) the necessity to supply **tantum,** (ii) the impersonal passive **obsisti** (*lit.*, ' it could be resisted '), (iii) **quantum** is an adverbial acc. of extent. Tr. ' as far as resistance could be offered by one person '.

ll. 17–18. **in primum aditum,** ' to the head '.

ll. 18–19. **insignis . . . terga.** **conspecta** agrees with **terga,** and **pugna** is abl. with **cedentium,** ' conspicuous among the seen backs of (those) withdrawing from the fight ', i.e. ' conspicuous among the cowards who were seen withdrawing . . .'.

ll. 19–20. **obuersis . . . armis.** Note the order, participle (**obuersis**) in agreement with noun (**armis**) separated by all the words that go closely with them. Ability to recognise this sandwiching,[1] so typical of Latin and possible only in a highly-inflected language, is a great help in translation, ' (conspicuous) by his armour (sword and shield) which he turned against the foe to engage in battle hand-to-hand '.

ll. 23–24. **quod . . . erat,** ' what was the most stormy moment of the fight ', object (with **procellam,** *lit.*, ' tempest ', here ' onset ', ' attack ') of **sustinuit.**

ll. 25–26. **reuocantibus qui rescindebant.** Note again the necessity to supply the antecedent to **qui, eis** *or* **illis** in agreement with **reuocantibus,** *lit.*, ' those who . . . calling (them) back '.

ll. 26–27. **circumferens,** ' darting '. **oculos,** ' looks '.

l. 28. **prouocare, increpare,** historic infinitives. Note the colon l. 29, followed by indirect speech.

---

[1] As it may loosely be called.

l. 29. **seruitia,** ' tools ': abstract for concrete. **oppugnatum,** acc. of the supine, expressing purpose.

ll. 31–32. **dum ... circumspectant. circumspectant,** historic present, with primary sequence **incipiant.**

l. 34. **quae cum,** ' which when ' =' when they '.

l. 35. **neque ... ,** ' and yet he none the less firmly ...'.

ll. 37–39. **cum ... sustinuit.** Note this example of what is called the inverse-**cum**-construction; i.e. the functions of the two clauses (temporal and main) are reversed and the **cum** clause is logically, though not grammatically, the main clause. In this construction **cum** is always followed by the indicative.

ll. 38–39. **alacritate ... sublatus,** ' (the shout) raised in their glee at the completion of their task '.

l. 40. **sancte** is an adverb. **ut** to be supplied before **haec arma.**

l. 42. **ita,** ' thereupon '. **multis ... armis,** ' though many missiles fell around him '.

ll. 43–44. **rem ... fidei,** ' having dared a deed destined-to-win (**habituram**) more fame than credence with posterity '.

ll. 45–46. **in comitio,** ' in the comitium ', an open space in the forum used for various assemblies.

ll. 46–47. **agri ... datum,** ' (as much) land as he could plough in a single day was given (him) '. **tantum** again to be supplied: cf. the note on Chap. 9, ll. 8–9; **agri,** partitive gen. Similarly **famae, fidei** above.

Note finally that Latin often says ' he did something ' as here ' he ploughed ' where we would prefer ' he could do ', i.e. ' he could plough '.

l. 48. **in magna inopia,** ' in (spite of) their great dearth '. **pro ... copiis,** ' in-proportion-to their private means '. Note this common meaning of **in,** ' in face of ', ' in spite of ' and cf. the note in Chap. 3, ll. 17–18.

ll. 49–50. **fraudans ... suo,** ' though he robbed himself willingly (**ipse,** *lit.,* ' himself ') of his own provisions '. **uictu suo,** abl. of separation.

CHAPTER 11

ll. 1–7. **consiliis. . . .** Make the abl. absols. main verbs in the *active* and start a fresh sentence with **ipse . . . posuit.**

l. 3. **in plano . . . ,** ' on the plain by the banks of the Tiber.' Note that Livy frequently uses adjs. as nouns, especially in oblique cases.

l. 4. **et** means ' both ' linking **ad custodiam,** ' for keeping watch ' and the purpose clause **ut . . . traiceret.** It can be ignored in translation.

ll. 4–5. **ne . . . sineret,** *lit.,* ' lest he should allow anything of corn being brought to Rome ', i.e. ' to prevent any corn from . . .'.

ll. 5–6. **praedatum,** acc. of the supine again (purpose). **per occasiones,** ' as opportunity offered '.

l. 7. **infestum** here means ' unsafe '.

l. 8. **non cetera solum,** ' not only their other property '. This and **pecus omne** are the subjects of **compelleretur,** but the verb agrees in number with the nearer subject.

l. 11. **hoc tantum licentiae,** ' this so much of licence (i.e. all this licence) was granted '. **metu, consilio** are abl. of cause, ' not so much from fear as policy '.

ll. 12–13. **intentus in,** ' eager for '.

ll. 14–15. **in paruis . . . seruabat,** *lit.,* ' a careless avenger in small matters, was keeping himself (as) a stern punisher for greater (things) ', i.e. ' not bothering to excite vengeance in trifling matters, he was keeping himself for the infliction of a much heavier and weightier blow '.

l. 16. **edicit. . . .** Supply **ut** before **postero die,** to introduce the indirect command.

ll. 16–17. **porta Esquilina,** see the map; abl. of route.

l. 17. **auersissima.** The Etruscans are on the west side of Rome, the Esquiline Gate on the east.

l. 18. **scituros . . . ratus,** ' thinking that the enemy would learn of it '.

l. 19. **seruitia infida,** ' disloyal slaves '. Note the abstract for concrete again.

l. 19. **transfugerent,** subj. in subordinate clause directly or virtually in indirect speech.

l. 19. **et,** ' and in fact '. Note this meaning of **et** at the beginning of a sentence.

l. 20. **multo plures,** ' many more '. Note **multo,** abl. of the measure of difference (found with comparatives).

ll. 20–21. **ut . . . praedae,** *lit.,* as-was-natural (**ut**)[1] with-a-view-to (**ad**) the hope of all the booty ', i.e. ' as was natural when they expected to capture the booty in-one-swoop '.

l. 23. **ad secundum . . . uia,** ' at the second milestone on the Gabinian road '. The latter led from Rome via the Esquiline Gate.

ll. 24–25. **ad portam Collinam.** For the Colline Gate, consult the map.

l. 25. **praetereat.** The present subj. suggests that **donec** means here ' so long as ', not ' until '.

l. 25–26. **inde . . . reditus,** ' then to put themselves in the way (i.e. to bar their passage), to prevent their retreat to the river '.

l. 27. **Naeuia porta,** abl. with **egressus.**

l. 28. **Caelio monte,** ' by way of the Caelian Hill ', abl. of route. He would then leave the city by the porta Caelimontana (see map).

l. 31. **in Lucretium.** If we retain the reading **Lucretium** of the MSS., we shall have to assume that the Etruscans who had sighted **Valerius'** forces first turned from them to face **Lucretius** and thus offered their rear to Herminius' troops who had been waiting in ambush. Many editors, however, assume that **Lucretium** is an obvious mistake for **Valerium.**

l. 32. **hinc . . . illinc:** the former refers to **laeua,** ' on the left ', the latter to **dextra** ' on the right ', and thus is given from the Roman point of view.

l. 34. **neque pares =et non pares** *or* **impares,** ' and they were no match for the Romans '. **uiribus,** abl. of respect, ' in strength '.

[1] Note this use of **ut** =**ut par erat,** ' as was natural '.

CHAPTER 12

l. 1. **frumenti** is dependent upon **inopia.**

ll. 2–3. **sedendoque . . . spem Porsinna: habebat spem = sperabat. sedendo,** ' by sitting ' = ' by remaining encamped '.

1. 3. **cum C. Mucius. . . .** Inverse **cum** clause, for which see the note on Chap. 10, ll. 37–39. The verb (indicative) is **constituit** l. 11, This **cum** clause is broken by a long relative clause **cui . . . fuderit,** and resumed by **ita.**

l. 5. **seruientem,** ' being in slavery ', = ' at the time of their servitude '.

l. 6. **liberum,** ' free ', = ' in their freedom '. Insert ' yet ' before this word to get the contrast which Latin achieves merely by the juxtaposition of words, phrases, or clauses (asyndeton).

l. 8. **fuderit,** primary sequence again.

ll. 9–10. **eam . . . ratus,** ' having thought that that outrage (was) to-be-avenged ', i.e. ' thinking that he ought to avenge . . .'.

It might be helpful to make **ratus** the main verb, and to begin a fresh sentence at **primo.**

ll. 11–13. **ne . . . forte deprehensus . . . ut transfuga,** ' lest . . . he might by chance be caught and dragged back by the Roman sentries as a deserter '. Note: (i) Latin has perf. part. pass. and *one* finite verb for English *two* finite verbs (ii) **ut =** ' as '.

ll. 13–14. **fortuna . . . adfirmante,** abl. absol., best translated here as a causal (' as ' ' since ') clause, ' especially as the state of the city at-that-time would confirm such a charge '.

ll. 16–17. **non . . . ultor,** ' not as a free-booter nor to avenge[1] (**ultor**) their raids in our turn '.

l. 20. **cum. . . .** As usual, English would prefer to make the introductory **cum** clauses main verbs and begin a new sentence with **timens.**

ll. 21–22. **pari fere ornatu,** ' in much the same sort of dress '. **multa ageret,** ' was busy '.

[1] Cf. introduction, p. xvi.

ll. 23–24. **ne . . . esset**, 'lest by not-knowing the king he himself might disclose himself who he was'. Cf. the New Testament literal translation of what is really a Greek idiom, 'I know thee who thou art'. The subject of the indirect question is by anticipation made the object of the main verb.

ll. 24–25. **quo . . . facinus**, 'whither fate by chance led the deed'. Supply 'following' before 'whither ' = 'where'.

ll. 26–31. **Vadentem. . . .** Grammatically **uadentem** is in agreement with the understood object **eum** of **retraxissent**. Make a literal translation and then translate **uadentem** as a temporal clause, 'as he strode', and make the **cum** clause the main verb, beginning a new sentence with **ante**.

ll. 28–29. **cum concursu . . . retraxissent.** See the note on Chap. 5, ll. 9–11. ' Rushing towards the shouting, the king's attendants seized and dragged him back '.

l. 29. **destitutus**, 'brought forward and placed'.

ll. 32–33. **nec . . . caedem**, 'and there is no less (of) courage (to me) for death than there was for murder', i.e. 'I have no less courage . . .'.

l. 33. **et . . . et**, 'both . . . and'. **fortia** is object of both verbs **facere** and **pati**. With the latter the meaning is somewhat strained: 'to do brave deeds and to suffer bravely'.

ll. 35–36. **idem . . . decus**, 'of (men) seeking the same glory'.

l. 36. **accingere**, 2nd sg., pres. imperat. pass., 'gird yourself ready for'.

l. 37. **in singulas horas**, 'from hour to hour'.

ll. 38–39. **iuuentus Romana**, 'we, the Roman youth'.

ll. 39–40. **nullam . . . timueris.** Note that ne (**nullus**) + perf. subj. expresses a negative command,—a more colloquial use than **noli** (**nolite**) + the infinitive.

l. 40. **uni**, dat. sg., in agreement with **tibi**. **res**, 'the struggle'.

l. 41. **ira**, abl. with **infensus**. **minitabundus**, adj. for adv., 'threateningly'.

ll. 43–44. **quas . . . iaceret**, 'what threats of treachery he (i.e. Mucius) was hurling in riddles at him (i.e. Porsenna)'.

l. 44. **tibi,** ' for yourself ' (with **sentias**).

l. 46. **accenso . . . foculo,** dat., after the compound verb **inicit,** ' into the fire that had been lit for the sacrifice '.

l. 46. **quam,** ' it ' (i.e. his right hand) direct obj. of **torreret,** ' he allowed to burn '.

ll. 46–47. **uelut . . . animo,** ' as if his consciousness were bereft of feeling '.

ll. 46–49. **cum . . . prosiluisset . . . iussisset.** Once again, we can drop the **cum,** and make these pluperfect subjunctives main verbs. Insert ' and ' before **inquit.**

ll. 50–51. **iuberem . . . esse,** *lit.,* ' I should bid you be blessed because of your valour ', i.e. ' I should bid you, " well done " '. **macte** may be *either* a vocative of a perf. part. pass. which was treated in this particular phrase as indeclinable, *or* an adverb. **uirtute** is an abl. of cause.

l. 51. **ista uirtus,** ' such courage as yours '.

l. 52. **iure belli liberum,** ' free from the rights of war ', agrees with **te,** as do also **intactum, inuiolatum.**

The phrase means that Mucius might go free from the power which war gave Porsenna over him as his prisoner of war. **iure,** abl. of separation.

l. 54. **quando,** ' since ', the enclitic **quidem** always stresses the preceding word.

l. 55. **ut tuleris,** ' that you may find-yourself-to-have won '. The perfect subj. in this purpose clause represents the action as single *or* completed. **quod . . . nequisti** is the object of **tuleris,** ' what you could not (win) . . .'.

l. 58. **ut cuiusque ceciderit primi,** ' as (the lot) of each man first (i.e. next) will have fallen (i.e. falls) '.

l. 59. **suo quisque tempore,** ' each in his (appropriate) time ', is in apposition with the subject **ceteri.**

CHAPTER 13

ll. 1–3. **Mucium dimissum legati secuti sunt.** See the note on Chap. 5, ll. 9–11. Begin, ' after the dismissal of M.'.

l. 1. **Scaeuolae** is a dim. of **scaeua,** ' left-hand '. Note that it is attracted into the case of the relative pronoun **cui.**

l. 3. **adeo mouerat eum. . . .** Note the order of this sentence, fairly common in Latin:[1] (1) active verb (2) direct object (3) subject or subjects with dependent clauses (relative etc.). To translate literally makes the English clumsy and top-heavy: it is often better to turn into the passive and thus retain the Latin order: ' he had been so deeply stirred both (et) by the chance of the first danger (i.e. by what had happened in his first danger) from which . . . , and by the extreme peril as often to be faced (i.e. which, he would have to face as often) as there were conspirators left . . . '.

l. 5. **texisset,** subjunctive in virtual indirect speech: it gives the thoughts of Porsenna.

l. 7. **ferret = offerret.** See introduction p. xvi. **ultro,** ' voluntarily '. **ultro,** usually, as here, suggests going a step further than might have been expected.

l. 7. **iactatum.** Supply **est** and **a Porsinna.** Similarly with **impetratum** in l. 11.

ll. 10–11. **de agro . . . restituendo,** i.e., the territory which legend said the kings Romulus and Ancus had taken from the people of Veii. See Livy Book I, Chaps 15.5 and 33.9.

ll. 11–12. **expressa . . . Romanis,** ' and the necessity . . . was wrung from the Romans '. **Romanis** is dat. (cf. Chap. 1, l. 11) with **expressa.**

l. 16. **quae** is attracted into the gender and number of the predicate **prata.** So also the verb. Strict use would say **qui** to agree with antecedent **agrum.**

l. 18. **ad publica decora,** ' to win honours for their country '.

l. 21. **dux uirginum,** ' at the head of a troop of girls '.

l. 25. **alias . . . facere,** ' (he said) he did not value the rest highly '. Note: (i) **alias = ceteras.** (ii) **magni,** genitive of **value.**

ll. 26–27. **supra . . . esse,** ' he said (**dicere,** historic infin.) that

[1] Especially where an event or feeling affects people.

that deed was beyond (=surpassed) (the deeds of) men like Cocles and Mucius '.

l. 27. **et prae se ferre,** 'and declared '; *lit.,* 'bore in front of himself '.

ll. 27–28. **quem ad modum** = **ut** in the sense, 'although '.

l. 29. **sic,** 'yet '. **deditam,** 'surrendered ' = 'if she were surrendered '. Note that **quem ad modum,** which introduces a comparative clause is here in acc. +infin., probably by attraction from the fact that the main clause **sic** ... is in that construction. Strict usage would expect it to have the verb in the subjunctive (subordinate in indirect speech).

l. 30. **utrimque** ... **fides,** ' the promise was kept (*lit.,* stood firm) by both sides '.

l. 31. **restituerunt.** The obj. is **eam,** ' her ' understood and **pignus pacis,** ' (as) a pledge of peace ', is in apposition.

ll. 33–34. **laudatam** ... **dixit.** See the note on Chap. 5, ll. 9–11.

l. 33. **parte obsidum,** ' with half the hostages '.

l. 34. **legeret,** indirect command, ' let her choose '.

l. 35. **elegisse** ... **dicitur.** Note the personal construction: she is said to have chosen ', where we prefer the impersonal, ' it is said that she chose '.

l. 35. **quod** ..., 'a choice which was becoming for her as a maiden and in-accordance-with the unanimous view of the hostages themselves likely-to-win-their approval (**probabile**) '.

l. 37. **eam aetatem** ... **quae,** explanatory of the choice, ' that that age (i.e. the girls of that age) ... which (i.e. who) '.

l. 40. **in summa sacra uia,** generally explained as where the Sacra via crossed over the hill of Velia.

CHAPTER 14

ll. 1–4. **huic** ... **uendendi.** The skeleton of the sentence is: ' not-in-accordance-with (**abhorrens**) this peaceful departure ... (is) the custom handed down ... (which) remains among other formal practices, viz., (the custom) '' of selling king P.'s goods '' '.

Note: (i) the dat. (instead of the commoner abl.) used after **abhorrens.** (ii) at public sale of property (booty or confiscated), there was the practice of assuming that Porsenna's goods were being sold. Livy now attempts an explanation of this formula.

ll. 4–7. **cuius originem . . . ,** *lit.,* ' it is necessary that the origin of this custom either arose during the war and was not given up at the peace, or grew up from a beginning more kindly than this notice suggests, viz., of selling an enemy's goods '. Begin: ' this custom must have originally arisen . . .'.

l. 8. **proximum . . . traduntur,** *lit.,* ' the nearest to the truth of what is handed down (is) ', i.e. ' the most credible of the traditional explanations is '.

ll. 9–10. **conuecto . . . commeatu.** Note: (i) sandwiching. Cf. note on Chap. 10, ll. 19–20. (ii) the abl. absol. is explanatory of **opulenta,** ' the camp well-supplied with provisions brought in . . .'.

l. 11. **inopi tum urbe,** abl. absol., ' the city (being) then destitute '.

l. 12. **ea** agrees grammatically with ' camp ', but really refers to the contents. **uēnisse** from **uēneo.**

ll. 14–15. **gratiam . . . regiae,** *lit.,* ' the term indicating gratitude for the gift rather than an auction of the king's property ', i.e. ' as the term indicated . . .'.

ll. 17–18. **ne exercitus . . . uideretur.** Note personal construction again: we prefer, ' lest it might seem that the army . . .'.

l. 19. **oppugnatum,** acc. of the supine to express purpose. **Ariciam** may be the object of the supine, but as this use is not very common, it may be preferable to take it with **mittit,** ' to Aricia ', (acc. of the goal of motion).

l. 21. **a Cumis.** The flourishing town of Cumae, originally a Greek colony, played an important part in the history of this period, especially in resisting Etruscan expansion. For the use of the preposition, cf. the note on Chap. 16, l. 12.

ll. 25–27. **effuseque . . . adortae sunt,** ' and wheeling about (**conuersis signis**), attacked in the rear, the enemy having streamed past ', i.e. ' after the enemy had streamed past, they wheeled and attacked them in the rear '.

l. 27. in medio, i.e. ' between the two armies ', i.e. of Cumae, and of the Latins. prope iam uictores, ' almost in the hour of victory '.

l. 28. pars, being a collective noun, is often used with verbs in the masc. pl., e.g. delati sunt.

ll. 29–30. et fortuna . . . supplicum, ' both in the state and with the appearance of suppliants '. fortuna, specie, abls. of description, more commonly found with an adj., although in this case the gen. supplicum seems to fulfil that role.

ll. 30–31. diuisi in hospitia, ' were assigned as guests to different hosts '.

l. 33. hospitum urbisque caritas, ' affection for their hosts and the city '. Note the objective genitives.

l. 34. Tuscum uicum. This street led from the forum down by the west side of the Palatine hill.

CHAPTER 15

l. 2. eo anno, i.e. in 506 B.C., in the consulships of P. Lucretius and Valerius Publicola.

l. 6. honoratissimus quisque, ' each most respected ', the regular Latin for ' the most respected '. Note that this phrase, though grammatically sing. has a plural verb, missi (sunt).

ll. 6–8. non quin . . . quam, lit., ' not because an answer could not briefly be given, that kings were not being (=would not be) received, for this reason chosen men of the fathers had been sent to him rather than '.

Note: (i) quin = quod non. (ii) potuerit, primary sequence. (iii) recipi, pres. infin. where we would prefer future. (iv) patrum, partitive gen.

Translate: ' it was not because they could not give a brief reply viz. that the royal family . . . , that they had sent to him chosen members of the senate rather than . . .'.

ll. 10–11. **in tantis ... beneficiis,** *lit.,* 'in so great mutual benefits ', i.e. ' when there were great benefits on both sides '.

l. 12. **Romani.** ... Insert 'while' before **Romani.** For the asyndeton see the note on Chap. 12, l. 6.

l. 13. **in perniciem suam faciles,** *lit.,* ' good-natured to their own destruction ', i.e. ' to be so good-natured as to destroy themselves'.

l. 13. **negarent,** 'said "no" '. **cui.** Supply the antecedent, ' (to one) to whom '.

ll. 17–18. **ut ... sit.** Note again the order: relative clause precedes and contains the antecedent. See note on Chap. 9, ll. 8–9. *Lit.,* ' that the same end be for the city as (**qui**) would be the end for freedom in that city '; i.e. ' that when freedom in that city was finished, so too would finish the city itself '.

Finally note, **erit,** fut. indic., although in a subordinate clause in indirect speech. Strict usage would demand **esset.** Occasionally, however, Livy retains the original tense and *mood.*

l. 19. **ut.** ... order for translation: **(se) orare ut patiatur (eam) esse liberam.**

l. 22. **eadem ... agendo,** ' by pleading the same things in vain ', i.e. ' by the same useless pleas '.

ll. 26–27. **obsidum ... erat,** ' what of hostages (partit. gen.) was remaining ', i.e. ' all the remaining hostages ', is the object of **reddidit.**

l. 27. **foedere.** ... See Chap. 13, ll. 10–11. **icto,** comes from the verb **ico,** defective mainly in its present stem.

l. 29. **exsulatum,** acc. of the supine to express purpose. This construction will not be commented upon again.

CHAPTER 16

l. 3. **mole. moles,** *lit.,* ' mass ', then anything massive like a ' pier ', ' mole ' (cf. Chap. 5, l. 5), is here used metaphorically for ' power ', ' effort '.

ll. 3–4. **aduersus eos,** *lit.,* ' against them ', i.e. ' to oppose them '.

ll. 4–6. **ne. . . . quid** has the partitive gen. **repentini periculi** dependent upon it, ' that no sudden peril might arise at the same time from Tusculum . . . '.

The latter was an important Latin town 15 miles south-east of Rome, built on a strong site, 2,000 ft. above sea-level. We learn from the previous chapter that its ruler was the son-in-law of Tarquin ' the Proud '. Later, the town became a firm ally of Rome and the first Latin city to obtain Roman citizenship.

ll. 7–8. **seditio . . . orta.** Note ' the sandwiching '.

l. 8. **aliquantum uirium,** ' a considerable part of their strength ': **uirium,** partitive genitive.

ll. 9–10. **Appio Claudio.** Note again: this complement agrees in case with the relative **cui** and not with **nomen,** the logical subject.

l. 11. **a turbatoribus belli,** *lit.*, ' by the stirrers-up of war ', i.e. ' by those who were agitating for war '.

l. 12. **ab Inregillo.** In Livy we often find a preposition with names of towns instead of the abl. alone for ' place whence ', a use which is typical of early Latin and found increasingly in Latin prose from the time of Livy onwards.

The site of this town is unknown.

l. 12. **magna . . . manu.** Note: (i) the perfect part. of the deponent **comitor** has a *passive* meaning, ' accompanied ', (ii) **clientium.** From this passage, it appears that the patron-client relationship, whereby a strong economic group gives protection and the use of land in return for personal service, was not confined to Rome, (iii) **manu,** abl. of the instrument.

ll. 14–15. **Vetus Claudia tribus . . . ,** 'after new tribesmen had been added later, those who came from this territory were called " the old Claudian Tribe ".'

This passage, the meaning of which is disputed, is perhaps best explained as follows: the name ' Old Claudian Tribe ' came to be used by those who came up to Rome for elections from the district across the Anio (**ex eo . . . agro,** the original seat of the tribe), to distinguish them from the members of the tribe who might live in different parts of Italy, as was inevitable, when by 241 B.C., the number of tribes being fixed at thirty-five, new tribesmen had to be allocated, no matter where they lived, to one of the existing tribes.

In this case: **uenirent** is an example of Livy's use of this mood in a frequentative or iterative sense in temporal and relative clauses.

ll. 16–17. **in . . . peruenit,** ' came to be regarded as one of its leading members '.

l. 18. **cum,** ' when '.

l. 19. **inde,** *lit.,* ' thence ' =' from that quarter ', *or* ' from them '.

l. 23. **anno,** abl. of the measure of difference, used with comparatives and words like **post** and **ante.** **post** is here an adverb; **Agrippa . . . consulibus,** abl. absol.

ll. 24–25. **gloria . . . exiguis,** abls. of description. Begin a fresh sentence here with; '(he was a man) of great reputation, (but) of such scanty private means . . . '.

Livy is probably mistaken here: the public funeral was given to Publius Valerius as a mark of honour, not because he was too poor to have left the money to pay for his own funeral.

l. 27. **duae coloniae Latinae.** Strictly speaking, Latin colonies at this time were federal foundations in which the Latin towns and Rome took part. They had two aims, to act as outposts and to satisfy land-hunger.

ll. 30–31. **omne Auruncum . . . est,** ' all the Auruncan war was driven upon (i.e. was concentrated upon) Pometia '.

l. 32. **caedibus temperatum est.** Note the passive use (impersonally) of an intransitive verb: turn into the active and make personal: e.g. ' it was refrained from acts of slaughter ', becomes ' they refrained from . . .'.

ll. 34–35. **ne ab obsidibus quidem . . . abstinuit,** *lit.,* ' not even from the hostages who three hundred in number had been received, did the passion of war refrain '.

Retain the order by turning into the passive: ' not even the hostages of whom . . . , were spared in the passions aroused by the war '.

CHAPTER 17

l. 2. **ui**, 'by sudden assault': **uineis . . . operibus**, 'with mantlets and other siege-engines'. The former were made of hides stretched on wooden frames and gave some protection from the enemy's missiles to the attackers as they tried to undermine or break through the enemy's defences.

At this time ' siege-engines ' would not be as elaborate or highly-developed as they became in later Roman campaigns. Perhaps only simple forms of battering-rams would be used.

l. 3. **In quos.** . . . Note once again this Latin period: subject, perf. part. of deponent in agreement, **cum** + pluperf. subj., main verb. English would prefer probably *three* main verbs: e.g. ' The Aurunci rose up against them (**in quos**), (inspired) more by a hatred (which-was) now implacable than . . ., rushed out, the majority armed with . . . , and spread slaughter and fire all around them (*lit.*, ' filled all with . . .'.)

l. 7. **et.** Note that we say ' or ' in such phrases.

ll. 9–10. **Romam . . . reditum (est).** Note: (i) impersonal passive of an intransitive verb: make *active* and *personal*, ' the (Romans) returned'. (ii) **male gesta re**, a useful phrase for ' after this failure *or* defeat'.

ll. 11–12. **interiecto . . . spatio**, ' when no great (=a short) time had been put between (=had elapsed)'.

ll. 12–13. **quod . . . satis esset**, ' such as was sufficient'. The subjunctive is consecutive.

l. 13. **cum . . . tum**, ' not only . . . but also '.

l. 15. **mole**, ' huge engines '.

ll. 15–16. **in eo esset . . . miles**, *lit.*, ' (it) was in that (situation) that the soldiers were making-their-way onto the walls ', i.e. ' the soldiers were on the point of . . .'.

ll. 16–18. **nihilo minus foeda Aurunci passi (sunt)**, ' the A. suffered no less a terrible (fate) ', i.e. ' the fate of the A. was just as terrible '. **quam** will then mean ' as '.

ll. 18–19. **sub corona . . . alii**, ' the rest of the colonists were sold as slaves '. Note: (i) alii = ceteri, (ii) uenierunt from ueneo, (iii) sub corona. Prisoners-of-war wore a garland (corona) when they were put up for sale.

l. 20. ob iras grauiter ultas, ' for the wrongs which they had avenged '. Note ultas, perf. part. of a deponent verb, in passive meaning: cf. comitatus, Chap. 16, l. 12.

CHAPTER 18

ll. 2-3. per ludos, ' at the games '. per lasciuiam, ' in wanton sport '.

l. 4. concursu hominum, lit., ' at the rushing together of the men '. Translate, ' when men rushed (to the scene) ', especially if cum in l. 2 has been dropped and raperentur made a main verb.

ll. 5-6. paruaque ..., ' and from an insignificant incident, the situation seemed to look to (=to tend to) a fresh outbreak-of-war '.

l. 6. Supra belli Latini metum occurs here in the MSS which many editors omit as a marginal comment on the following sentence, which has been later incorporated into the text. As it stands, it means, ' beyond the fear of (=caused by) a Latin war '.

ll. 6-7. id quoque accesserat, lit., ' this also had been added ' (accedere is often used as the pass. of addere), i.e. ' there was also this additional fact that (quod) '.

ll. 7-8. triginta populos. These are the thirty cities who formed the Latin League.

l. 9. in hac ... ciuitate, lit., ' the state being troubled (abl. absol.) in this apprehension of such great (dangers) ', i.e. ' as the state ... in its apprehension ...'.

l. 10. primum, adv., ' for the first time '. creandi, ' of appointing '. In the early years of the Republic, the consuls could take the initiative in appointing a dictator to cope with a military crisis. Later, it became the practice for the Senate to issue a formal decree and to suggest the person to hold this important office (six months).

ll. 10-13. sed ... satis constat. Note: (i) quibus consulibus parum creditum sit nec ... creatus sit are indirect questions dependent upon **nec satis constat,** ' there is not sufficient agreement '. (ii) **quibus consulibus** is dat., dependent upon **parum creditum sit,** an intransitive verb used *impersonally* in the passive. Translate personally and in the active, ' as to which consuls they distrusted '. (iii) **quia . . . essent** gives the reason why they were distrusted: **essent,** subjunctive in virtual indirect speech, ' because (they said) they were . . .'.

The MSS include **nec quo anno** before **nec quibus consulibus,** but it is omitted by many editors[1] as a gloss to **consulibus.**

l. 14. **auctores.** For Livy's sources, see the introduction, p. xiii.

l. 15. **magister equitum,** ' master of the horse ', a subordinate official, nominated by a dictator on his appointment, originally to command the cavalry, but later to represent the dictator either in battle or in Rome.

l. 16. **consulares,** acc. pl. **legere** =**legerunt,** subject, the senators. **ita . . . lata.** This is very uncertain, for in the early days of the Republic, not many men could have held the consulship. Moreover, Livy has already admitted his own doubts and he is quite wrong in giving the right to choose to the senate. See the note on l. 5 above.

l. 18. **Largium qui . . . erat.** This statement betrays more confusion, because we are told by Livy at the beginning of this chapter that this same year 501 B.C., Largius was consul for the first time.

ll. 18–20. **erat, fuerat.** Why are these verbs in the indicative, although they seem to be in subordinate clauses in indirect speech?

l. 19. **M.'** =**Manium.**

ll. 20–21. **moderatorem . . . appositum,** ' was joined to the consuls to control (them) (as) their superior '. For the translation of **moderatorem,** see the introduction, p. xvi. On the appointment of a dictator, the normal magistrates continued in office but their powers were subordinate to the superior imperium of the dictator.

l. 21. **quin** is here an adverb and means, ' nay '.

---

[1] Following the scholar Madvig.

ll. 21–22. **si maxime uellent,** ' if they specially wished '.

ll. 24–25. **praeferri secures,** ' the axes borne before him ', i.e. the dictator, against whose right to execute there was at this time ' no right of appeal to the people ', as had been granted by the Lex Valeria de provocatione, as a measure of protection against the consuls. See Chap. 8, ll. 4–7. In accordance with this law the consuls' lictors bore only the rods within the city's boundaries, the rods and axe outside.

l. 26. **ad dicto parendum,** ' for obeying commands '.

ll. 28–29. **neque . . . auxilium,** *lit.,* ' for neither as in-the-case-of the consuls inasmuch as (**qui** causal) they were of equal power (was there) the help of the other (consul) nor the right of appeal (to the people) nor any help anywhere except in the care for obeying '.

As there were two consuls of equal authority, a citizen could always appeal against an action or decree of one consul to his colleague the other consul, who, if he were disposed, could veto his colleague's action.

l. 30. **creatus Romae dictator,** ' the appointment of a dictator at Rome '.

l. 32. **Quibus orantibus . . . ut,** ' on their requesting the dictator and the senate to . . .'.

l. 34. **responsum (est),** ' the answer was given '.

l. 34. **adulescentibus** is dat. dependent on **ignosci** which is transitive in English, but intransitive in Latin and therefore can be used in the passive only *im*personally.

ll. 34–35. **senibus,** insert ' but '; an example of asyndeton.

ll. 36–37. **quod . . . erat,** ' what (of) expense had been incurred for the war ', is the object of **praestare,** ' to guarantee '.

l. 39. **tacitae indutiae,** ' a tacit suspension of hostilities ' (*lit.,* ' truce '). The phrase means that there was no formal armistice.

CHAPTER 19

ll. 1–6. **Consules. . . .** This chapter opens with short sentences which, in all probability, Livy has taken direct from one of his sources, the annalists.

l. 6. dilatum (est). Latin sometimes says 'was postponed', where we prefer 'could be postponed'. Cf. Chap. 10, ll. 46–47.

l. 6. A. Postumius dictator. Note that Postumius had not been consul, yet he is appointed dictator. Cf. what Livy says in Chap. 18, l. 16.

l. 7. magnis copiis. In military phrases, the troops with which a march is made are put in the abl., generally without cum when an adj. is used as here.

l. 8. ad Lacum Regillum. This is now identified with a volcanic depression near Tusculum, modern Frascati, 15 miles south-east of Rome.

l. 11. sustineri ... confligerent, *lit.*, 'anger could not be restrained but that they straightway engaged in battle', i.e. 'in their anger the Romans could not be restrained from ...'.

l. 12. quam cetera, *lit.*, 'than the rest (of battles)'; we might say for the whole sentence: 'therefore the engagement far exceeded all others in its severity and bitterness'.

ll. 13–14. ad regendam rem, 'to direct operations'.

l. 14. modo goes with non.

ll. 17–19. in Postumium ... instruentemque. Retain the Latin order by translating this participial phrase by an 'as' clause, 'as P. was encouraging and ...'.

ll. 19–20. quamquam ... grauior, *lit.*, 'although somewhat burdened now in respect of age and strength', i.e. 'although now bowed down by advancing years and (loss of) strength'.

aetate, uiribus, abls. of respect.

l. 21. concursu ... est, *lit.*, 'was taken back into safety by a rush of his men', i.e. 'was got back safely by his men who had rushed in to the rescue'.

ll. 23–24. nec fefellit ueniens, *lit.*, 'coming he did-not-escape-the-notice-of', i.e. 'his charge was not unnoticed by the Tusculan commander'.

l. 25. tantaque ... fuit, 'and so great was the violence of their coming (=of their charge) with lances levelled at each other'.

l. 26. **Aebutio,** dat. of disadvantage, where we would prefer the gen. Similarly **Mamilio.**

traiectum sit. The perfect subj., as usual in result clauses, expresses the immediate result or a single action.

l. 31. **cohortem,** 'a company'. The use of **cohors** is an anachronism, for it was not until the time of Marius (105 B.C.), that the legion was divided into ten cohorts. Before him, there were thirty maniples in each legion.

l. 32. **L. Tarquini filius.** His name was Titus. Another son, Arruns, had been killed in the fighting described in Chap. 6.

l. 32. **ea quo....** We should expect the relative clause (**quo** + comparative) to be balanced by a main clause **eo** + comparative; the abls. **quo, eo** are measure of difference), 'the more ..., the more ...'.[1] But in this case, there is no **eo** or comparative.

Translate: 'and it (=these) since they fought ... on account of the loss of ..., they succeeded-in-renewing ...'.

CHAPTER 20

l. 2. **conspicatus.** Make a main verb and insert 'and' before **domestica.**

ll. 4–5. **ut cuius ... forent.** Note: (i) the relative clause precedes and contains the antecedent **familiae.** (ii) **eiecti reges,** 'the expulsion of the princes'; **interfecti (reges),** 'the slaying (of them)' are subjects of **erant** and **forent** respectively, **decus** being the complement; 'that the slaying of the princes might be the distinction of the same family whose distinction had been their expulsion'.

ll. 8–10. **Valerium....** The Latin order (obj. subj. verb) may be retained if we begin as follows, 'Valerius was charging ... when someone ...'.

ll. 9–10. **nec quicquam ... retardato,** 'and as the horse was in no way (lit., not in-any-way) checked by the rider's wound'.

l. 13. **talem uirum,** 'so brave a hero'.

[1] Cf. Chaps. 35, l. 27, 51, l. 21, 55, l. 22.

l. 13. **citato agmine,** 'at full speed'. Livy frequently uses **agmen** (strictly 'column on the march') for any body of soldiers.

l. 15. **quam ... manum,** 'a picked body which'. **delectam manum,** inside the rel. clause, agrees with **quam,** whereas we should have it *outside* and in apposition with **cohorti suae.**

It is most unlikely that Roman generals had bodyguards at this time, for the institution of such a general's cohort is attributed to Scipio Africanus Minor in 134 B.C.

l. 16. **ut quem....** Note again the relative clause precedes: the antecedent (**eum**) has to be supplied: 'to treat (as) an enemy (anyone) of their army whom they saw ...'. **uiderint,** perf. subj., primary sequence for **uidissent** which strict usage would demand. It represents an original fut. perf. indic.

l. 17. **metu ancipiti,** *lit.,* ' by a two-fold fear ', i.e. from the enemy and the general's body-guard.

l. 24. **secum rapit,** 'hurriedly took with him'.

l. 24. **agmine,** 'in a body'.

l. 25. **legatus** means 'officer' here.

l. 28. **et** means 'both' and can be ignored.

l. 29. **occiderit,** and **exspirauerit,** l. 32, perf. subj. in consecutive clauses giving the actual immediate result.

ll. 29–30. **inter spoliandum ... hostis,** 'while in-the-act-of-stripping the enemy's body'. The acc. of the gerund or gerundive is rarely used after prepositions other than **ad.**

Strictly speaking, the death of Herminius was only indirectly the result of the violence of his attack.

l. 31. **inter primam curationem,** *lit.,* 'amid the first treatment (of his wounds)', i.e. 'as his wounds were first being treated'.

l. 33. **fesso iam pedite,** abl. absol., 'now that the infantry were exhausted'.

l. 35. **in primum,** 'to the front'.

l. 35. **pro antesignanis.** The 'front-rank fighters were so called because in the actual fighting the standards of the first line (**hastati**) were placed behind the maniples which composed it. The

principes formed the second line and the **triarii** the third (in reserve).

l. 37. **aequato genere pugnae,** ' their kind of fighting equalled ' = ' on equal terms in the fighting '.

l. 38. **partem,** ' a share '.

l. 40. **equiti** is a collective singular.

l. 41. **nec . . . nec.** Note that the negative **nihil** is subdivided here by **nec . . . nec** which therefore means ' either . . . or '.

l. 42. **aedem Castori.** The temple of Castor and Pollux was commonly called **aedes Castoris,** the twins (brothers of Helen) being known as the Castores. It was built in the forum, being dedicated in 484 B.C. Cf. Chap. 42.

There was another legend (probably of Greek origin) that the two heroes actually took part in the battle on the Roman side. See Dionysius Halicarnassus, *Ant. Rom.* (6, 13, 1–2).

ll. 43–44. **qui . . . intrauisset,** ' who were the first and second to enter . . .'. Note: (i) the Latin idiom **primus intrauit,** ' he (was) the first to enter '. (ii) **intrauisset** represents an original fut. perfect indic. Postumius said: ' I shall give rewards . . . who . . . will have entered '.

CHAPTER 21

l. 1. **triennio,** ' in the (next) three years', abl. of time within which.

l. 3. **aedes Saturno.** This was built at the north-west end of the forum at the foot of the Capitoline hill. The eight columns which can still be seen belong to a reconstruction of the first century B.C. This temple of Saturn came later to be used as a sanctuary, a treasury, and a record office (for the measures passed by the Popular Assemblies).

l. 4. **Saturnalia.** Saturnus was probably in origin an old Italian deity of sowing (**serere**).[1] His festival of thanksgiving began on Dec. 17th and from the second century B.C. onwards became a

[1] Thus this festival may be much older than Livy suggests.

carnival with much licence and excessive eating and drinking. It was destined later still to influence the celebrations associated with our Christmas.

institutus is attracted into the gender of the complement **festus dies,** ' as a holiday '.

l. 6. **ad Regillum ... inuenio;** i.e. in 496 B.C., not 499 as described in the previous chapter.

ll. 9–10. **tanti ...** , ' such great uncertainties of times entangle (the historian) (i.e. the historian gets so involved when there are so many doubts as to dates) with the magistrates arranged differently in different sources that ...'. For these sources, see the introduction, p. xii.

ll. 12–13. **in tanta ... auctorum,** *lit.,* ' in so great an age not only of events but also of authorities ', i.e. ' when not only events ... are concealed in the past '.

l. 17. **ad Aristodemum tyrannum.** Aristodemus is regarded as an historical figure who helped to break the Etruscan control of Latium at the battle of Aricia (505 B.C.). He had seized power at Cumae after repulsing Etruscan forces as early as 524 B.C.

ll. 19–20. **cui ... erat.** Note: the intransitive verb **inseruio,** used impersonally in the passive. As usual make it personal and active; e.g. ' whom they had until that day treated with the utmost (**summa ope**) consideration '.

ll. 20–21. **fieri coepere. coepere** = **coeperunt.** The normal rule is for **coepi** to be used in the *passive* when it has a passive infinitive dependent upon it. Here **coepere** remains in the active, probably because **fieri** is not felt to be truly passive.[1]

l. 21. **Signia colonia.** Note the apposition and cf. **urbs Roma,** ' the city of Rome '.

It appears that the original colonists had been driven out by the Volsci. They now return from Rome where they had taken refuge, with new colonists.

ll. 23–24. **Romae....** Tradition ascribes to Servius Tullius two important reforms, (1) the registration of property (i.e. land),

[1] An early Latin form **fiere** suggests that the verb may have originally been active.

(2) a grouping of the people by wealth, for military purposes. In (1), the people were registered in four city tribes in Rome and sixteen country tribes in the countryside surrounding Rome. As Rome's territory expanded, so did the number of ' country ' tribes, until by 241 B.C. the number had reached thirty-five. After this there was no further increase in numbers, but new citizens, no matter from what part of Italy they came, were registered in one of the existing tribes.

These tribes were the units for the census, taxation (**tributum**) and the military levy.

Livy now states that the ' country ' tribes were raised in 496 B.C. to seventeen.

l. 24. **aedes M.** This temple lay at the foot of the Aventine hill, overlooking the Circus Maximus. Mercury was the god (or patron saint) of traders.

<h3 style="text-align:center">CHAPTER 22</h3>

l. 1. **Latino bello,** abl. of time within which, ' during the war with-the-Latins '. et =' both ' and, as so often, can be ignored.

l. 3. **quae mitterent;** the subjunctive expresses purpose, ' to send '.

ll. 3–4. **ni maturatum . . . esset.** The real apodosis is unexpressed, i.e., ' and they would have sent them '.

l. 6. **hac ira,** abl. of cause, ' owing to resentment at this '. Note: **hac** used instead of the objective gen. **huius.**

l. 7. **consilii poenam,** ' punishment for their design '.

l. 8. **armorum immemores,** *lit.,* ' unmindful of arms ', =' without a thought of offering armed resistance '.

l. 8. **obsides,** ' as hostages '.

l. 9. **a Cora atque Pometia.** As Pometia has already been destroyed in the war with the Aurunci (Chap. 17), it is surprising to find it mentioned here. It is, therefore, generally accepted now that Livy has included in Chaps. 17 and 22 two versions of the same event. Further evidence of this is given by the number of 300 hostages (cf. Chap. 16, l. 35).

l. 11. **suum ingenium,** ' their native character '. **suum** refers to
Volcis which is logically, if not grammatically, the subject of the
sentence.

l. 15. **ira odioque . . . ,** *lit.*, ' the defeat recently experienced at
Lake R., held back the Latins through anger and hatred against
anyone whoever urged war, not even from violating the envoys '.
Note: (i) **ira odio,** abls. of cause. (ii) **quicumque suaderet.** See
note on Chap. 16, ll. 14–15 (end).

A possible translation might begin: ' owing to the defeat . . . the
Latins were so filled with . . . against . . . , that they did not even
refrain from . . .'.

l. 17. **comprehensos. . . .** See note on Chap. 5, ll. 9–11.

l. 20. **adeo fuit gratum,** ' (their action) was so pleasing . . .'.

l. 22. **negatum fuerat.** Livy seems to use **fuerat** for **erat** in
compound tenses, without any difference of meaning.

l. 24. **facto,** ' in-what-they-had-done '.

l. 25. **donum,** ' (as) a gift '.

ll. 26–27. **qui captiuorum,** i.e. ' those of the captives who '.
magna . . . multitudo is nom., and therefore in apposition with the
preceding relative clause.

l. 29. **liberaliter . . . sua,** ' because they had been treated and
cared for so generously in their adversity '.

l. 31. **alias, ante,** are adverbs.

CHAPTER 23

l. 1. **et ciuitas. . . .** It is probable that in the early years of the
Republic there was some economic retrogression, due to little or
no expansion of Roman territory (such as had occurred under the
kings), loss of productivity[1] owing to frequent enemy raids, and
the decline of the overseas trade that had been built up under the
Etruscan kings with their free communications with Etruria.
Furthermore in the community of Rome which was predominantly
agricultural and therefore dependent upon what could be produced

---

[1] See later in the chapter, l. 21.

from the soil, a bad season could have disastrous effects upon the peasantry who, under the laws of debt then prevalent when lenders must have been few, rates of interest high, and the penalties for insolvency ruthless, had to borrow seed-corn or stock on the security of their land, if they had sufficient, or on that of their own person and of those of their families. So it might well happen that a Roman freeman who could not meet his debts either by his land or by his personal service, might eventually be sold to a slave-dealer.

Throughout the struggle of the orders, during the next two centuries, the plebeians felt the harshness of the laws of debt to be one of their main grievances.

ll. 4–5. **dimicantes,** ' while they fought '.

l. 9. **magno natu quidam,** ' an old man '.

ll. 11–12. **foedior . . . perempti; perempti** agrees with **corporis,** ' more terrible was the state of his person destroyed by pallor and leanness '; i.e. ' more terrible was his bodily appearance with its deathly pallor and emaciation '.

l. 12. **ad hoc,** ' in addition to this '.

ll. 12–13. **promissa . . . oris,** ' his unkempt beard and hair had given his face the look of a wild beast '. **promissa** from **promitto,** in the meaning, ' I let grow '.

l. 13. **in.** See the note on Chap. 10, l. 48.

l. 14. **ordines duxisse,** ' that he had led the ranks ' = ' that he had been a company-commander '.

l. 16. **testes,** ' (as) witnesses of ' = ' that bore witness to ', in apposition to **cicatrices** which were **aduerso pectore,** ' all in front '.

l. 17. **Sciscitantibus,** abl. absol., ' them asking ', = ' when they asked '. **unde;** supply **esset** for this indirect question, *lit.,* ' whence was . . .' = ' the reason for his condition and unsightly appearance '.

l. 19. **prope in contionis modum,** ' almost as if it were a public meeting '.

ll. 20–23. **se militantem aes alienum fecisse** is the skeleton of the sentence; ' that he had contracted debt while-on-service in the Sabine campaign' (**Sabino bello**).

l. 21. **caruerit, incensa fuerit.** Primary sequence again.

ll. 22–23. **tributum ... imperatum (fuerit),** ' (and) the war tax had been levied at a time unfavourable to him '.

ll. 23–25. **id ... aliis,** ' that (debt), increased by interest, had stripped him first of the farm that had been his father's and his grandfather's and then of the rest of his property.' **fortunis** would include movables, such as stock, implements and furniture. **aliis = ceteris.**

l. 26. **non in seruitium.** A **nexus** did not become the slave of the creditor, but he had to work off his debt by service and work. The speaker is suggesting, however, that this might be as bad as, if not worse than, slavery.

l. 27. **ostentare,** historic infinitive.

ll. 28–29. **ad haec ... auditaque,** ' at this seen and heard '; i.e. ' at the sight of this and at the story they had heard '.

l. 30. **se tenet,** ' remained '.

l. 31. **uincti solutique,** ' both chained and unchained '.

l. 31. **in publicum,** ' into the streets '.

l. 32. **Quiritium.** The ancients themselves derived **Quirites** from the name of the Sabine town Cures and saw in its use with Romani a recollection of the traditional union of the Romans and Sabines by Romulus in one community. But the probable derivation of the word suggests it means either ' wardsmen ' from **curia,** or ' a gathering of men ' (**co-viri**). In general usage **Quirites** came to be employed of the Romans in their civilian role.

ll. 32–33. **Nullo ... comes,** *lit.,* ' in no place was there lacking a willing companion of the outbreak ', i.e. ' everywhere arose men willing to take part in . . .'.

l. 34. **curritur,** impersonal passive, ' men were running '.

l. 35. **suo,** ' to themselves '. **qui patrum,** ' any of the fathers who '.

l. 36–37. **nec temperatum manibus foret,** impersonal pass. again: ' nor would they have refrained from violence '.

l. 40. **deformitatemque aliam,** ' and other hideousness' =' and other hideous sights '.

l. 40. **haec se meritos dicere** (historic infin.), ' they said, these (were the rewards) they had won '—the sentiment is, of course, ironical.

l. 41. **exprobrantes ... militiam,** *lit.,* ' each one, making a reproach of his military service, one here, another there (**alius alibi**)', i.e. ' as each one reproached them with his military service in different places '.

l. 42. **postulare,** historic infin. So also **putare** in l. 49.

ll. 43–44. **futuri ... consilii,** ' as men who intended to determine and control the policy of the state '.

futuri. Livy uses the future participle to express purpose.

ll. 49–50. **et patrum qui abessent abesse,** ' and the absent fathers were absent '.

ll. 51–52. **nec dubie ... suas,** ' and their miseries were without doubt (**nec dubie = et non dubie**) a mockery to them '. **ludibrio,** predicative dative.

ll. 52–53. **iam prope erat ut,** *lit.,* ' by now it was almost that ' = ' the situation had deteriorated to such an extent that . . .'.

l. 53. **iras,** ' angry passions '.

ll. 53–55. **cum ... ueniunt,** inverse **cum** clause. Cf. note on Chap. 10, ll. 37–39.

l. 53. **morando,** supply ' whether ' before this gerund.

l. 55. **frequenti curia,** abl. absol.

ll. 55–57. **non modo ... conueniebat.** Note that in the expression **non modo non—sed ne ... quidem,** provided the two negative phrases have a verb in common, the **non** is generally omitted.

l. 58. **imperio ... agendam,** *lit.,* ' that the matter was to-be-done by consular authority ', i.e. ' that the situation should be dealt with by the (use of) consular authority '.

ll. 58–59. **uno ... arrepto.** Translate this abl. absol. by an ' if ' clause. **quieturos.** This fut. infin. act. is dependent upon **censebat.**

l. 61. **cum ... tum,** ' not only ... but also '.

CHAPTER 24

l. 1. **Inter haec,** ' meanwhile '. **maior ... terror.** Supply the verb, ' arose '.

ll. 3–4. **Quae audita,** *lit.,* ' which heard ', nom., subject of **fecere;** translate, ' this report '.

l. 5. **exsultare, dicere, confirmare** are historic infinities: **plebes** is the subject of the first two and **dicere** has a dependent acc. + infin. **deos adesse.**

l. 6. **ultores,** ' as avengers ' with **superbiae patrum** dependent; ' to punish the proud arrogance of the fathers '.

l. 7. **alius alium,** ' one the other ' is the regular Latin for ' one another'. **confirmare** means here, ' they encouraged' and is followed naturally by indirect command.

l. 7. **ne ... darent,** i.e. to the consul when he held the military levy. After **darent** we have acc. and infin. with ' they said ' understood.

ll. 8–9. **militarent ... caperent,** indirect command: ' let the fathers serve ...'.

l. 10. **praemia.** The rewards are the **ager publicus,** ' state-land ' enlarged from time to time by the acquisition of land from a defeated enemy. **Ager publicus**[1] was used either as common land for pasture or divided in small-holdings leased by the community to the tenants. No doubt the patricians had more than their fair share of its use.

l. 11. **et ... et,** ' both ... and '.

ll. 12–13. **cui ... populare erat,** ' whose character was more likely to-win-the-people (**populare**) (than that of his colleague) '.

l. 13. **orare,** historic infin.

ll. 14–15. **misso senatu. misso** = dimisso. Cf. the note on Chap. 13, l. 7.

l. 15. **in contionem prodit,** ' went forth to address the people '.

---

[1] By this time Roman territory was about 350 square miles, twice as much as any other Latin city.

ll. 15–16. ibi . . . , *lit.*, ' there he pointed out that it was for a care (predicative dat.) to the fathers that it be consulted to the people ', i.e. ' that the fathers were anxious that the interests of the people be consulted '.

l. 17. de . . . ciuitatis, ' concerning that very large part, but yet (only) a part of the state '. Note that ille is often strengthened by quidem, which here for further emphasis, is placed after maxima.

ll. 18–20. nec posse bello praeuerti quicquam, *lit.*, ' nor can anything be attended to before war ', would probably be better in English as the active, ' nor could they attend to . . .'.

ll. 20–24. nec . . . consuluisse, ' nor, should there be some respite,[1] would it be on the one hand honourable for the people not to have taken up (i.e. to refuse to take up) arms for their country, unless they received payment first, or at all seemly for the fathers to have consulted . . .'.

Note: (i) that Latin uses the indicative ' it is honourable ' where we prefer, ' it would be . . .'. This indicative is the same as that in the apodosis of conditional clauses with verbs denoting *power, possibility, duty*, and the like, where we should normally have the subjunctive. (ii) the first aut (l. 20) is followed not by a second one, but by neque (l. 22).

l. 22–23. per metum . . . uoluntate, ' under intimidation rather than later of their own free-will '.

ll. 24–25. contioni addidit fidem, ' increased their confidence in his words '.

l. 25. edicto quo edixit ne quis, ' by a proclamation that no-one . . .'. Livy inserts quo edixit to introduce the indirect command ne quis. . . . It can be ignored in English.

ll. 26–27. quo minus . . . fieret, ' in order that he might not have the chance of giving in his name to the consuls '.

l. 28. possideret, from possido (3).

l. 29. liberos . . . moraretur, ' (or) (was) to detain his children or grandchildren ', i.e. by making them be responsible for paying off the debt by working for him.

---

[1] By the Volscians postponing their hostile intentions.

The important new provision is of course, **donec in castris esset.**
A creditor could take no action to recover his debt, while the debtor
was on active service.

l. 30. **qui aderant nexi**, i.e. **nexi qui aderant.**

l. 30. **profiteri**, historic infin., ' gave in '.

l. 31. **proripientium** depends upon **concursus fieri**, *lit.*, ' there
was a rush of men bursting forth . . .', i.e. keeping the order of the
Latin, ' everywhere . . . , men burst forth from the houses now
that the creditor had not the right to detain them and rushed into
the forum . . .'.

l. 33. **ut . . . dicerent.** Livy uses **sacramento dicere**, *lit.*, ' to
speak in accordance with the oath ', where Caesar says **sacramentum
dicere**, ' to take the military oath '.

ll. 34–35. **neque . . .** , ' and the valour and service of no others
was more conspicuous . . .', i.e. ' and no others were more conspicuous in their . . .'.

<h4 style="text-align:center">CHAPTER 25</h4>

l. 2. **si qua . . .** , ' in case there might be any . . .'.

l. 7. **ab omni parte**, ' on every side '. ' Place whence ' gives the
point of view from which: English uses a different preposition in
these phrases: cf. **a tergo**, ' in the rear '.

ll. 8–13. **cum consul . . . emittit.** ' Inverse ' **cum** clause, cf.
Chap. 10, ll. 37–39.

Note the periodic construction of this clause:

(1) **quamquam clamabant** with dependent **ut** clause.

(2) Nom. of perf. part. of dep. vb., **moratus.**

(3) **postquam** ' when ' clause.

(4) abl. absol. **dato . . . signo.** Note also sandwiching.

(5) **emittit.**

As a literal translation is impossible, it will be necessary to break
it up into shorter sentences. One suggestion, possible among
many, is to drop **cum** and make **moratus** a main verb, beginning a
fresh sentence at **postquam.**

l. 10. **experiendi . . . causa.** Note: (i) the gen. of the gerund may have a direct object. (ii) **causa,** ' for the sake of ', *follows* the genitive (**experiendi**) it controls.

l. 14. **fugientibus** is probably dat. (of disadvantage) with **terga.** We say, however, ' in their flight '. **terga caesa (sunt),** *lit.*, ' their backs were cut down ', i.e. ' they were cut down from behind '.

l. 16. **legionibus circumdatis,** abl. absol., 'the legions having been thrown around ', becomes ' was surrounded by the legions' with **castra** as the subject.

ll. 16–17. **Volscos . . . expulisset,** cf. the note on Chap. 13, l. 3.

l. 17. **inde etiam,** ' from it also '.

l. 20. **praedae,** ' to plundering ', i.e. ' to plunder '.

l. 20. **inde . . . ,** ' from this (booty) the needy soldiers obtained some slight relief '.

Actually Livy tells us in Chap. 17 that Suessa Pometia had been razed to the ground. See the note on Chap. 22, l. 9.

l. 22. **decedentem,** ' (him) making-his-way-back', i.e. ' as he was on his way back '.

l. 23. **Ecetranorum Volscorum.** The position of this Volscian community is unknown.

l. 25. **ex . . . consulto,** ' in accordance with a decree of the senate '. Theoretically the senate which came to consist more and more of ex-magistrates was only an advisory body. But its power increased until it became the real governing body in Rome as was inevitable when officials held office for only one year, and Rome's power and influence spread, first in Italy and then in the Mediterranean.

CHAPTER 26

l. 2. **tumultus,** ' a rising '—a word which the Romans applied to unorganised raids or movements of tribes and peoples.

l. 5. **uillas,** ' farm-houses '.

l. 9. **nec restitit,** ' offered no resistance to '.

ll. 9–10. **Sabina legio,** 'the Sabine troops'. **Legio** originally meant ' the levy ' of Roman troops, for at this time the Roman forces were not organised in legions nor in cohorts. Livy also uses it of non-Roman forces in the sense ' troops ', ' forces '.

ll. 10–12. **fessi . . . habuere.** Note: (i) **cum . . . tum,** ' not only . . . but also '. (ii) **magna pars** in apposition with the subject of **habuere.** (iii) **quod . . . esset,** consecutive subjunctive, ' had scarcely enough strength for running away '.

l. 14. **in magna . . . pacis,** ' when hopes were now high that peace had been won on every side '. Note: (i) **partae** from **pario- ere.** (ii) for this qualifying use of **ut,** cf. Chap. 11, ll. 20–21.

ll. 15–16. **ni . . . indicentes,** ' declaring war unless (the Romans) evacuated Volscian territory '. Note: (i) **decedatur,** impersonal pass. (ii) the subj. is due to subordination in virtual indirect speech, for ' declaring war ' =' saying that they would declare war '.

ll. 17–18. **cuius fama . . . uisi,** ' the report of its having been seen not far from Aricia '. Note the sandwiching.

ll. 18–19. **tanto . . . Romanos,** *lit.,* ' roused the Romans with such great confusion '.

l. 19. **consuli,** pres. infin. pass. of **consulo,** ' I consult '. **ordine,** ' in due form '; the abl. of manner without an adj., is used with a few nouns that have developed an adverbial meaning.

ll. 19–20. **pacatum responsum,** ' a peaceful answer '. **arma ipsi capientes,** ' when they themselves were taking up arms '.

l. 21. **itur,** impersonal passive again: ' they marched '; cf. **debellatum est,** ' they finished the campaign '.

CHAPTER 27

l. 2. **Romanus,** collective singular.

l. 2. **promissa . . . senatus,** ' (the fulfilment of) the consul's promises and of the senate's pledge '.

l. 3. **cum,** ' when in the meantime ' is followed normally by the imperfect subj., but here by the historic infin. **dicere.**

l. 3. **et . . . et,** ' both . . . and '. Note that the abl. of cause **insita superbia** ' from his innate arrogance ' is balanced not by a similar phrase, but by a purpose clause, ' to nullify his colleague's pledge '.

l. 5. ius . . . dicere, ' pronounced judgments in cases of debt '.

l. 7. quod . . . inciderat, ' whenever this happened to any soldier '. Note that a subordinate clause describing iterative action has perfect or pluperfect indic. for the English present and imperfect.

l. 7. collegam, i.e. Servilius.

l. 9. illi, dat., ' (it was) in his (teeth) (that) each one cast . . .'.

l. 11. referret. Supply the object: ' the dispute '.

l. 11. auxilio, dat. of purpose, ' should be a help, (both as) consul to his fellow-citizens, (and as) a commander to his men '.

ll. 12–13. mouebant . . . haec. Turn this sentence in the passive. See Chap. 13, l. 3.

ll. 14–15. adeo . . . nobilium, *lit.*, ' for, for the other side (i.e. of the creditors) was not only his colleague violently inclined but (also) . . .'. The Latin order may be retained if we translate as follows: ' for so violently was the other side supported not only by his colleague . . .'. adeo means ' for ' when it adds an important or satisfactory reason to an assertion. Cf. Chaps. 27, ll. 51–52 and 49, l. 42.

ll. 15–16. medium se gerendo, ' by steering a middle course '.

ll. 18–19. breuique . . . odium, ' and, in a short time, it was clear that he had equalled the hatred of A. (=that he aroused as much hate as A.) '

Note: (i) apparuit =' it was clear '. (ii) aequasse, = aequavisse. (iii) Appi, objective gen.

l. 20. dedicaret, deliberative subjunctive in an indirect question. As Chap. 21, l. 24, tells us that the dedication had already taken place, Livy must be following another authority here.

ll. 21–24. utri . . . suscipere: eum is the antecedent of utri which is dative. *Lit.*, ' to which of them the dedication had been given by command of the people, that one the senate ordered was to be . . .'.

Begin: ' the senate ordained that whichever of the two consuls should be given . . . , was to be in charge of the corn-supply . . .'.

pro pontifice, ' in the presence of the pontifex (maximus) '.

From what we know of the early history of Rome, it is clear that there were years in which there was a serious shortage of food (partly due to the ravages of war and the consequent neglect of the farms). Hence it became necessary to import corn, probably from Cumae and Sicily. As Mercury was the god of trade, it is natural that the dedication of his temple should also coincide with the institution of a guild of traders, most of whom may have been concerned in the corn-trade.

l. 25. **primi pili centurioni,** ' a senior centurion '. Strictly speaking, the use of this expression is an anachronism, for it was not until the time of Marius (100 B.C.) that the Roman army was organised into the legions, cohorts, and centuries which are so well-known to us from the pages of Caesar.

ll. 25–27. **quod facile . . . ignominiam,** *lit.,* ' which could easily be seen to have been done (**factum esse**) not so much with-a-view-to (**ad**) honouring one (**eius**) to whom treatment had been given higher than his rank warranted (**suo**) as (**quam**) with-a-view-to humiliating the consuls '.

Note: (i) **appareret,** potential subjunctive. (ii) **data esset** is attracted into the subj. by the influence of **appareret** and its dependence in a relative clause on **factum** (**esse**).

l. 27. **saeuire,** historic infin.

ll. 29–30. **et longe . . . grassabantur,** ' and they went-into-action along a path (**uia**) far different from that on which they had first begun '.

ll. 31–32. **cum . . . uidissent,** ' whenever . . .'. **uidissent,** subj. expressing repeated action, frequent in Livy. Cf. introduction, p. xv.

l. 32. **decretum,** i.e. the judgment of the consul which handed over the debtor to the power of the creditor.

l. 34. **cum decresset** (=decreuisset). See preceding note.

ll. 34–35. **ui agebatur,** *lit.,* ' it was done by violence ': translated by all editors as: ' violence was the order of the day '.

l. 36. **singuli,** ' individual (creditors) '. **uerterant,** ' had shifted '.

l. 39. **furente . . . ,** ' while A. raged and stormed at the selfish action of his colleague '.

l. 40. **populari silentio,** ' by his inactivity aimed-at-making-him-popular (**populari**).'

l. 41. **ad id quod non dixisset,** *lit.,* ' in addition to this, namely that he had not given ', i.e. ' in addition to his refusal to give '.

l. 42. **ut . . . haberet,** noun clause, object of **adiceret;** *lit.,* ' was adding (the fact) that he did not even hold . . .'. i.e. ' was besides not even holding . . .'.

l. 46. **multitudo licentia accensa,** ' the crowd inflamed by their freedom (from control) '.

l. 49. **non dubium** ' not in doubt ', i.e. the people would have supported his appeal.

ll. 51–52. **adeo . . . inuidiam,** *lit.,* ' for his courage was more than enough to withstand unpopularity ', i.e. ' for he had courage more than sufficient to . . .'.

l. 52. **crescere,** historic infin., with **malum** as the subject; ' from that (time) the trouble grew (worse) daily, not only with unconcealed outcry but (also) what was much more dangerous (*lit.*), with withdrawal and secret meetings ' (i.e. ' with the people withdrawing into secret meetings ').

CHAPTER 28

l. 3. **Esquiliis,** ' on the Esquiline ', abl. of place where without a prep. This local abl. occurs in Livy (a poetical use) with nouns, other than the names of towns. The Esquiline is the eastern plateau, formed by the Cispian and Oppian hills. At this time it was used as a cemetery.

l. 4. **in Auentino.** Here there was a small trading community which acted as a centre for plebeian activities. No doubt it would contain Greek traders who had had experience of a more developed democracy than Rome as yet had produced.

ll. 4–5. ne . . . ageret, ' lest (while) in the forum they might be confused by (the need to take) sudden decisions and do everything . . .'.

l. 6. ut erat, ' as (indeed) it was '.

l. 7. sed . . . non licuit, ' but it was not possible to debate their report (lit., it reported) normally '.

l. 7. adeo. See note on Chap. 27, ll. 14–15.

ll. 8–9. indignatione . . . si . . . , lit., ' by the indignation of the fathers if . . .'. i.e. ' of the fathers who were indignant that . . .'.

l. 9. quod. . . . Note the relative clause precedes: ' (that) the consuls should throw upon the senate the unpopularity of an action (eius) which should be carried out by the authority of the consuls '.

l. 11. profecto is an adverb. magistratus, ' (real) magistrates '.

l. 12. futurum fuisse, ' there would be '. Note that imperfect and pluperfect subj. act. become fut. part. act. + fuisse in the infin. Cf. the note on Chap. 1, ll. 9–10.

l. 12. nisi publicum, ' except that-organised-by-the-state '.

ll. 13–15. nunc . . . rem publicam, ' now the country was broken up and divided into a thousand senate houses and public meetings '—a rhetorical exaggeration. cum alia . . . concilia is bracketed as a gloss on section 1 and explanatory of curias contionesque.

l. 16. id enim . . . consulem, ' for to-be-a-man (id) was more than to be consul '.

ll. 17–18. discussurum fuisse, ' would have scattered '. See the note on l. 12 above.

ll. 18–20. correpti. . . . Begin: cum consules correpti (' thus reproved ') percontarentur quid ergo uellent se facere.

l. 19. nihil enim . . . lit., ' for (they said) they would do nothing more slack or more gentle than it pleased the fathers ', i.e. ' for they would act in every way as vigorously and energetically as the fathers determined '.

l. 20. **decernunt.** Subject is **patres.**

l. 23. **iuniores.** According to Livy I, 43, when he describes the Servian reconstruction of the Roman levy, the classes (according to wealth) consisted of an equal number of units,[1] seniors (46–60 years) and juniors (17–45 years). The latter would form the striking force of the army, the former to act as a reserve and to protect the city.

l. 25. **negare,** historic infin., ' said that the people could not . . .'.

l. 26. **habituros (esse)** . . . , ' they (i.e. **illos** understood) would never have . . .'.

l. 27. **libertatem reddendam.** . . . The gerundive (passive in Latin) often needs a translation into the active to suit our idiom: ' they should restore freedom . . . '. **prius quam arma danda.** Note the idiom here: if the main verb is in the acc. +infin., as here, the dependent **prius quam** clause *may* be in the same construction.

l. 30. **uidebant** governs both the preceding indirect question in the meaning ' the consuls realised ' and also the following acc. + infin., ' they saw '.

l. 32. **et,** ' and besides '. Cf. Chap. 11, l. 19.

l. 33. **prius quam . . . experirentur.** The subj. is usual in temporal clauses where there is an additional idea of purpose or anticipation, ' before they had recourse to extreme action . . .'.

l. 35. **minimus quisque natu,** ' all the youngest '.

l. 37. **ad quod . . . deesset,** *lit.,* ' for which to-be-defended, the courage was lacking ', i.e. ' for the defence of which they lacked the courage '. **deesset:** subj. in virtual indirect speech.

CHAPTER 29

l. 1. **vtraque re . . . experta,** ' having sufficiently examined both (courses of) action '; i.e. (1) of persuading the fathers to appease the plebs. (2) of holding the levy. Note: **experta,** another example of a deponent perf. part. used in a passive sense. See Chap. 16, l. 12.

[1] Called centuries.

l. 2. **ne . . . negetis.** With **praedictum,** supply **id esse a nobis,** ' lest you deny it to have been warned beforehand by us ', i.e. ' in order that you cannot say we have not given you due warning '.

l. 4. **nobis** is dat. with **adsint,** ' be by our side while we . . .'.

ll. 4–6. **acerrimi . . . rem agemus,** ' we shall act (guided) by the decision of the most severe, since such is your will '.

l. 7. **dedita opera,** ' deliberately '. Ignoring the usual procedure of conducting a levy, the consuls pick on one of the ringleaders of the mutinous plebeians.

l. 8. **aliquot hominum** depends on **globus,** subject of **constitisset.**

ll. 11–12. **qui . . . aderant,** ' (those) of the fathers who were present in support of the consuls '.

l. 13. **ab lictore . . . prohibito,** ' from the lictor who had merely been prevented from arresting the man '. The full translation is, '. . . prevented from doing (**facere** understood) nothing else than arrest '.

l. 15. **in qua . . . ,** ' in which, however, there were no stones or weapons used (*lit.*, without a stone, without a weapon), (but) more shouting . . .'.

ll. 17–18. **senatus . . . consulitur,** ' the senate was summoned (=met) amid uproar, and its proceedings were conducted in (still) greater uproar '.

ll. 18–19. **quaestionem . . . fuerant,** ' for those who had been manhandled demanded . . .'.

l. 19. **decernente . . .** ' (while)[1] all the most violent (members) gave-their-views not so much by speeches as by . . .'.

l. 23. **ordine . . . coepit,** ' the business of the house began to be conducted in an orderly manner '.

The usual procedure was for the president (usually the consul) to put a motion before the senators: if there was a debate, he would call upon the senior members to give their opinions. Then he would put the motion or motions, if there were amendments, to the vote. In this case three proposals are put before the senate.

ll. 23–24. **P. Verginius . . . uolgabat,** ' P. Verginius was for not

[1] Asyndeton.

making the relief common to all '; *lit.*, ' was for not-making the thing common '. Note the conative force of the imperfect tense and how it is translated.

ll. 24–26. **de iis tantum agendum censebat,** ' he thought that they should deal only with those '. **agendum (esse),** neuter gerundive of **ago,** used impersonally in the passive.

ll. 24–25. **fidem secuti,** *lit.*, ' having followed the pledge ', i.e. ' relying on the pledge '.

l. 26. **T. Largius:** supply **censebat.**

l. 27. **ut merita . . . exsoluerentur,** *lit.*, ' that services should be merely paid for ', would be better in the active: ' merely to pay for . . .'.

ll. 28–29. **nec sisti . . . consulatur; sisti** is the pres. infin. pass. impersonal, *lit.*, ' it could not be stayed ', but we can say, ' the situation could not be prevented-from-deteriorating, unless regard were had for all '.

ll. 29–30. **quin . . . sedari,** ' nay if the treatment of debtors varied (*lit.*, the treatment of different (debtors) is different), the discontent was (=would be) aggravated . . .'.

ll. 32–33. **non miseriis . . . turbarum,** ' said (it was) not by their wretched plight but by their freedom from discipline (that) so much of the people had been stirred up '.

l. 34. **adeo** emphasises here the preceding word: ' it was precisely this evil that . . .'.

ll. 35–36. **quippe . . . imperium,** ' for the consuls could only threaten but not govern '; *lit.*, ' for threats, not the power to rule were of the consuls '.

l. 38. **iam,** ' immediately ': **hic** goes with **furor.**

l. 39. **mihi** is an excellent example of what is called the ethic dat., ' let him, I pray, strike a lictor who knows . . . ': *or*, ' I should like to see him strike a lictor . . .'.

l. 40. **ius de tergo uitaque,** *lit.*, ' the right about the back and the life ' = ' the right to scourge and to execute '.

CHAPTER 30

l. 2. **Vergini Largique**: supply **sententiae uidebantur**.

l. 2. **exemplo**, abl. of cause, ' because of the precedent '.

l. 4. **quae . . . tolleret**, ' since it (**quae** causal) destroyed all credit '.

ll. 4–5. **medium . . . utroque**, ' the one most midway (between the two extremes) and moderate in both directions '.

l. 6. **factione respectuque** are abls. of cause, ' owing-to the party spirit and consideration for private interests '.

l. 7. **A. uicit**, ' Appius won the day '.

l. 8. **prope. . . .** Cf. the note on Chap. 23, ll. 52–53.

l. 9. **quae res**, i.e. **res quae**, ' an appointment which '.

ll. 11–12. **curae . . . patrum**, *lit.*, ' it was for a care (predicative dat.) to . . . ', i.e. ' the consuls and the . . . were anxious that . . .'.

l. 12. **sua ui uehemens**, ' strong (enough) by-reason-of-its own powerful authority '.

l. 13. **M'. Valerium.** He was the brother of Valerius Publicola: hence the reference to **fratris lege** in l. 14.

l. 16. **nihil triste nec superbum**, ' no stern or tyrannical action '. Note that a general negative (**nihil**) may be continued by **nec**, subdivided by **neque . . . neque**[1] or strengthened by **ne . . . quidem**.[2]

l. 18. **conueniens** is neut., in agreement with **edictum**; the edict the dictator proposed practically corresponded with that of Servilius, and although the latter had failed the people, yet (**sed**) they believed that they could have greater confidence in the man (Valerius) and his office (**homini et potestati melius rati credi**).

l. 19. **credi**, pres. infin. pass. (impersonal).

ll. 20–21. **quantus . . . effectae.** Note: (i) the necessity to supply the antecedent (**tantus**). (ii) the relative clause precedes as usual. Begin: ' ten legions were mustered, a force (as great) as never before ' = ' the greatest force they had ever had '.

l. 21. **inde**, *lit.*, ' thence ', ' from there ' = ' from them '.

l. 26. **capere . . . sinerent.** It is extremely unlikely that Rome

---

[1] Cf. Ch. 49, ll. 11–12.   [2] Cf. Ch. 61, l. 18.

possessed any hegemony at this time among the Latin peoples, such as she may have claimed during the last sixty years of the regal period. The battle of Lake Regillus had been fought by the Latins against Rome, not to restore the Tarquins, as legend and Livy tell us, but to secure the freedom of the Latins from any Roman claims, and it was not such a glorious Roman victory as to give the Romans any decisive advantage. Thus in assuming that the Latins this time could not make war without the permission of the Romans, Livy is transferring to this period a principle which Rome later adopted in her successful organisation of Italy.

l. 28. **is** is attracted into the gender of the complement **finis.** Cf. Chap. 4, l. 8.

ll. 31–32. **et ipse,** ' likewise '.

l. 33. **ad . . . castra,** ' to bring their camp nearer (the Romans) '.

l. 34. **quisque,** i.e. **exercitus. infestis signis,** ' in battle formation '.

ll. 36–37. **effusi et contemptim,** ' straggling and carelessly ' i.e. ' in straggling and careless formation '. Note the combination here of participle and adverb.

ll. 37–38. **nec . . . nec.** The second **nec** somewhat irregularly qualifies the participle **passus,** instead of the second coordinate verb **iussit.** The sense will be clear if we make **passus** a main verb and insert ' but ' before **defixis.**

l. 38. **defixis pilis,** ' with spears grounded '. Livy is guilty of another anachronism, because the **pilum** (a hurling spear) was not the normal equipment until much later.

l. 39. **ad manum,** ' within reach '. Note the indirect speech after the colon. **rem gerere** ' (he ordered them) to finish the business '.

ll. 40–45. **Volsci. . . .** As usual, drop **cum** and begin a new sentence with or without ' and ' at **postquam.**

l. 41. **uelut,** ' apparently '.

ll. 42–43. **postquam . . . factam,** ' when they realised that their attack was fully met '.

ll. 43–44. **haud secus quam,** *lit.,* ' not otherwise than ', = ' just as '.

l. 48. **facile ... fessos,** 'easily caught up with the exhausted (Volsci) '.

ll. 48–49. **castris ... persecuti,** *lit.,* ' having pursued to Velitrae the enemy deprived of his camp '. See note on Chap. 5, ll. 9–11.

ll. 50–51. **plus ibi sanguinis factum (est),** ' more blood was shed there '.

l. 51. **promiscua ... caede,** i.e. in a massacre that spared no-one, women, children and the old.

CHAPTER 31

l. 2. **ubi ... fuerat,** ' where (i.e. amongst whom) by far the most of war had been (i.e. the Romans had by far the most important operations) '.

l. 2. After **fundit,** the MSS have **fugatque,** bracketed by the editors of the O.T.

ll. 4–5. **quam ... firmauerant,** *lit.,* ' which, while the wings deployed themselves too far, they had strengthened with ranks (stationed) too little suitably inside ', i.e. ' which, in deploying the wings too far, they had not strengthened enough with men in depth '.

l. 5. After **ordinibus,** the MSS have **aciem,** removed by most editors as a gloss to **quam.**

l. 9. **inuehitur. ueho** and its compounds are often used in the passive like a deponent in the meaning ' go ', ' ride '.

l. 10. **ad spectaculum,** ' to watch the games '. This distinction, unique in the privilege (normal for a magistrate) being passed on to his descendants, is mentioned in an inscription (C.I.L. i, 284).

ll. 10–11. **sella curulis.** The ' curule chair ' was a chair of honour inlaid with ivory, the use of which was granted to the highest magistrates.

l. 11. **Volscis deuictis,** dat. with **ademptus (est),** ' from the V ...'.

l. 12. **ab urbe,** i.e. from Rome. The colonists were Roman citizens.

l. 14. **inuito quidem consule,** abl. absol., ' against the wishes of the consul '.

subeundum erat, impersonal and passive in Latin becomes personal and active in English, ' they had to approach '. **iniquo loco,** ' over unfavourable ground '.

ll. 15–16. **sed milites . . . ,** ' but the soldiers alleging that he was prolonging the campaign (*lit.,* the thing was being prolonged) . . .'. The soldiers suspected that the consul deliberately avoided engaging the enemy in order to delay the return of the army to Rome until after the dictator's term of office (6 months) had elapsed. In this way, the men could not compel the dictator to carry out his promises to them.

l. 18. **forte temere,** ' by chance, blindly ', i.e. ' relying on blind chance '.

ll. 18–19. **in aduersos . . . erigeret,** ' (him) to lead his forces straight up the heights that-faced-them (**aduersos**) '.

ll. 19–20. **id male commissum,** ' this badly-conceived operation '.

l. 20. **ignauia,** abl. of cause, ' owing to . . .'.

ll. 20–21. **priusquam . . . ueniretur.** Note: (i) impersonal passive. (ii) subjunctive in temporal clause denoting purpose *or* anticipation: ' before the Romans could come within range (*lit.,* to the hurling of a lance) '.

l. 23. **in auersas ualles,** ' into the valleys on the other side '.

l. 24. **ibi,** ' there ', i.e. in the camp.

ll. 25–26. **de . . . decesserat,** *lit.,* ' about the issue of domestic affairs, neither from the fathers nor from the people had anxiety departed ', i.e. ' neither the fathers . . . had lost their concern for the issue of their problems at home '.

l. 27. **cum . . . tum,** ' not only . . . but also ', *or* ' both . . . and '.

l. 28. **quae = ea quae. quae** introduces a purpose clause, ' the means to baffle not only the people but also the dictator himself '.

ll. 30–32. **omnium . . . placeret,** ' the very first business (*lit.,* of all business the first) he handled was on behalf of the victorious people and he put the question (**rettulit**) as to what the senate wanted done (*lit.* what it pleased to be done) about those-bound-for-debt '.

l. 33. **non placeo . . . auctor,** ' I do not please you, (i.e. I do not win your support) (as) one-who-supports civic harmony '.

l. 34. **mediusfidius,** is an abbreviated oath, a contracted form of **me dius (deus) fidius adiuvet,** ' so help me the god of faith (i.e. Jupiter) '.

ll. 35-36. **quod . . . attinet,** ' as far as I am concerned '.

ll. 37-38. **discordiae . . . externum.** Note the asyndeton here and again in l. 39.

l. 39. **priuatus, dictator,** ' as a . . . , as a . . .'.

l. 41. **apparuit . . . ,** ' the reason was clear to the people, that he (**eum** understood) . . .'.   **suam uicem,** adverbial acc., ' for their sake '.

ll. 43-44. **quoniam . . . praestaretur,** ' since it was not due to him that it (the pledge) was not carried out '.   Note the impersonal use of **stare** ' it is due to ' with **per** and a **quominus** *or* **ne** clause, or with **quin,** as here (the only example).

stetisset is subjunctive, because it is virtually in indirect speech, ' because (as they believed) . . .'.

CHAPTER 32

l. 1. **timor patres incessit,** *lit.,* ' fear entered the fathers ', i.e. ' the fathers were filled with fear '.   Cf. Chap. 13, l. 3.

ll. 1-5. **dimissus foret, habitus esset, iurassent.** All these subjunctives give the thoughts in the minds of the senators.

ll. 4-5. **quoniam . . . iurassent,** ' since they had sworn unto the words of the consuls ', i.e. ' they had sworn obedience to the consuls '.

ll. 5-6. **per causam . . . ,** ' on the pretext of the renewal of hostilities by the A.'

ll. 7-9. **agitatum . . . sacramento,** ' it is said there was discussion about assassinating the consul that they might be freed from their oath '.

ll. 9–11. doctos . . . , indirect speech.

l. 9. doctos, ' having been informed ' i.e. ' on learning '.

ll. 9–10. exsolui, ' could be discharged '. See the note on Chap. 10, ll. 46–47.

ll. 10–11. in Sacrum montem, ' to the " Mount of Curses " '. This is the first of three secessions or ' general strikes ' on the part of the plebeians, who, to gain their aims, withdrew from the life of the community. Unfortunately there is little agreement in the authorities available to us about the details of this first secession. For example, Piso, as Livy states, placed the scene on the Aventine hill, and we may be tempted to see in the ' Mount of Curses ' a graphic reference to the solemn oath the people took to kill anyone who violated their own magistrates, the newly created tribunes. In other words the ' Mount of Curses ' is the Aventine over again, associated as it had been with the plebeian cause. See Chap. 28, l. 4.

ll. 12–13. ea . . . , ' this report is more generally adopted than (that) of which . . .'.

l. 15. castris; take with sese tenuere, l. 17, ' they remained '.

l. 16. sumendo, ' taking '. Note again this modal use of the gerund. See introduction, p. xvi.

l. 19. timere, historic infin; subject plebis relicta ab suis.

l. 20. Supply utrum, ' whether ', before manere.

ll. 21–22. quamdiu . . . fore. Note that rhetorical questions in the third person become acc. + infin. in indirect speech. Note again that Livy retains the primary tenses of direct speech secesserit and exsistat, l. 23.

l. 22. futurum (esse), ' would happen '.

l. 25. ducere, historic infin. patres is the understood subject.

ll. 25–26. eam . . . esse, lit., ' it (i.e. concordia) must be won for the community by fair (means), by foul ', i.e. ' they must win it . . . by fair means or foul '.

l. 28. inde, ' thence ', ' from there ', i.e. ' from them ', i.e. from the plebeians. His plebeian origin is most unlikely, as he was a senator. The story of Menenius is fictitious. The Oxford Classical Dictionary says: ' it is either a fable common to the peoples of Aryan stock or the adaptation of an allegorical tale elaborated by Greek sophists '.

ll. 29–31. is ... fertur. Note: (i) personal construction with fertur ' he is said ' for English ' it is said that he '. (ii) with nihil aliud supply fecisse. 'to have done nothing else (quam narrasse) than to have narrated', i.e. 'simply to have told the following fable', (hoc).

ll. 31–33. tempore quo ... lit., ' at the time at which in man, not as now all things were agreed together, but to individual members its own purpose to each was, its own speech was ', i.e. ' once upon a time the individual members in man had each their own purpose, their own power of speech, for they did not as now all agree together '.

l. 33. indignatas; insert ' and ' here: ' and the other parts thought it unfair ...'.

l. 35. uentri, dat., ' for the (good of the) belly '. Insert ' while ' before uentrem.

ll. 35–36. nihil aliud: supply facere and see note on ll. 29–31 above.

ll. 37–38. nec ... nec. Livy uses nec more often than neu to introduce additional negative purpose clauses.

l. 39. os, nom. datum, ' (the food when) given '.

l. 38. conficerent, ' chew '; lit., ' make-an-end-of '.

l. 38. Many MSS have nec dentes quae conficerent. Some editors remove quae, but Walters in the O.T. suggests the addition of acciperent.

l. 38. hac ira, abl. of cause, ' by reason of this anger '.

l. 39. una is an adverb.

l. 40. ad extremam tabem, ' to the last (stages of) emaciation '.

l. 42. nec ... eum, lit., ' that it (eum) was no more nourished than it nourished '; i.e. ' that it nourished (others) as much as it received nourishment itself '.

l. 42. **reddentem,** ' (by) sending '.

ll. 43–45. **hunc . . . sanguinem,** 'this blood by which . . . , divided . . . and enriched by the digested food '.
Note the indicatives **uiuimus uigemusque,** in a relative clause in indirect speech. We may explain this as an addition by Livy, i.e. the words were not spoken by Menenius, or as another example of Livy's retention of the original mood.[1] Cf. note on Chap. 15, ll. 17–18.

l. 45. **comparando,** ' showing by this (**hinc**) comparison '. Cf. note on l. 16 above.

CHAPTER 33

l. 1. **coeptum.** See the note on Chap. 21, ll. 20–21. *Lit.,* ' it was begun to be discussed ', i.e. ' discussions began to be held '.

ll. 1–2. **concessum . . . condiciones ut,** 'and agreement was reached upon the terms that' . . . **sacrosancti.** See Chap. 32, ll. 10–11.

ll. 3–4. **quibus . . . esset,** 'to whom there was the right of bringing help against the consuls ', i.e. ' and they should have the right to . . .'. The tribune could say, **ueto,** ' I forbid ', to protect any citizen who appealed to him against arbitrary actions of the consuls.

l. 4. **cui** is the dative of **quis,** ' any '. **capere,** ' to hold '.

l. 5. **plebei** =**plebis,** gen.

l. 6. **sibi creauerunt,** ' co-opted '.

ll. 6–7. **in his . . . auctorem** depends upon **convenit,** ' there is agreement ', understood from **minus convenit** l. 8 ' there is less agreement '.

ll. 7–8. **de . . . fuerint,** ' who the other two were ', *or* ' about the identity of the other two '.

ll. 8–9. **Sunt qui . . . dicant,** ' some say '.

l. 10. **sacratam legem,** ' the enactment of inviolability '.
This last statement is probably correct. All we now know for

[1] i.e. if we assume that the use of the 1st person plural is appropriate to Menenius as well as to Livy.

certain about the early history of the ' tribunes of the people ' is
that by 449 B.C. the number had become ten.

l. 13. **foedus.** For this very important treaty, its terms, and its
significance, see the introduction, p. xxi.

ll. 15–16. **compulsos . . . persecutus.** See the note on Chap. 5,
ll. 9–11.

ll. 19–20. **et consilio . . . promptus,** ' active both in counsel and
in action ', i.e. ' as active in counsel as he was in action '.

l. 21. **Coriolano.** Note the agreement in case with **cui.** Cf.
Chap. 15, ll. 17–18.

The whole of this story is now regarded as purely legendary.[1]
The author of the article in the *O.C.D.* rejects the usual possibilities
for the origin of such legends (e.g. aetiological explanation for a
custom or building, glorification of a patrician family, imitation of
incidents in Greek history), and baldly states that this story
' reflects the period when Rome suffered severely from famine and
Volscian pressure '.

ll. 21–26. **cum . . . fuit.** Note in this period: (i) **exercitum . . .
obsidentem . . . intentum** is object of **inuasissent.** (ii) sandwiching,
especially from **atque** to **intentum.**

Begin as follows: ' while the R. army was besieging . . . and was
fully occupied with the townsfolk . . . , suddenly the V. legions
which . . . attacked them and at the same time. . . . It was in this
crisis that Marcius was by chance on guard '.

l. 24. **imminentis** is bracketed in the *O.T.* as a gloss.

ll. 24–25. **ab Antio.** See Chap. 16, l. 12.

l. 29. **ferox,** adj. for adv., ' boldly '.

ll. 29–30. **ignem arreptum iniecit.** See the note on Chap. 5, ll.
9–11, ' he snatched up a firebrand on-the-spur-of-the-moment
(**temere**) and threw it . . .'.

l. 31. **mixtus . . . ,** ' mingled with the wailing of the women and
children which had arisen as is usual at the first alarm . . .'.

l. 32. **et** means ' both ' and can be ignored.

[1] The custom of giving titles to victorious generals from the towns or
countries they had conquered did not develop until much later.

l. 33. **utpote . . . urbe,** ' seeing-that the city had been captured. **utpote,** ' seeing that ', is most commonly used to reinforce the causal use of the relative pronoun. Its use with a participle is rare.

l. 35. **tantum,** ' to such an extent '. **sua laude,** ' by his (glorious) exploit '.

ll. 36–39. **nisi . . . ictum,** ' if we had not as evidence the treaty with the Latins inscribed on a bronze stele, (a treaty which was) concluded by Sp. C. alone in the absence of his colleague '.

This bronze stele was still in existence in the first century B.C., until Sulla's building operations (80 B.C.) probably caused its removal from its position in front of the Rostra. Dionysius (vi, 95, 2) gives the terms or a summary of them.

l. 38. **monumento,** ' as evidence '; predicative dative.

l. 40. **memoria cessisset,** 'it would have gone from memory', i.e. ' it would have been forgotten '.

The meaning of this sentence is not very clear. Livy seems to argue that, if the treaty with the Latins was struck by Cassius alone, it must have been because his colleague Commius was absent from Rome, and, again, if he were absent, he must have been waging war with the Volsci. It can also be assumed that Commius was not mentioned by the annalists in their account of the Volscian wars.

Note that Livy retains the pluperfect subj. act., i.e. the original tense and mood of the apodosis (unfulfilled condition, past time), although it is usual to turn it into the periphrastic perf. subj., when dependent on a sentence which requires the subj., e.g. here **cessurum fuerit.** Cf. Chap. 1, ll. 9–10.

l. 43. **huic . . .** *lit.,* ' for this negotiator . . . the expense for his funeral was lacking '; i.e. ' this man who . . . did not leave enough money to pay for his funeral '. Cf. Chap. 16, ll. 24–25.

l. 46. **sextantibus . . . in capita,** ' contributing a sextans[1] per head '. Actually there was no coinage at this time in Rome.

---

[1] *Lit.,* $\frac{1}{6}$ of a pound of copper.

CHAPTER 34

l. 4. **ex incultis . . . agris,** ' in consequence of the lack of cultivation during the secession of the people '.

ll. 5–6. **qualis . . . solet,** ' (such) as usually comes to a besieged city ' (*lit.*, ' to [those] besieged ').

l. 6. **uentum.** Supply **esset** and note impersonal passive: ' it would have come to the destruction (by starvation) ', i.e. ' it would have meant death by starvation for the slaves, at least, and for the plebeians, had not . . .'.

l. 7. **dimissis,** ' by sending out (agents) '.

l. 9. **dextris . . . litoribus,** ' by the shores on the right from Ostia ', i.e. ' northwards as you sail up the coast from Ostia '.

A similar abl. of route in **laeuo . . . mari,** ' and southwards along by the Volscian coast '.

l. 10. **quaesitum,** acc. of the supine (purpose); object is **frumentum** (understood).

l. 10. **ad Cumas,** ' to (the vicinity of) Cumae '. ' To Cumae ' would normally be **Cumas.** But see note on Chap. 16, l. 12.

l. 12. **coegerant:** object (*understood*) is ' the Romans '.

l. 13. **pro,** ' as security for '.

l. 15. **potuit,** subject **frumentum.**

ll. 18–19. **incommodo . . . vexati forent,** *lit.*, ' by a campaign (which might have been) disastrous considering the scantiness of their supplies they would have been distressed ', i.e. ' a campaign which . . . supplies would have added to their distress '. For **in,** cf. Chap. 10, l. 48.

l. 21. **remisisset,** intransitive use of this verb in the meaning ' abate ', ' slacken '. The mood is due to attraction, i.e. because it is a clause dependent upon another subjunctive.

ll. 23–24. **Norbam . . . ,** ' they sent a new colony to N. in the hill-country '.

l. 24. **quae . . . esset,** purpose clause.

l. 27. **quanti,** genitive of value.

l. 29. **extorta patribus essent,** ' had been wrung from the fathers '.

l. 31. **annonam ueterem,** ' corn at the old price '.

ll. 33–34. **sub ... redemptus,** ' (I) sent beneath the yoke as though I had been ransomed from brigands '—a rhetorical exaggeration, borrowed from the practice by which an army that capitulated was forced to make a symbolic entry into captivity by passing under the **iugum,** i.e. two spears stuck upright in the ground, with a third lashed horizontally across them.

ll. 35–36. **patiar, feram,** deliberative subj., ' am I to endure ... , am I to put up with '.

ll. 35–36. **Tarquinium ... tulerim,** ' who could not put up with T. (as) king '. The subjunctive is similar to that in relative clauses, expressing cause or concession. As Coriolanus is described as a youth at the siege of Corioli, it is difficult to see how he could have assisted in the expulsion of Tarquin or even been a prominent member of the Senate.

l. 39. **tertio anno,** ' in the third year (from now) ', i.e. ' three years ago '. As we normally find **ante** in expressions of time of this kind, many editors add **ante** after **anno.**

ll. 40–42. **hoc malo ... prohibeant,** ' (that when they have been) tamed by this suffering they will prefer to till their fields (*lit.*, rather be tillers of the fields) rather than in armed secession to prevent (the fields) being tilled (*lit.*, armed prevent ...) '.

ll. 43–46. **faciendumne ... sibi,** ' whether it was expedient (*lit.*, it was to-be-done) as I believe it could have been, namely that (**ut**) by means of terms for lowering the price-of-corn, the fathers should rid themselves (*lit.*, take from themselves) both of the tribunes' authority and all the (plebeians') rights imposed (upon them) against their will '.

CHAPTER 35

l. 2. **ira,** nominative.

ll. 2–3. **peti ... ,** ' they were now being attacked (they said) ... '.

l. 4. **quae sola alimenta,** i.e. **sola alimenta quae.**

ll. 5–6. **nisi . . . satisfiat,** *lit.*, 'unless reparation were given (to him) from the backs . . .', i.e. 'unless the Roman people made reparation to him with lashes on their backs'; the implication is that if the tribunes were removed, the consuls would be able to scourge without check or control.

l. 8. **in exeuntem e curia,** 'as he was leaving the senate-house'.

ll. 8–9. **ni . . . dixissent,** 'if the tribunes had not just-in-time appointed a day (for his trial)'. It is extremely doubtful whether, at this early date in Rome's history, the assembly of the people (**concilium plebis**) could act as a High Court of Justice as the assembly by centuries (of the whole nation) could in hearing appeals in capital cases. All we can be reasonably certain about is that the patricians seem to have recognised the right of the tribunes to bring an impeachment against patricians, in cases where they could be accused of having injured the tribunician power or encouraged others to do so (cf. Coriolanus), and that this right was based on the physical force of the plebeians, as indeed the power of the tribunes was from the first.

ll. 12–13. **auxilii . . . ius,** *lit.*, 'the right of help, not of punishment', becomes in English, 'the right to help, not to punish'.

ll. 13–14. **plebis, non patrum esse,** 'belonged to the people, not the fathers'.

l. 15. **ut . . . patribus,** 'that the fathers had to finish with (the matter) by sacrificing one man to punishment, (*lit.*, by the punishment of one man)'.

l. 15. **aduersa inuidia,** abl. absol., 'hatred fronting them', i.e. 'in the face of (the people's) hatred'.

ll. 16–17. **qua . . . uiribus,** *lit.*, 'both (**qua**) each his own (strength) and (**qua**) the strength of the whole order'.

l. 18. **temptata res est.** Make active, 'they tried'; **si,** '(to see) if'.

l. 18. **dispositis clientibus** goes very closely with **absterrendo;** a literal translation is clumsy; 'they could, clients posted here and there, by frightening away . . . bring their-plan-to-nought'; say: 'by posting clients . . . they could frighten away . . . and so bring . . .'. At this time, a client was a free-man who entrusted himself to a patron and, in return for his protection and aid, rendered to his patronus certain services in his public and private life. The relationship between the two was regarded as most sacred.

ll. 20–21. **quidquid . . . diceres,** *lit.*, ' you would say whatever there was of fathers (was) on trial ', i.e. ' you would have said that the whole body of the fathers . . .'. Note: ' you would say ', more graphic than ' you would have said '.

ll. 22–23. **unum sibi civem . . . donarent,** ' (that) if they were unwilling . . . , they should grant one citizen, one senator to them as-a-favour, though guilty '.

ll. 23–24. **die dicta,** ' on the day appointed (for the trial) '.

l. 24. **perseueratum est,** impersonal pass., ' feelings hardened (against him) '.

l. 25. **absens,** ' in his absence '. This right to go into voluntary exile may probably from the earliest time have been granted to those threatened by criminal proceedings on a capital charge. It thus became a substitute for the death penalty. Later it became a widespread practice of avoiding a trial on any criminal charge.

l. 27. **benigniusque. . . .** Supply eo[1] with **benignius,** to balance quo[1] maior, ' and they treated him daily the more kindly, the greater appeared his anger towards his fellow countrymen and (the more) frequently now his complaints . . .'.

l. 33. **consilia conferunt,** ' they consulted together '.

l. 34. **plebem suam,** i.e. the Volsci.

l. 37. **arte agendum (esse),** ' it was to-be-done by stratagem ', i.e. ' they must use stratagem '.

ll. 37–38 **in . . . odio,** *lit.*, ' in a hatred weakened . . .', i.e. ' where hatred had weakened in the lapse of time '.

CHAPTER 36

l. 1. **ex instauratione,** ' in consequence of their being repeated '. ' Great Games ' (**ludi magni**) were celebrated, if a general had

[1] Ablatives of the measure of difference.

vowed them in return for victory and the victory had been gained. In all religious observance, the ritual had to be perfectly performed: should there be any flaw, the ritual would have to be repeated from the beginning.

ll. 2–3. **ludis mane,** ' early in the morning on the day of the games '.

ll. 3–4. **seruum sub furca caesum egerat,** ' had driven his slave as he flogged him bearing the punishment yoke '. **caesum** is here— a rare use—the equivalent of the pres. part. pass. which does not of course exist in Latin.

ll. 4–5. **medio circo,** abl. of the route, ' through the midst of the circus '.

l. 5. **uelut** = **uelut si,** ' as if '. **religionem,** ' the sacredness (of the games) '.

l. 8. **praesultatorem,** *lit.*, ' the chief dancer ', refers to the slave who had been flogged through the circus.

l. 10. **iret, nuntiaret,** ' let him go ', ' let him announce '.

l. 11. **religione,** ' from religious fear '.

ll. 11–13. **uerecundia . . . ,** ' yet the awe (he felt) for the dignity of the magistrates overcame him (i.e. was too much tor him), (for he feared) lest he might end up a byword and a laughing-stock '.

l. 13. **magno,** abl. of value, with **illi stetit,** ' cost him dear '.

l. 16. **aegro animi,** ' to (him) sick at heart '. **animi** is locative.

l. 17. **satin'** = **satisne: spreti numinis,** ' for scorning the divine will '.

ll. 19–20. **cunctantem . . . ,** ' (him) hesitating . . .', i.e. ' as he nevertheless hesitated and put off (going) '.

l. 21. **debilitate subita,** *lit.*, ' with sudden crippling ', i.e. ' and suddenly crippled him '.

l. 22. **admonuit,** ' made (him) think '.

l. 23. **consilio . . . adhibito;** make this abl. absol. a main verb, ' he called . . . (and) when (**cum**) . . .'. For the family council see Chap. 41, ll. 35–36.

l. 30. **captus . . . membris,** ' paralysed in all his limbs '. Note ablative of respect.

ll. 30–37. qui . . . eum . . . est: order for translation: **traditum est memoriae eum** (the man) **qui . . . esset, functum officio redisse domum pedibus suis.**

CHAPTER 37

l. 3. **Volscorum.** It is impossible to accept this visit as other than legendary.

ll. 3–4. **priusquam . . . ludi.** If this temporal clause is strictly temporal, as it may well be, the subjunctive is explained in the introduction, p. xv.

l. 5. **esse quae,** ' that there were (matters) which '.

l. 7. **quod sequius sit,** ' (such a thing) as is somewhat discreditable '. **sequius,** *lit.,* ' worse ' is a comparative of **secus,** used predicatively here. **quod = tale ut id:** hence the consecutive subjunctive.

l. 8. **criminatum,** acc. of the supine (purpose) governing the preceding acc. +infin., which, passive in Latin, would be better as active in English: e.g. ' that anything (wrong) has been done by them ', becomes, ' that they have done anything wrong '.

l. 9. **cautum . . . admittant,** ' to see that they do not commit (it) '.

l. 9. **nimio . . . uelim,** ' for more than I should like '.

l. 14. **ciuitas,** abstract for concrete; i.e. ' city ' for ' citizens '.

ll. 14–15. **quid . . . sit.** Cf. the note in l. 8 above and turn into the active. **per eandem occasionem,** ' when a similar opportunity arose '.

l. 19. **in animo est,** ' I intend '.

l. 21. **rem . . . certo,** ' this vague warning supported by so reliable an authority '.

ll. 22–23. **auctor . . . movit,** ' the source (of the story) as often happens rather than the story itself (**res**) roused (them) to take precautions, even if (they were) superfluous '.

l. 25. **qui . . . iuberent,** ' to order ' (purpose).

ll. 26–27. discurrentes . . . hospitia, 'as they hurriedly scattered to their hosts to pick up their things '.

l. 27. proficiscentibus . . . oborta, 'as they were leaving they began to be filled with indignation ': *lit.*, 'indignation welled up (for them) setting out '. proficiscentibus, is dative of person interested.

l. 28. ut . . . contaminatosque, 'like criminals and outcasts '. ab ludis with abactos esse.

CHAPTER 38

l. 2. ut quisque ueniret, iterative subj., see introduction, p. xv 'as . . .'. querendo indignandoque, modal use of the abl. of the gerund. See introduction, p. xvi.

Make excipiens, a main verb, 'he received them ', and insert 'and ' before et ' which means ' both ' and can be ignored.

l. 4. secunda irae, 'that supported their anger '.

l. 5. per eos, ' by means of their influence '. aliam, ' the rest '.

l. 7. ut,' supposing that '. ueteres . . . Volscorum, in apposition with alia. populi Romani, subjective gen., i.e. ' wrongs inflicted by the R. people '.

l. 9. tandem. Note this use of tandem with questions or commands =' I pray ', *or* ' I ask '.

ll. 11–12. an non . . . esse, ' or did you not feel that they triumphed over you today? '.

ll. 12–13. uos . . . fuisse, ' that your departure (*lit.*, you departing) was a spectacle (predic. dat.) to all—to the citizens . . .'.

l. 14. traductos (esse), *lit.*, ' were lead past ', i.e. like prisoners in a triumph; translate: ' were led in shame '. per ora hominum, ' before the gaze of the onlookers '.

ll. 15–17. quid eos . . . putatis: order for translation: quid putatis eos existimasse qui . . . , ' what do you think were the thoughts of those who . . . , who . . . who . . .'.

l. 16. uidere = uiderunt.

l. 17. **nisi ... esse,** ' except that assuredly there was some sin '.

l. 19. **uiolaturi simus,** ' we should defile '. **quo** introduces a consecutive relative clause and according to the rule, the present subj., **uiolemus** in the apodosis of a conditional clause, when dependent on an **ut** clause becomes periphrastic, i.e. fut. part. + **sim** (Primary), or **fuerim** (Historic). Cf. note on Chap. 1, ll. 9–10.

l. 19. **piaculumque merituri,** ' and incur the punishment of heaven '; *lit.*, ' and deserve expiation '; i.e. have to make an offering for sin (by being punished) for the defilement of the religious nature of the games.

l. 19. **ideo ...,** ' on this account only that we were being driven away ...'. This acc. + infin. is dependent upon **existi-masse,** l. 17.

l. 22. **hoc.** We should expect this to be **haec,** i.e. attracted into the gender of the predicate **profectio.** Cf. Chap. 10, l. 5.

l. 22. **et,** ' and after all this ', a meaning **et** sometimes has in introducing a question.

l. 24. **moriendum omnibus fuit,** ' you would all have had to die '.
Note that in conditional clauses unreal in past time, the apodosis, if it consists of **possum, debeo,** gerundive =' ought ', and periphrastic future, has the indicative, not the subjunctive.

l. 25. **magno ... malo,** ' to the great cost of those ...'. It is an abl. absol.

l. 27. **instigando,** modal use of the abl. of the gerund again, equivalent to a pres. part. act. **quisque** belongs to it.

ll. 28–29. **omne ... deficeret.** It is incorrect of Livy to use the verb ' revolt ' of the Volscians who had no form of alliance or treaty with Rome, and could not therefore be regarded as allies on an equal footing, let alone as subject ones, for whom alone such a verb is suitable.

CHAPTER 39

l. 1. **omnium populorum,** i.e. the peoples who were members of the Volscian community.

ll. 5–6. **ducibus . . . esse,** ' that the Roman state (**rem =rem publicam**) was stronger in its leaders than in its army '.

l. 9. **nouella.** Cf. Chap. 33, sections 4–9. As Satricum is not mentioned there, **nouella** refers only to the last three.

ll. 10–11. **inde . . . transgressus** in the MSS. occur between **tradidit** and **Satricum** but make the topography impossible to explain, as the Via Latina lies to the north-east of the Via Appia, and the towns mentioned are to the south-west. Most editors follow the suggestion of Conway and Walters and place them here.

transuersis tramitibus, ' by cross-roads '.

l. 13. **a Pedo.** See the note on Chap. 16, l. 12.

l. 16. **qui seruarent,** purpose clause.

ll. 16–17. **siue infensus siue ut . . . oreretur.** Note that Livy offers a reason (**infensus,** ' whether because he was angry with the people ') and a purpose, **ut . . . oreretur,** as alternatives.

l. 19. **iam ferocem per se plebem,** ' a people already on their own account headstrong '. **criminando,** ' by accusing ', i.e. ' by their accusations '; object to be supplied is ' of the nation's leaders ' from **in primores ciuitatis.**

l. 20. **sed. . . .** After the apodosis in l. 8 we should normally expect the protasis ' if ', or ' if not ', but the flow of the sentence has been partially interrupted by the parenthesis **adeo . . . instigabant.**

l. 21. **quamuis** is here an adverb, not a conjunction, and is to be taken with **suspectos . . . inter se,** ' however suspected and hostile (they were) to each other ', i.e. ' in spite of their mutual suspicion and hostility '.

l. 22. **id,** anticipatory subject of **conueniebat,** the real subject being the **quod** clause: ' this only was not agreed ', i.e. ' the only disagreement was that . . .'.

l. 24. **plebes,** insert ' while '—asyndeton.

l. 26. **eos. . . .** The Latin order (acc. present participles with dependent relative clause, then subject and verb) may be retained, if we begin: ' while they were reviewing the levies (and) distributing garrisons . . . , a huge mob (of people) demanding . . . first terrified them . . .'.

ll. 27–28. **per muros . . . loca,** 'about the walls and the other places where (*lit.*, in which) they had decided (*lit.*, it had pleased) there should be pickets and sentries '.

l. 31. **acceperunt relationem,** ' listened to (=gave a favourable hearing to) the proposal '.

l. 34. **redderetur** represents a fut. indic. in direct speech. **posse . . . pace,** ' there could be discussions about peace '.

l. 35. **per otium,** ' in inaction ', i.e. ' without doing anything '.

l. 36. **memorem . . . appareat,** ' mindful of (=he would not forget) the wrong done him by his fellow-citizens (**ciuium** subj. gen.) and the kindness of his hosts (but) he would strive that it be clear . . .'.

l. 38. **animos,** ' his spirit ' (i.e. of Coriolanus).

ll. 39–40. **suis . . . uelatos,** *lit.,* ' veiled with their proper badges ', i.e. ' wearing the proper caps and fillets '.

uelare is generally used in connection with the fillets or special headgear used in religious ceremonies.

CHAPTER 40

ll. 2–3. **id publicum consilium. . . .** Supply **utrum** to introduce the double indirect question, dependent upon **parum inuenio,** ' I do not find ' =' I cannot find '. Cf. Chap. 10, ll. 46–47.

l. 5. **duos paruos ex Marcio,** ' her two little sons by Marcius '.

ll. 6–7. **quoniam . . . possent:** the subj. is due to the **quoniam** clause being dependent on the **ut** clause after **peruicere.**

l. 8. **uentum est,** impersonal passive: in English, personal and active, ' they came '.

ll. 10–12. **ut qui nec motus esset,** ' as one who had not been moved '.

ll. 10–11. **publica . . . religione,** ' by the majesty of the state in-the-person-of-its envoys nor by the great holiness of religion when-presented to his eyes and mind in-the-person-of-its priests '.

l. 16. **tibi,** dat. of the person interested =' your '.

ll. 17–18. **Coriolanus . . . ab sede sua,** ' Coriolanus sprang in dismay almost like a madman, from his seat (and) '.

l. 18. **cum . . . complexum,** ' when he offered his embrace to (=offered to embrace) her as-she-moved-to-him **(obuiae)** '.

ll. 19–21. **sine (ut) sciam:** Livy uses **sinere** with the subjunctive (instead of the more usual infin.) in four passages only, all of which occur in direct speech. This use is probably colloquial, as we find this construction often in Plautus and Terence.

Supply again (cf. l. 2 above) **utrum** before **ad hostem;** similarly before **captiua.**

l. 22. **in hoc,** is emphatic by position: to be rendered by a periphrasis in English: ' is it to this that . . .? '

l. 24. **tibi,** dat. of the person interested, = ' your ' as in l. 16 above: ' did not your anger subside as you passed (our) boundaries . . .'.

l. 25. **quamuis . . . perueneras.** This is the only instance in which Livy uses **quamuis** with the indicative—a usage explained by some commentators as poetic.[1]

On the other hand, as the indicative after **quamuis** becomes commoner in Livy's prose contemporaries and, by the post-Augustan period, seems almost regular, it looks as if Roman writers no longer felt the full force of the word's etymology.

l. 26. **non =nonne? succurrit,** ' come unto your mind '.

ll. 28–29. **nisi peperissem, . . . oppugnaretur.** Note the difference in tense between protasis and apodosis which must be clearly brought out in translation: ' if I had not borne (you), Rome would not now be attacked '.

l. 30. **libera . . . essem,** ' I should be on-my-death **(mortua)** a free woman in a free country '.

l. 32. **nec ut . . . sum. ut** with **ita** (expressed or understood as here), sometimes compares actions that are adversative: **ut,** then = ' though ', ' while '.

l. 32. **de his uideris.** Note: (i) **his** referring to Volumnia and her children and contrasted with **ego** in l. 28 above. (ii) the fut.

[1] First occurs in Lucretius (among the poets).

perf. is sometimes like the future used in a sense simliar to a polite imperative: e.g. ' please see to these here '.

l. 34. **uxor . . . amplexi,** ' his wife and children having embraced him ', subjects with **fletus. . . . comploratio** of **fregere.** Translate: ' the embraces of his wife and children '.

l. 35. **comploratio sui patriaeque.** Note the objective genitives ' lamentations for themselves and their country '.

ll. 38–39. **inuidia . . . leto,** *lit.,* ' (the historians) relate that he (**eum** understood) perished, overwhelmed by the unpopularity of the affair (=that arose from this incident), some (say) by one death, (others by another) '. ' The historians say . . . incident, but give different accounts of his death '.

l. 39. **Fabium.** See the introduction, p. xiii.

ll. 41–43. **refert . . . ,** ' he reports at least that he (when) at an advanced age often made use of this saying—that exile . . .'.

l. 43. **laude sua,** an unusual abl. (of respect?) with **inuideo;** ' the fame rightly theirs '.

l. 45. **uiuebatur,** impersonal pass., ' life was lived '; **sine,** ' without ' =' free from ' here.

l. 45. **monumento . . . esset,** *lit.,* ' so that it could be for a memorial ' (predic. dat.): i.e. ' to keep alive its memory '.

ll. 50–51. **Volsci Aequine . . . darent,** ' as to whether the Volsci or the Aequi should provide . . .'. **darent,** deliberative subj., in indirect question, dependent upon the verbal notion in **certamine.** For the omission of **utrum,** cf. ll. 2–3 and ll. 19–21 above.

ll. 53–54. **haud . . . certamine,** *lit.,* ' in a contest no less disastrous than obstinate ', i.e. ' as obstinate as it was disastrous '.

ll. 55–57. **Sicinio . . . ,** *lit.,* ' to Sicinius, the Volsci fell as his-sphere-of-activity . . .'. i.e. ' Sicinius got the Volsci as his field of operations . . .'. The appointment would be by lot or agreement. Note the verb **euenit** agrees in number with the predicate **prouincia.**

ll. 57–58. **Cum V. . . . est,** ' the fighting with the V. ended with the honours even '.

CHAPTER 41

l. 2. **cum Hernicis . . . ictum.** In the valley of the Trerus which separated the Volsci from the Aequi, lived a people called the Hernici. Though possessing little territory, they had grouped their few cities into a league. Rome and the Latins now formed an alliance with them and so drove a wedge between their two powerful enemies, the Volsci and the Aequi.

Livy's statement that the Hernici were conquered and lost two-thirds of their territory cannot be accepted, as Rome, hard pressed as she was by Etruria and the Volsci, was not in a strong enough position to force hard bargains on supporters as useful to her as the Hernici.

ll. 2–3. **partes duae,** ' two-thirds '.

l. 3. **inde,** ' of this land '.

l. 4. **adiciebat,** ' he was for adding ' *or* ' he proposed to add '. Note this meaning of the imperfect.

l. 5. **agri . . . publicum . . . ,** ' a considerable (amount) of land, which (although it belonged to the state (**publicum**)) . . .'.

ll. 5–6. **possideri a priuatis.** While we do not know the extent of **ager publicus** at this time, it became the practice later for the Romans to increase the **ager publicus** by depriving their defeated enemies of a third of their land. As far as we know, **ager publicus** was used as commons for pasture or allotted in small holdings for cultivation. What is clear is that the patricians made full use of their political and social privileges to possess more than their fair share, and this caused great hardship at a time when the small amount of land available (both private and public) must have made life difficult in any case both for patrician and plebeians.

ll. 8–9. **sed . . . struere,** ' but anxiety on-behalf-of-the-state was in the fathers (i.e. but the fathers also felt anxiety . . .) that the consul by his largess was creating a powerful position dangerous to liberty'.

l. 10. **lex agraria. . . .** Modern historians believe that the account by Livy and Dionysius of the land problem in 5th-century Rome has been influenced in its details by the agrarian legislation of

Tiberius and Gaius Gracchus (133 B.C.–123 B.C.), which ushered in the age of revolution and civil war in the 1st century B.C.

ll. 10–12. nunquam . . . agitata, *lit.*, 'never from then right up to our own day without the greatest disturbances discussed ', i.e. ' and since then right . . . day, it (i.e. a lex agraria) has never been discussed . . .'.

l. 13. auctoribus patribus, 'with the active support of the fathers '.

l. 14. fastidire . . . socios, ' to take offence that the bounty had been made common (and) extended (*lit.*, gone forth) from the citizens to the allies '.

MSS. readings vary. Many have isse, one egisse, and others esse. exisse may be the best correction. Conway and Walters think that a ciuibus in socios may possibly be part of a scribe's gloss., or suspect that a ciuibus egisse conceals an original ambitiose (cf. l. 27).

ll. 16–17. pestilens . . . esse, ' that his colleague's bounty would be (*lit.*, was) dangerous '. The subject of audiebat is ' the people '.

ll. 18–21. quid ita . . .; adsumi . . . Latinum depends upon quid ita enim attinuisset, ' for what would have been the purpose (*lit.*, that the allies and the Latin name be admitted) of admitting the . . .'. Similarly with Hernicis . . . reddi (*lit.*, ' that a third of the captured land be restored to the H. a short time before enemies ') i.e. ' of restoring to the H. . . .'.

ll. 21–22. nisi ut . . . , ' except that . . .'. hae gentes includes both the Hernici and the Latins.

Two points need to be mentioned: (i) socios et nomen Latinum is applicable only to later Roman history, when Rome had incorporated within her community most members of the Latin league and bound to herself by alliance the other communities in Italy. Within the latter group was another under the title Nomen Latinum which consisted of a few of the original Latin communities which had not been incorporated, and the important Latin colonies which, mainly of Roman citizens, were established at important points on the great Roman trunk roads. Unlike the socii, the Latin Name had the important rights of the ius commercii and the ius conubii. (ii) The best MSS. have attinuisset: some have attinuisse,[1] a normal use of the infinitive in a rhetorical question of the 3rd person in indirect speech.

l. 22. popularis, predicate after coeperat (esse).

l. 24. ut certatim, ' as though in rivalry '.

l. 24. dicere like indulgere, l. 24, is historic infin.

l. 25. dum . . . adsignentur, ' provided they were allotted to no-one except a R. citizen '. ne cui, *lit.*, ' not to anyone '.

l. 27. eoque, ' and for that reason '. ciuibus uilior, ' cheaper to the citizens ' = ' lost caste in the eyes of his fellow-citizens '.

l. 28. iubere, ' urged (the Senate) '.

l. 30. haud secus quam, ' not otherwise than ' = ' just as if it were '.

ll. 30–31. praesentem mercedem regni, ' payment in cash for royal power '.

l. 32. uelut abundarent omnia, ' as if they had everything in abundance '.

l. 33. in animis hominum which occurs in the MSS. is bracketed by the editors of *O.C.T.*, as a gloss on insitam, copied later from the margin into the text.

l. 33. quem, coordinating relative = et eum, to be taken with damnatum necatumque (esse).

ll. 35–36. sunt qui ferant, ' some say '. patrem. The Roman father (pater familias) possessed sovereign authority (including ius uitae necisque) over all members of his household, wife, children, daughters-in-law and grand-children. Custom, however, and the family council[2] tended to exercise some restraint on his autocratic powers.

l. 37. peculium, ' the private property ', originally given by the pater familias to his wife, son, daughter or slave.

l. 37. signum, ' a statue ', i.e. of Ceres.

l. 40. quaestoribus. It is generally agreed that at the beginning of the republic, the consuls nominated two quaestors to help them

---

[1] ' perhaps rightly ' *O.C.T.*　　　　[2] See Ch. 36, l.23.

especially in judicial enquiries. Later the number was increased to four, appointments were made by the **comitia tributa,** and the office opened to plebeians in 421 B.C.

ll. 40–41. **diem . . . perduellionis,** 'that a day was appointed for him to appear on a charge of treason '.

l. 42. **Telluris**—a very old Roman goddess of fertility. Her temple was not built until 268 B.C.

CHAPTER 42

l. 3. **ea cupiditas,** 'their desire for it ', i.e. the agrarian legislation. For the use of the demonstrative, cf. **hac ira** in Chap. 22, l. 6.

ll. 6–7. **in publicum,** 'into the state treasury '. The citizen-levies of Rome and the neighbouring communities served without pay in the border warfare which at this time constituted most of the fighting. The soldiers, however, did expect some recompense, irregular though it was and possible only when victory had been won, viz., a generous share in the booty.

l. 9. **tenuere,** 'secured '. At this time the consuls were drawn from the patricians, who alone had the right to propose candidates. In addition, the retiring magistrate, as president of the elections, could also reject patrician nominations. Thus, liberty of voting was greatly restricted.

l. 12. **bello,** abl. of cause, ' owing to the war '.

l. 16. **fusos,** ' (the enemy) in-their-rout '; *lit.*, ' routed '.

ll. 16–17. **Castoris aedis.** See the note on Chap. 20, l. 42. The three columns of the temple which can still be seen in the forum belong to a later period, for the temple was rebuilt several times, the most important reconstruction being in 117 B.C.

l. 17. **idibus Quintilibus,** ' on the fifteenth of July '.

l. 19. **duumuir.** Normally the magistrate who had vowed the temple, dedicated it. When this was impossible, **duumuiri** were appointed and one of them in this case was the son of Postumius.

l. 20. **et eo anno,** ' in that year too '.

l. 21. **plebi.** Note this old form of the gen. sg.

l. 22. **celebrabant,** ' tried to assert '. See the note on Chap. 3, l. 10. **patres,** i.e. the patricians.

ll. 22–23. **satis . . . furoris,** ' that (there was) enough and to spare of frenzy unpaid ', i.e. ' without their paying for it '.

ll. 23–24. **largitiones . . . inuitamenta,** ' grants (of land), that proved incitements to violence '. Note that **-que** sometimes adds a phrase explanatory of the previous one. For **horrebant,** cf. Chap. 9, l. 30.

ll. 25–26. **ea pars,** i.e. the Senate.

l. 28. **accusatione Sp. Cassi,** causal abl., with objective gen., ' because of the accusations made against Sp. C.'.

l. 29. **consules dedit,** ' got (elected as) consuls '.

ll. 30–32. **uana . . . facti,** ' the (proposed) law came to nothing (**uana**) and of-no-account (**uani**) became its proposers in putting forward a bounty of no effect '.

ll. 32–34. **nomen . . . habitum,** ' was held in high repute after three successive consulships which-had-been-tested uninterruptedly (**uno tenore**), so-to-speak (**uelut**) in struggles with the tribunes '.

expertos, another example of the perf. part. of a deponent, used in a passive sense.

ll. 34–35. **ut bene locatus,** *lit.,* ' as if well placed ', i.e. ' like a good investment '.

l. 38. **accessere.** Note that **accedo** is often used as the passive of **addo** (3); ' there were added to . . .', i.e. ' in addition to the already general (**omnium**) uneasiness of mind, there occurred . . .'.

ll. 41–43. **motique . . . fieri,** ' for the divine will thus moved-to-anger, the soothsayers gave no other reason (when) consulted officially and privately now by (inspecting) entrails, now by (observing the flight of) birds than that the rites were not being duly done (i.e. the failure to perform religious rites in due form) '.

ll. 42–43. **nunc extis, nunc per aues.** In addition to the interpretation of dreams and inspired possession of prophets (both familiar to us from the Old Testament), the ancients had two other common methods of divination, the inspection of the entrails (especially the liver) of sacrificed animals (extaspicy), and augury, perhaps the oldest of them all, i.e. the observation of the flight of birds and of other actions that were interpreted symbolically (number, cries, eating).

l. 43. **qui . . .** , ' these causes-of-alarm, however, had this out-come—the condemnation of O. . . . for unchastity and her punish-ment '; *lit.*, ' that O. . . . having been condemned . . . was pun-ished '.

The punishment was to be buried alive.

CHAPTER 43

l. 6. **Ortonam.** It has not been possible to identify the site of this town.

l. 7. **pleni,** *lit.*, ' full (of) ', i.e. ' sated with '.

l. 10. **redibat . . . mos,** ' and there returned to the people (though) not of their own accord the practice '; i.e. ' and the people though . . . resumed their practice . . .'.

l. 13. **iniungendae** depends upon **tempus,** ' the time for impos-ing '.

ll. 13–14. **susceperat . . . impediendam,** *lit.*, ' had undertaken the military operations to-be-hindered ', i.e. ' had undertaken to hinder . . .'.

ll. 14–15. **tota . . . potestatis,** ' the full unpopularity felt to-wards the tribunician power '. Note the objective gen. Perhaps **tota,** ' full ', would be best translated as an adv. ' fully ' with **uersa est.**

l. 16. **ipsius collegae.** We are not sure how many tribunes there were at this time (the numbers given are two, four, and five), but this incident, whether it is fact or fiction, illustrates the im-portant principle of ' collegiality '; i.e. the power of all magistrates (with or without imperium) was limited by the fact that similar magistrates, having the same powers, could therefore nullify the actions of a colleague. As the *C.A.H.* says (VII. 444), ' it speaks volumes for the political sense of the Romans that the possession of the veto by so many offices did not lead to the breakdown of orderly government '.

In the later history of Rome especially in the 2nd and 1st centuries B.C., the senate maintained its political power by being able to win over by bribery or other pressures some members of the tribunate, who then used their veto to bar any legislation that was against senatorial interests.

l. 18. **scribitur = conscribitur.** See introduction, p. xvi.

ll. 18–19. **ducendus.** . . . As the reading of most MSS. in which Fabius is to be sent against the Veientes, and Furius against the Aequi—is inconsistent with Chaps. 44 and 46, the *O.C.T.* re-arranges the words to remove the inconsistency.

l. 24. **quantum in se fuit,** ' as far as it was able '. Note: (i) **tantum** has to be supplied.   (ii) the use of **se** which, though grammatically unusual in that it does not refer to the subject of the main clause, is understandable, in that this expression **quantum . . . fuit** had become stereotyped.

l. 24. **prodebat.**   Beside its conative use, the imperfect also expresses *intended* and *expected* actions: ' was for betraying ', i.e. ' was likely to *or* was ready to betray '.   The subject of this verb is **exercitus,** ' troops ', in l. 23.

ll. 25–26. **quas . . . plurimas.**   English would probably prefer to take **plurimas** with the antecedent **artes;** ' in-addition-to the numerous other qualities of-a-general which he showed . . .'.

ll. 28–32. **nec illos . . . instructos,** *lit.,* ' nor them (i.e. the in-fantry), even if no exhortation of a detested leader, not even their own feeling-of-disgrace, nor the immediate dishonour to-their-country, (nor) the danger later if courage returned to the enemy, could compel (them) to quicken their pace or, if nothing else, to stand in their ranks (**instructos**) '.

Note: (i) **nec** negatives the whole sentence (ii) the sentence will be less clumsy in English, if we begin: ' as for the infantry, even if no . . . (could move them), not even their . . .'.

l. 33. **maestique,** adj. for adv., ' and sadly '.

ll. 36–38. **adeo . . . superent,** *lit.,* ' to such an extent could the skill with which to rule their fellow citizens be more often lacking to men of outstanding qualities than (that) to defeat the foe '. It will sound better if we make ' men . . . qualities ' the subject with ' could lack ', as the verb used transitively.

defuerit is a perfect subj., potential.

l. 42. **creant;** subject **patres.** The use of **datur** suggests that for the selection of his colleague, the patrician allowed the voters in the **comitia centuriata** some choice.

CHAPTER 44

ll. 2–3. **uelut . . . Sp. Licinio,** ' as if Sp. Licinius had been successful '. Note: (i) **uelut** = **uelutsi.** (ii) the impersonal use of **procedit** (with dat.): *lit.,* ' it turns out well for someone ' = ' someone is successful '.

l. 5. **dicere,** historic infin.

ll. 5–6. **in praesentia . . . perpetuum,** ' at that time in fact (**re**), (but) for all time by the precedent (established) '.

in praesentia, ' at present ', ' at this time ', is used here of the past, to emphasise the present as it then was in contrast to the future.

ll. 7–9. **neque . . . qui uelit,** ' for they would never be short of a tribune willing ', *lit.,* ' for nor ever would there be lacking (a tribune) who wished '. Cf. the note on Chap. 43, l. 16.

l. 9. **bono publico,** ' for the good of the state ', abl. of manner.

l. 9. **quaesitam** agrees with **uictoriam** and **gratiam:** *lit.,* ' victory gained and favour gained '; better in the active, ' to gain victory for himself over a colleague and the favour of the better element '.

ll. 11–12. **uel . . . omnes,** ' even in-opposition-to all (the rest) '.

l. 12. **darent modo consules et . . . operam,** indirect command, ' only let the consuls and . . . see to it '.

l. 13. **minus** here = ' not '.

ll. 16–17. **ut . . . erat,** *lit.,* ' as to each of them personally there was something (of) claim against individual tribunes ', i.e. ' according as any of them had a personal claim on an individual (tribune) '.

ll. 20–21. quattuor . . . auxilio, ' with the help of four tribunes against one who-aimed-at-hindering the good of the state '.

Most MSS. have nouem for quattuor (i.e. IX for IV) which is due either to a scribe's mistake in copying or to a corrector who believed that the number of tribunes had always been ten. See the note on Chap. 43, l. 16.   In any case, Livy gives five as the original number in Chap. 33, ll. 5–6.

l. 23. quo, *lit.*, ' whither ', i.e. ' for which '; ' to (take part) in which '.

l. 24. non. . . . Note: (i) concitata agrees with auxilia, gratia then being abl.   (ii) Veientium, a good example of the objective gen., ' by good-will felt for the men of V.'.

l. 25. in spem uentum erat; ' they had developed hopes '.

l. 26. rem = rem publicam.

ll. 28–29. nisi . . . saeuiant, ' unless they themselves raged amongst themselves in strife ', i.e. ' unless they vented their passions against each other in faction and strife '.

ll. 29–30. id, eam, attracted into the gender of the predicate.

l. 30. labem, ' cause of decay '.

l. 31. ut . . . essent, ' so that great empires might be short-lived '.

ll. 31–32. diu . . . id malum.   Supply a Romanis.

l. 35. saeuire solitos (esse), ' were usually exasperated '.

l. 35. eosdem, ' the same '.   As idem is often used to emphasise the contrasted behaviour patterns of the same person, we can translate here: ' but in spite of this '.

ll. 36–37. qualicumque . . . statu, abl. absol., *lit.*, ' whatever (being) the state of the city ', i.e. ' no matter what the conditions in Rome '.

l. 37. manente . . . militari, abl. absol., ' provided military discipline remained (firm) '.

sisti potuisse, impersonal passive; ' they had been able to stand firm '.

l. 38. **non** with **parendi** to give ' of disobeying '. **morem** is the subject, **R. militem** the object of **sequi.**

l. 39. **proximo bello,** ' in the last campaign '. Cf. Chap. 43, ll. 30–35.

l. 42. **reditum (esse),** impersonal passive again. So also **instetur,** ' if they pressed on '.

l. 43. **suo milite,** abl. of the instrument (instead of the agent with prep. **a, (ab)),** sometimes found in military expressions.

ll. 43–44. **nihil . . . bellum,** *lit.,* ' nothing else was necessary that war be declared and (hostilities) shewn '. i.e. ' all that they had to do was to declare war and to shew hostilities '.

ll. 46–47. **multis . . . uictoresque,** ' who had experienced defeat and victory on many alternating (**in uicem**) occasions '.

CHAPTER 45

l. 3. **terrebat** = **deterrebat,** ' deterred (them) '.

l. 4. **eo ubi,** *lit.,* ' to that place where ', i.e. ' in a position in which '.

l. 4. **duae acies,** i.e. the Roman and Veientine.

l. 5. **tam . . . auersi,** ' restrained (from joining battle) by so (grave) a danger from-two-quarters '.

l. 6. **iras,** ' angry passions '.

l. 8. **lacessere,** historic infin.; ' the Romans ' is the object.

l. 10. **ut nihil mouebant,** ' as they moved (the Romans) not-at-all ' = ' as they produced no reaction from the R.'

l. 10. **qua . . . qua,** ' both . . . and ', and again in ll. 16 and 60 below.

ll. 11–12. **simulationem . . . inuentum,** ' the pretence of civil faction had been found (as) a means against cowardice ', i.e. ' in pretending to be factious, they had found a means of concealing their cowardice '.

l. 13. **non confidere . . .**; supply **animo,** ' courage ': ' had no confidence in their valour more than lack-of-trust (**non credere**) in their men ', i.e. ' lacked confidence in their valour rather than trust in their loyalty '.

ll. 14–15. **nouum . . . ,** ' this was (they said) a strange kind of faction, peace and inaction amongst armed men, (i.e. when armed men confronted each other) '.

l. 15. **ad haec,** ' in addition to this'.

l. 15. **in . . . originisque,** ' at the newness of their race and origin '. The Etruscans were much older in their civilisation than the Romans. **iacere,** historic infin.

l. 16. **haec,** ' these taunts '.

l. 17. **haud . . . pati,** ' the consuls put up with (them) with indifference (*lit.,* ' not with difficulty ') '.

l. 18. **imperitae multitudini,** dat. of person interested, equivalent to ' of the . . .', with **pectora.**

ll. 19–20. **nolle inultos hostes. nolle,** historic infin., and **inultos,** passive in meaning. Cf. Chap. 16, l. 12.

ll. 20–21. **nolle . . . consulibus.** Note: (i) **successum** (**esse**), impersonal pass. (ii) **non . . . non** reinforce[1] (not cancel) the negative in **nolle;** ' they were unwilling that the fathers, or the consuls should gain a success '.

l. 22. **externa,** ' for the enemy '; **domestica,** ' for their own people '.

ll. 28–29. **adderent impetum,** ' they might add impetus to ' = ' might spur on further '. **incitato** is dat. with **militi.**

l. 29. **immaturam rem agi,** ' that the action proposed was premature '.

l. 32. **ut in hostem animaduersuros,** ' they would inflict punishment upon (him) as upon an enemy '.

ll. 32–33. **dimissis** is strictly dat. (person interested with **crescit ardor**), but it is best translated as abl. absol.

ll. 33–34. **quo . . . pugnandi,** ' the less they believed . . . , the

[1] Cf. the note in Ch. 30, l. 16.

greater their eagerness to fight '. Note the comparative clause, quo + comparative, normally balanced by eo + comparat. Here the comparative idea is in the verb crescit and eo is omitted as often in Livy.

l. 34. hostes, subject. accendunt; supply 'the Romans' as object.

l. 35. ut, ' when '.

l. 36. quippe is a conjunction here, ' for indeed '. hostes is the understood subject of insultaturos, se, i.e. Romans, the object in indirect speech which continues to l. 38.

l. 36. credi has its literal meaning here, ' were entrusted '.

l. 37. rem . . . erupturam, ' the incident would end-violently in the worst (form) of civil faction '.

l. 48. uelle . . . ipsi fecerunt, ' they have themselves brought it about that I do not know that they (eos understood) are willing (to conquer) ' = ' they have themselves caused my ignorance of their wish to conquer '.

l. 48. certum est, lit., ' it is fixed ', i.e. ' I am resolved '.

l. 50. iurant. We should expect the fut. perf. here.

l. 53. si fallat, ' if he broke (his vow) ': subjunctive due to virtual indirect speech.

ll. 54–55. Iouem . . . inuocat, ' he called (on himself) the anger of Father Jupiter . . .'.

l. 54. Gradiuum Martem. The origin of the title is disputed: it may be connected with gradior, ' I march '.

ll. 55–56. idem . . . iurat, ' the entire army took the same oath, one after the other (invoking it) upon himself '.

The formula idem in me was used by individual soldiers at the taking of the military oath, after the first to swear had taken the oath in full.

ll. 58–59. nunc . . . offerri, ' now each (cried, iubent understood) " let the bold-tongued enemy encounter them (sibi) when they were armed " '.

armati is nom. pl. and agrees by attraction with the subject of the main clause, although in sense it goes more logically with **sibi**.

l. 61. After **nomen**, the MSS have **Fabia gens**, rejected by most editors as a gloss.

l. 63. statuunt. The subject is ' the Fabii '.   **multis . . . infensos,** ' that-had-been-embittered in many political struggles '.

CHAPTER 46

l. 2. detrectant. Supply **pugnam** as the object.

l. 3. pugnaturos (esse), ' that (the Romans) would fight '.

ll. 3–5. maius aliquod haud desperundum esse facinus, ' that some greater crime was not-to-be-despaired-of ', i.e. ' that it was likely to expect some . . .'.   The crime is mutiny or desertion. **in tam . . . ancipiti,** ' when the (Romans') feelings were so provoked and the opportunity (existed) for both actions '.

ll. 8–9. Vix . . . fuit, ' the Etruscans hardly had time to deploy their line '.   **cum** introduces an inverse **cum** clause with indicative verb.   The pluperfect indic. is unusual.   Perhaps Livy wanted to emphasise the suddenness of the action.

ll. 9–10. pilis . . . emissis, ' throwing their javelins at random amid the first excitement rather than discharging (them) '.

l. 11. pugna . . . , *lit.,* ' the fighting had come to hands and to swords ', i.e. ' they had got to close fighting with their swords '.

l. 13. insigne with **inter primores.**

l. 13. spectaculo exemploque, predicative datives.

ll. 13–14. ex his Q. Fabium. . . . Note the basic order: object, **Fabium;** subject, **Tuscus;** verb, **transfigit.** We can retain this, if we begin: ' Q. Fabius . . . was leading his men to the attack on . . . , when a Tuscan . . . (got him) as he moved carelessly amid many a group of the enemy and transfixed him . . .'.

l. 18. praeceps . . . abiit.[1]   It is not easy to translate this. Perhaps: ' Fabius fell forward on to his wounded chest ' or ' F. fell fainting headlong over his wound '.

[1] A German scholar has conjectured **cadit**: i.e. ' his head fell onto his wounded chest '.

NOTES 197

l. 20. **Romanus,** collective sg. **cum** introduces inverse **cum** clause.

l. 21. **parma** is a small round shield, carried by the cavalry.

l. 24. **iniuratus,** concessive, ' although I have taken no oath '.

l. 26. **Caeso** is nom. with **Fabius.** Supply ' said ' as the verb.

ll. 27–28. **te impetraturum,** ' that you will prevail upon (the men)'.

l. 31. **in primum,** ' into the foremost (part of the field) '.

CHAPTER 47

l. 1. **nihilo segnius,** ' no more idly ', =' just as vigorously '.

l. 3. **ubi . . . uersata,** ' when almost the same (change of) fortune occurred '.

ll. 3–6. **nam. . . .** Note again the basic order: **ipsum consulem M.,** object, **milites,** subject, then verb; ' for like Q. Fabius on the other wing, so on this Manlius the consul in person was driving the enemy whom he had almost routed and his soldiers followed (him) . . . but when (**ut**) . . .'.

l. 8. **gradum rettulere.** Livy uses **gradum referre** for the more common **pedem referre** three times in this book.

ll. 8–11. **ni consul alter . . . rem . . . sustinuisset,** ' had not the other consul . . . restored the tottering situation '.

l. 13. **cognita ora,** *lit.,* ' the recognised faces ' =' the recognition of the faces '.

l. 14. **uanior,** ' less solid '.

ll. 14–16. **dum . . . oppugnanda,** ' in that, relying on their superior numbers, they had withdrawn their reserves and sent them . . .'. Note: (i) this use of **dum** +pres. indic., which is causal. (ii) the translation of **subtracta mittunt.** Cf. Chap. 5, ll. 9–11.

ll. 16–17. **in quae . . . facto,** ' having forced their way into it without much of a struggle '.

l. 18. **triarii Romani,** ' the Roman reserves '.

l. 20. **quo loco res essent,** ' in what place the things were ', i.e.
' (to report) the seriousness of the situation '.

ll. 22–23. **ad omnes . . . opposito,** ' by posting soldiers at all the
gates '. **uiam,** ' the way (out) '.

ll. 23–24. **ea desperatio,** ' desperation at this '. Cf. **hac ira,** Chap.
22, l. 6.

ll. 25–26. **quacumque** . . . **spes,** ' wherever hope pointed to a way
of escape '. For the subj., cf. introduction, p. xv.

l. 32. **ad extrema . . . foret,** ' the situation would have become
critical '.

l. 35. **in uictorem . . . consulem,** ' they fell in with the other
consul (who had been) victorious '.

l. 37. **parta,** from **pario -ere.**

ll. 37–38. **duobus . . . funeribus,** ' by the death of two distinguished men '.

ll. 38–39. **decernente . . . triumphum,** ' when the senate was
going to decree (him) a triumph '.

ll. 40–41. **pro . . . respondit,** ' replied that he would readily allow
(it) in-view-of its remarkable services in that campaign '.

ll. 41–42. **familia funesta, re publica orba,** abl. absols. which are
equivalent to causal clauses.

l. 42. **ex parte,** ' on its side ', i.e. by the loss of Cn. Manlius, the
consul. Note that **consule altero amisso** which are found in many
MSS. may have got into the text as a copyist's explanation of **ex
parte.** On the other hand, it may be part of the original, as fulness
of expression is characteristic of Livy's style.

l. 43. **publico . . . luctu,** ' (a laurel) which sorrow on behalf of his
country and of himself blighted '.

l. 44. **omni acto triumpho,** abl. of comparison, ' than every
triumph that had been celebrated '. **depositus triumphus,** ' his
refusal of the triumph '. For the translation, cf. the note on Chap.
6, l. 18.

l. 45. **in tempore,** ' at the proper moment '.

l. 46. **cumulatior rediit,** *lit.,* ' has returned more heaped up ', i.e. ' returns in fuller measure '.   Note this use of the perfect (sententious or gnomic it is called) for that which has been, and shall be.

ll. 47–48. **idem . . . laudator,** ' and delivered the funeral oration in the case of both alike '. When a Roman patrician died, it was customary to deliver a panegyric either on the deceased if he had done anything of note, or on his family and house, if he had not.

l. 49. **ferret,** ' won '.

l. 49. **eius quod,** ' of that (purpose) which '.

l. 51. **curandos,** ' to be looked after '.

ll. 53–54. **nec . . arte,** ' and this by no method except (what was) beneficial to the community '.

<h2 style="text-align:center">CHAPTER 48</h2>

ll. 2–4. **neque . . . quam ut,** *lit.,* ' urged care neither for war nor for the levy, nor for (anything) else sooner than that '.

Note: **aliam = alius rei,** i.e., obj. gen. like **belli** and **dilectus.** ' He was first concerned neither for . . . else but only that '.

l. 4. **iam aliqua . . . spe,** ' now that some hope of internal peace had to some extent begun '.

l. 5. **primo quoque tempore,** ' at the first possible opportunity '.

l. 7. **agrariae . . . auctor,** ' to propose a land-law '.

l. 8. **occuparent . . . facere,** ' (that) the fathers of themselves should be the first to do what-was-their-proper (**suum**) function '. Note this meaning of **occupare.**

ll. 9–10. **captiuum . . . darent** is explanatory of **munus suum.**

l. 10. **uerum . . . eos,** ' it was (only) right that they should possess (it) '.

l. 13. **uiuidum . . . ingenium,** ' those natural-gifts of Caeso, once so alive ', is the subject of the two infinitives in l. 12.

l. 15. **eo,** *lit.,* ' thither ', = ' there '.

ll. 16–17. **depopulandum,** *lit.,* ' to be ravaged ' = ' to ravage it.'

The use of the gerundive after **transit** is analogous to its use after **suscipere, curare.**

l. 18. **eo,** ' because of this ', abl. of cause. So also **temeritate** l. 19.

l. 20. **actum . . . foret,** ' and it would have been all up with the army '. Note this use of **agere** impersonally in the passive.

ll. 22–23. **res . . . uenerat,** *lit.,* ' the situation had come very near the shape of brigandage ', i.e. ' their action resembled those of brigands '.

l. 24. **in urbem,** i.e. of Veii. **Legionibus R.** is dative.

ll. 25–26. **bellum . . . eludentes,** ' alternately frustrating (their enemies') warlike operations by inactivity and their inactivity by warlike operations '.

l. 27. **et,** ' furthermore '.

l. 27. **praesentia,** adj. for adv., ' immediately '.

l. 29. **quiescentibus** agrees with **ab Aequis Volscisque,** ' on the part of the A. and V. who remained at peace no longer than (= only while) the recent pain of their latest defeat was passing away '. **transiret,** subj., because the clause is virtually in indirect speech.

l. 30. **moturos. bella,** the subject of **instabant** in l. 28, has to be supplied as the object of **moturos,**[1] ' or subsequently, as it was clear that the . . . and all E. would stir up trouble '.

l. 33. **animos,** i.e. of the Romans.

l. 34. **aut auerti . . . sinebat,** ' or allowed them (i.e. Romans) to turn away (i.e. turn their attention) elsewhere '. **poterat** and **sinebat** are sg., because the subject is still **Veiens hostis,** collective sg.

l. 36. **adsiduo . . . praesidio,** ' a body of troops that is not so much large as always on the spot '.

ll. 38–39. **auctores sumus,** ' we are guarantors ', i.e. ' we guarantee '.

---

[1] After **mox moturos,** the MSS have **se,** excluded by most editors, at the suggestion of the scholar Madvig.

l. 39. **ibi,** ' there ', i.e. ' in that family '.

l. 40. **nobis in animo est,** ' it is our purpose '; **nostrum . . . bellum,** ' this war as if (it were) our own family war '.

l. 42. **uacet,** jussive subj., ' let the state be exempt from . . .'. **illic,** *lit.,* ' there ' = ' in this cause '.

l. 45. **iussi armati:** with **iussi** supply **sunt** and take **armati** with **adesse.**

CHAPTER 49

l. 1. **Fabios . . . ferunt,** in our idiom we say; ' they praised the F. to the skies '.

ll. 4–5. **si sint, deposcant.** The two verbs form the protasis.

ll. 4–5. **duae gentes,** ' two (other) clans '.

l. 5. **haec,** ' the one (clan) ', **illa,** ' the other '.

l. 6. **populo . . . agente,** abl. absol., ' while the R. people enjoyed peace and quiet '.

l. 11. **signa ferri,** ' the standards to be borne ' = ' the march to begin '.

ll. 11–12. **nunquam . . . neque . . . neque.** Cf. the note on Chap. 30, l. 16.

ll. 14–15. **quorum . . . sperneres,** ' none of whom you would have rejected as commander '. For **sperneres,** cf. note on Chap. 35, ll. 20–21.

ll. 15–16. **egregius . . . senatus,** in apposition with **milites,** ' (who would have been) an outstanding senate at any time '.

l. 17. **sequebatur. . . .** Retain the order by turning into the passive: ' they were followed by a crowd partly of-their-own-people, (consisting) of kinsmen . . .'.

ll. 18–19. **nihil . . . animo. uoluentium** is in agreement with **cognatorum sodaliumque:** ' who had in their minds no ordinary thoughts, whether of hope or of anxiety but (only) what was grandiose '. Note: **nihil** followed by **nec . . . nec.** Cf. again ll. 11–12 above and the note on Chap. 30, l. 16.

l. 20. **alia** balances the first **alia**: ' partly (of those) aroused by concern for-the-state . . .'.

ll. 20–21. **fauore . . . stupens,** ' besides themselves in enthusiastic wonder '.

ll. 21–22. **inceptis . . . reddere,** *lit.,* ' to give back results equal to the attempts ', i.e. ' to return with a success that matched (the greatness of) their enterprise '.

l. 23. **praetereuntibus:** commentators explain this either as abl. absol., with **Fabii** as the understood noun, ' as the Fabii passed . . .', or as a dat. of advantage with **quidquid . . . occurrit,** referring it to the crowd; ' as the crowd passed . . .'. The participle however, probably refers both to the Fabii and the crowd, i.e. to the whole procession and can be taken either as a loose use of the abl. absol.,[1] or as dat. as explained above, ' as the procession passed . . .'.

l. 25. **quidquid . . . ,** ' they prayed to whatever gods met their gaze or (entered) their thoughts to escort that band with good fortune and success (and) restore . . .'.

ll. 28–29. **infelici . . . Carmentalis,** ' by the unlucky way, i.e. the right arch of the Carmentis Gate '. It is assumed here that there was a right and wrong way to march out by a gate and the Fabii chose the wrong one, as events showed. The gate was so called, because it was near the shrine of Carmentis, a Roman goddess of prophecy.

Ianus: the word originally either meant a gate or barbican and then was used of the deity that protected gates, and openings.

ll. 30–31. **communiendo praesidio,** ' for building a strong point '.

l. 36. **infesta hostium:** supply **omnia:** ' (everything) of the enemies' dangerous '.

ll. 36–37. **uagantes . . . finem,** ' by their movements along the border land of both sides '.

l. 41. **quamquam,** ' and yet '.

l. 42. **adeo.** See the note on Chap. 27, ll. 14–15.

---

[1] The crowd only being the subject of **precantur.**

ll. 43–44. **dum . . . introeunt . . . locant,** 'while the ranks were falling in . . . and (the leaders) were posting . . .'.

l. 44–45. **inuecta . . . ala,** *lit.,* 'a Roman squadron of cavalry having suddenly charged on the flank' = 'a sudden charge on their flank by a R. . . .'.

l. 46. **locum,** 'the opportunity'.

l. 47. **saxa Rubra** is on the Via Flaminia, north of Rome.

ll. 48–50. **cuius . . . paenituit. cuius** (co-ordinating relative) **impetratae** (supply **pacis**) depends upon the impersonal **paenituit,** 'they grew weary of the peace they had been granted'. **ab =** 'owing to'. **ante . . . praesidium,** 'before the withdrawal of the R. garrison from Cremera'.

CHAPTER 50

l. 5. **certatum (est),** impers. pass., 'they fought'.

ll. 4–5. **aequo . . . signis,** 'in the open field, viz. in pitched battle'.

l. 6. **ut tum res erant,** *lit.,* 'as then things were' = 'by the standards of those days'.

l. 7. **tulit** = rettulit, simple for compound verb. See the introduction, p. xvi.

l. 8. **consilium ex re natum (est):** 'a plan was born from the situation' = 'the situation was responsible for a plan'.

l. 9. **gaudere . . . ,** 'they rejoiced even (seeing that) . . .'.

l. 10. **Itaque. . . .** This section describes the plan. **obuiam** with **praedantibus,** 'they drove flocks (*lit.,* flocks were driven) in-the-path-of the plunderers as if they (i.e. the flocks) had fallen in (with them) by chance'.

ll. 13–14. **subsidia armatorum missa,** 'armed men sent in support'.

ll. 17–19. **ad conspecta pecora,** 'at the sight of flocks'. **magno . . . interuallo,** 'beyond a great expanse of plain'.

l. 19. **rara,** 'here and there'; **arma,** 'armed groups'.

l. 20. **improuidi,** adj. for adv., ' rashly '. **effuso,** ' headlong '. **superassent,** ' had passed '.

l. 22. **ut . . . ,** ' as happens when terrified ', explanatory of **uaga.**

l. 27. **breuiore spatio; eo** to be supplied, to balance **quo magis;** ' the more the enemy advanced, the smaller the space in which they were compelled likewise **(et ipsi) . . .'.**

l. 28. **quae res,** ' this movement. **insignem faciebat,** ' made clear ': **multiplicatis . . . ordinibus,** ' their ranks multiplied in the narrow space ', i.e. ' for their ranks were increased in depth . . .'.

l. 31. **parem,** ' equally '.

l. 32. **nisi,** perf. part. of **nitor.**

l. 34. **ut,** ' when '.

l. 36. **subeuntes,** acc. pl., '(the enemy) advancing (against them) '.

l. 36. **uincebat . . . ,** ' and a few men with the help of a (good) position were winning the victory (and would have won it), had not . . .'. Cf. the note on Chap. 10, l. 4.

l. 37. **Veiens,** collective sg.

l. 41. **unum . . . relictum,** ' (that) one boy survived, almost mature in age ', i.e. ' grown-up to manhood '.

ll. 41–43. **stirpem . . . ,** ' destined-to-be **(futurum)** the parent stock for the Fabian clan, and to-be often the greatest help at home and in war to Rome at times of crisis *(lit.,* ' to the uncertain affairs of the R. people ') '.

This latter statement applies only to his descendants: Livy is thinking especially of Q. Fabius Cunctator whose steadiness rallied Rome in 217 B.C.

CHAPTER 51

ll. 5–6. **super . . . premente,** *lit.,* ' in addition to the war the scarcity of corn pressing (them) hard ', i.e. ' for they were hard pressed not only by the war but also by . . .'.

ll. 8–10. **ut . . . ,** ' that engagements took place at first at (the temple) of Hope, with no definite result, and later at . . .'.

NOTES 205

For **ad Spei,** cf. the English idiom: 'at St. Paul's'. The temple is said to have been built in the 1st Punic War on the Esquiline.

l. 10. **paruo momento,** *lit.,* 'by a small (determining) amount' ='by only a small turn of the scale'.

ll. 14–15. **abstinuere acie,** 'they refrained from (i.e. they avoided) regular fighting'.

l. 15. **et uelut ... Ianiculo,** 'and from the Janiculum, as from their stronghold'.

ll. 19–20. **Secuti ... pecora,** 'Having pursued the flocks which had been driven out purposely here and there (*lit.,* for enticing) to entice them on'.

Note **dedita opera,** ='purposely'.

l. 21. **maior.** ... Note the omission of **eo. plures,** l. 20, i.e. than the Fabii.

l. 21. **ex hac ... ira,** 'the fierce anger that-arose from (**ex**) this disaster'.

l. 23. **adorti sunt.** Subject, 'the Veientines'.

l. 25. **et ipse,** 'likewise'.

l. 27. **nonnihil,** 'in some degree'; **et ...,** 'because he was made confident by his success in the battle of the day before'.

ll. 28–29. **magis ... consilia,** 'but more because the lack of corn drove (him) into plans however rash, provided they were speedy'.

l. 30. **aduerso Ianiculo,** 'straight up the J.'.

l. 33. **cum,** 'since'. This sentence suggests that Verginius attacked the enemy on their flank or from the rear.

l. 34. **occidione occisi (sunt),** 'were cut to pieces'.

ll. 34–35. **temeritate felici,** 'by a rash action that-had-a-lucky result'. **oppressum (est),** 'was decisively ended'.

CHAPTER 52

l. 1. **laxior etiam annona,** 'also an easier market in corn'.

ll. 1–4. **et aduecto ...** 'both because grain was ... and because what had remained concealed was brought out, when ...'.

ll. 2–3. **postquam . . . abiit,** *lit.,* 'when fear for his future scarcity had gone from each one for himself'; i.e. 'when each man lost his own fears for his personal shortages'.

l. 4. **ex,** 'as a consequence of'. **lasciuire,** historic infin.

l. 5. **postquam . . . deerant,** 'now that they (i.e. trouble) were missing abroad'.

l. 6. **quaerere,** historic infin. The subject 'the people' can easily be supplied from the previous subject: 'the minds of the people' **(animi).**

l. 6. **suo,** 'their (natural)'.

l. 7. **in resistentes,** with **patres.** **plebem** is the understood object of **incitare,** hist. infin. like **agitare,** l. 6.

l. 10. **diem dicunt.** See Chap. 35, ll. 8–9. Livy does not mention the charge: it may have been that of having been responsible for the loss of so many plebeians in the battle which followed the disaster of the Cremera (Chap. 51).

l. 10. **inuidiae,** predicative dat. **amissum . . . praesidium,** 'the loss of the post at the Cremera'.

l. 12. **ea,** i.e. **inuidia,** 'this unpopularity'. **oppressit,** 'overthrew (him)', i.e. 'caused his overthrow'. **cum,** 'although'.

l. 15. **cum . . . anquisissent,** 'although they had begun the enquiry on a capital charge'.

l. 16. **dixerunt,** 'they imposed'. **duorum . . . aeris,** 'of 2,000 (pounds) of copper'. See the note on Chap. 33, l. 46.

l. 16. **ea . . . uertit,** 'that changed into (a-matter-affecting) his life'.

l. 19. **alius deinde reus,** 'then another (patrician) was accused'.

l. 22. **precibus . . . patrum,** 'with his own entreaties or (those) of the fathers'.

l. 25. **crimini,** predicative dat., with **huic,** 'the ground of the accusation against him'.

l. 27. **refutando exprobrandoque.** Modal use of the abl. of the gerund again. As the whole sentence is too long for English idiom, make them main verbs: 'he resisted . . . and reproached . . .'. Begin at l. 30 with 'In this way by his boldness . . .'.

ll. 28–30. **cuius . . . haberet,** ' and (it was) by his father's sense of duty (that) the people had been formerly restored (and) now possessed those very magistrates, those very laws by means of which they were then making (=which enabled them to make) such savage attacks '.

l. 30. **haberet:** subj. due to virtual indirect speech. **saeuiret:** subj. by attraction.

l. 32. **participando laudes,** ' by sharing (with him) the credit he had won for himself '.

l. 33. **adeo . . . animum,** ' to-such-an-extent had their feelings changed '; *lit.,* ' they (i.e. the people) had changed . . .'.

CHAPTER 53

l. 1. **Veiens bellum,** means ' the war with the Veientines ': hence **quibus.**

l. 6. **tantam . . . iniecit,** we say: ' threw them into such great confusion '.

ll. 6–8. **dum . . . uim,** ' while they were running out in scattered companies (*lit.,* scattered in companies) by various ways to ward off the Romans' attack '.

Note that **dum** +pres. indic. is sometimes retained, when dependent on other subjunctives or infinitives.

l. 11. **tamquam Veiis captis,** ' as if V. had been captured '.

l. 13. **Romanos . . . castra,** ' the R. who were directing the whole of their attack on the camp '; *lit.,* ' with all their attack directed against the camp '.

l. 14. **auersi turbatique.** ' The Romans ' is the subject.

ll. 14–15. **utroque . . . signis,** *lit.,* ' the standards turned in both directions ', i.e. ' wheeling in both directions '.

l. 20. **per se ipsi,** ' entirely by themselves '.

l. 23. **praeter . . . res,** ' in addition to recovering . . .'.

l. 24. **ab Roma.** Cf. the note on Chap. 16, l. 12.

l. 25. **credo,** parenthetical, i.e. the verb has no grammatical influence on the rest of the sentence.

ll. 24–25. **mos non placebat,** 'the practice did not meet with their approval'. What the practice was is explained in the following acc. + infin.

ll. 27–29. **nullum . . . dimicarent,** 'although no kind . . . was not inflicted ', i.e. ' although every kind . . . was inflicted upon the V., yet they could not be driven into giving battle '.

CHAPTER 54

l. 3. **petentibus,** ' to (them) requesting ', = ' at their request '.

l. 4. **imperato,** ' demanded ' *or* ' exacted '. Note this use of **impero** as a transitive vb. = ' demand ', ' exact ', ' requisition '.

It is very difficult to believe that Rome was so strong at this time to make such demands.

ll. 4–5. **paci . . . domi,** *lit.,* ' to the peace abroad immediately was made continuous the faction at home ', i.e. ' peace abroad was immediately followed by . . .'.

ll. 5–6. **agrariae . . . stimulis,** ' owing to the tribunician goads of . . . ', abl. of cause: i.e. ' goaded by the tribunes in the . . .'.

l. 6. **nihil,** adverbial, ' in no way '.

l. 8. **abeuntes magistratu,** ' as they quitted their office '.

l. 9. **arripuit,** not ' seized ', but ' summoned (before the people)'.

l. 13. **rei ad populum,** ' on being accused before the people '.

l. 14. **sordidati.** In Greek and Roman trials, it was customary for the defendant to use every means of exciting pity, i.e. by wearing old clothes as here, or by bringing in his wife and numerous children.

l. 14. **non plebem;** supply ' canvassing ' from **circumeunt.**

l. 14. **non plebem . . . patrum,** ' the younger patricians as much as the people '.

l. 15. **suadent, monent.** Latin often uses two synonymous verbs where we prefer adverb, verb; here: ' they earnestly warned (them) '.

l. 16. **abstineant:** supply **ut.**

l. 16. **uero** is used in emphatic statements to introduce a climax as here: ' in truth ' *or* ' in a word '.

l. 18. (ut) **putent . . .** , ' to think that the consular fasces . . . were nothing else than (=exactly the same as) the display at a funeral '.

ll. 18–19. **claris . . . destinari**, ' (for) wearing (*lit.*, veiled in) (such) splendid regalia like sacrificial fillets, they were marked for death '.

l. 20. **iam . . . inducant**, ' let them, as things now were, be convinced that the consulship . . .'. **nunc** is used to emphasise **iam** in the meaning ' as things now are '.

l. 21. **ab** is used here with **t. potestate** because the latter is personified.

ll. 22–23. **consuli omnia agenda esse,** ' the consul had to do everything '.

l. 23. **si se commouerit,** ' if he moved (an inch) '.

ll. 24–25. **si . . . crediderit,** ' if he believed there was any other (element) (in the state) but the people '.

l. 27. **patres,** ' (some) senators '. There is no need to suppose that they would be only the younger ones.

l. 28. **seductaque . . . conscientia,** *lit.*, ' (meetings) withdrawn from the knowledge of more ', i.e. ' so secret that the majority knew nothing about them '. The majority refers more to the senate than to the people.

ll. 29–30. **iure . . . reos,** ' that the accused were to-be-rescued rightly or wrongly ', i.e. ' that they must rescue the accused . . .'.

ll. 30–31. **maxime placebat,** ' found the most favour '.

l. 31. **quamuis audaci,** ' however reckless '.

l. 33. **mirari,** ' they were surprised ', historic infin.

ll. 33–34. **quod . . . descenderet.** The subj. is due to virtual indirect speech: ' because, as they saw, the tribune did not come down into the forum '. The forum lies in the low ground between three hills, Palatine, Capitoline, and Quirinal.

l. 35. **credere,** ' they believed ': **queri,** ' they complained '.

210 LIVY, BOOK TWO

ll. 36–37. **qui ... fuerant,** ' those who had presented themselves
at the tribune's vestibule ', i.e. to attend him on his way to the
forum.

l. 38. **quod, ' this news ':** co-ordinating relative and object of
pertulit.

l. 40. **ita ... alio,** ' just so they gradually disappeared their
different ways ': *lit.,* ' some somewhither, others otherwhither '.

ll. 41–42. **quam ... monitos:** order for translation: **monitos
morte collegae quam sacratae leges haberent nihil auxilii.**

sacratae leges is pl. for sg.: in Chap. 33, l. 10, it is referred to as
lex sacrata. The inviolability of the tribunes depended not upon
any statute, but upon the oath taken by the people to slay anyone
who used violence towards them.

ll. 42–43. **nec ... laetitiam,** ' the fathers were not at all restrained in the way they showed their pleasure '.

ll. 43–46. **adeoque ... potestatem,** ' to such an extent did no-
one repent for the crime that even the innocent wished to be
thought guilty *(lit.,* to seem to have done (it)) and men openly
asserted *(lit.,* it was openly asserted) that (it was) by punishment
that they should tame the power of the tribunes *(lit.,* the power of
the tr. was to be tamed) '.

Livy and the tribune's contemporaries naturally assumed that
Genucius had been murdered. But sudden death has always been
common amongst mankind, and it is possible that Genucius died
of natural causes.

CHAPTER 55

l. 1. **sub,** ' just after '. **hac ... uictoria,** ' this victory, of so
pernicious a precedent '.

l. 5. **actum ... sua.** See Chap. 48, l. 20.

ll. 5–6. **rursus ... reditum,** indirect speech with **reditum (esse)**
impersonal passive; ' they had gone back to the (bad) old days '.

l. 6. **una,** adv.

ll. 7–8. **aliud ... patribus,** *lit.,* ' something else was to be done, it was to-be-planned how to resist the fathers ': i.e. ' they had to do something else, viz. plan how . . .'.

Note: (i) **cogitandum** is explanatory of **aliud agendum.** (ii) **resistatur,** impersonal passive.

l. 11. **apparere consulibus,** ' attended the consuls '.

l. 11. **et eos ipsos . . . ,** ' and even they were plebeians '. For the lictors, see the introduction, p. xvii. At this time the consuls had six, not twelve.

ll. 12–14. **nihil . . . facere,** ' nothing could be (*lit.*, was) more contemptible, nothing weaker, if there were (men) to make it contemptible; each man made such matters (=the power of the consuls) great and dreadful for himself '.

For Latin ' was ' =English ' could be ', see the note on Chap. 10 ll. 46–47.

The meaning here is that everything is as strong or as weak as men's imagination makes it so.

l. 14. **alii alios,** ' one another '.

l. 16. **quod . . . duxisset;** ' because he had been a centurion ', to be taken after **negaret . . . debere.**

l. 16. **negaret.** The use of the subjunctive can be explained, because the subjunctive is frequently used in causal clauses to give the alleged reason (without a verb of speaking). Although a verb of speaking is used here (**negaret**), Livy uses the subjunctive mood. See Gildesleeve and Lodge, section 541, note 3.

l. 16. **militem,** ' an ordinary soldier '.

l. 23. **circumscindere,** historic infin.: so also **spoliare:** ' tore off (his clothes) and stripped (him) '.

l. 24. **et . . . et;** ' both . . . and ', co-ordinates expressions which are unlike, i.e. **praeualens,** ' a strong man himself ', and an abl. absol. **adiuuantibus aduocatis,** ' with the help of his supporters ', but both explain the abl. absol. **repulso lictore** which should be translated as a main verb in the active: 'repulsed the lictor (and) . . .'.

ll. 25–26. **ubi . . . clamor,** *lit.,* ' where there was a very fierce shout of (men) indignant for him ',[1] i.e. ' where men were shouting most indignantly on his behalf '. Take this sentence after the main clause.

l. 26. **eo**, ' to that place ', antecedent of **ubi**, l. 25.

ll. 28–29. **nihil est quod exspectetis**: here **quod** = tale **ut**, ' of such a kind that ', to introduce a consecutive clause: tr. ' there is no point in your waiting for '.

ll. 29–30. **quibus . . . est**, *lit.*, ' for whom themselves there is need of your help ', i.e. ' who need . . . for themselves '.

ll. 31–33. **apparebatque . . . iuris**, ' it was clear that there was danger that-anything-might-happen, that nobody would hold anything sacred, either of public or private right ' (*lit.*, ' that nothing would be sacred to anyone ').

For the double negative **nihil . . . non . . . non**, see the note on Chap. 30, l. 15.

l. 33. **tantae**, *lit.*, ' so great ' = ' violent ' here.

l. 34. **facile**, ' readily '.

ll. 34–35. **parum . . . maiestatem**, ' that their position of dignity (was) little secure (=insecure) '.

l. 37. **exerceret uictoriam**, ' was likely to use his victory '.

The subj. in indirect question represents a present indic. which in the direct question was used of intended action.

l. 38, **in senatum uocari**: **uocari** is impersonal passive: ' a meeting of the senate to be held '.

ll. 39–40. **multis . . . sententiis**: this abl. absol. might be concessive ' although ', or purely temporal ' after ', ' when '.

ll. 40–42. **quibus . . . placuit**, *lit.*, ' whom it did not please ', (i.e. ' who did not want) a struggle (**certari**) by means of the anger of the fathers (i.e. between the angry fathers) against the recklessness of the people (i.e. and the people when in reckless mood) '.

CHAPTER 56

ll. 1–2. **proximis comitiis**. There are many difficult questions in the early history of Rome and one of them is the origin of and

[1] For Volero.

the method of the election of the first tribunes. Our ancient authorities do not help: Livy gives us no information, while Cicero states that they were elected in the **comitia curiata**[1] (assembly-by-wards), the oldest of all the Roman assemblies. What seems to be fairly certain is that in 471 B.C., the patricians officially recognised the tribunes and the right of the plebeians to meet and elect their tribunes probably by tribes. This meeting was the **concilium plebis tributum;** the tribal grouping meant that the small farmers and proprietors of the adjoining districts could be represented, whereas in any other earlier meetings of the people, the city plebeians and clients of patrician families would predominate in a grouping based on wards. Cf. Cicero's statement above. This **concilium plebis tributum** is what Livy means in l. 8, **tributis comitiis.**

l. 2. **plebi** = gen. Cf. Chap. 42, l. 21.

ll. 4-5. **eum ... tribunatum,** ' that he would devote his tribuneship to harrying the consuls of the previous year '. This use of **permittere** is not found elsewhere: it is derived from the meaning ' give one's horse the rein '.

ll. 6-7. **post ... consulibus.** The abl. absol. **priuato dolore habito** ' his personal resentment placed ', should be made a main verb: ' he put his ... resentment second to (**post**) the interests of his country (and) without attacking-the-dignity of the consuls by-as-much-as-a word (*lit.,* the consuls violated not even by a word) '.

l. 8. **tributis comitiis.** Strictly speaking, the **comitia tributa** was an assembly of all the citizens: it probably was founded much later than our period in imitation of the **concilium plebis tributum.** From what has been said above, it seems probable that Livy means by this expression the **concilium plebis.**

ll. 9-10. **haud ... ferebatur,** *lit.,* ' no trivial matter was proposed under (this) title at first sight not-at-all alarming '.

ll. 10-12. **sed quae ... auferret,** ' but (one) which would take from the patricians ...'. The subjunct. is consecutive. Cf. Chap. 17, ll. 12-13.

[1] This assembly gradually lost most of its power to the new **comitia centuriata,** and later still to the **comitia tributa.**

per clientium suffragia. See the note on ll. 1–2 above. The clients would vote as their patrons directed.

ll. 13–16. **nec quae ... posset.** Note: (i) **ut ... collegio** is dependent upon **adduci posset.** (ii) **quae una ... erat** is in apposition to the **ut ... collegio** clause: *lit.*, ' and that any from the (tribunician) college should use his veto, could not (**nec,** l. 13) be prevailed upon by ... or of the leading citizens,—which alone was power for resisting'. Begin as follows: ' and the only effective means of resistance: viz., the use of the veto by one of the tribunician college could not be brought into play by the influential persuasion either of ... or ...'.

ll. 16–17. **res tamen ... extrahitur,** ' yet the problem, (made more) difficult by its very importance, was drawn out by (party) strife over the whole year '.

ll. 18–19. **ad ... uenturam,** ' thinking that the matter would go to extremes in the struggle '.

ll. 19–21. **iam inde ... plebi,** ' hateful to and hating the people right from that time (**iam inde**) of the struggles between their fathers '.

a paternis certaminibus is in apposition with **iam inde.**

ll. 23–24. **principio ... agebatur,** ' at the very beginning of the year they discussed the law (*lit.*, it was discussed about . . .) before all else '.

ll. 24–25. **ut,** ' while '. **sic,** ' yet '.

Translate: ' while the originator of the law Volero urged it (**auctor erat**), yet his colleague Laetorius gave support (**auctor erat**) (that was) not only more fresh but more vigorous '.

l. 26. **ferocem. . . .** Turn into the passive: ' he was made confident by . . .'.

l. 26. **aetatis eius,** ' of that day '.

l. 29. **abstinens,** ' refraining from '.

l. 31. **exorsus.** Make a main verb. Begin a fresh sentence at **cum.**

l. 33. **contenderet,** ' maintained '.

ll. 33–34. **rudis ... animoque,** ' his rough soldier's tongue could not support (*lit.*, was not sufficient for) his outspokenness and anger '.

l. 35. **quando . . . loquor.** Supply **tam**: an omission found elsewhere in Livy.

l. 36. **quam . . . praesto,** 'as I (can) make good what I have spoken '.

l. 38. **templum,** i.e. the platform in the **comitium**: *lit.*, an area properly marked off and consecrated by augurs' rites.

ll. 39–40. **in contione,** ' in *or* at the meeting '. It is not a **comitia** because many are present who are not entitled to vote.

l. 40. **submoueri,** ' (all) to withdraw '. **qui . . . ineant,** ' those who were voting '.

l. 44. **negare . . . nisi,** ' said that a tribune had no power over anyone except . . .'.

ll. 45–46. **nec illam ipsam . . . Quirites,** ' nor could he (i.e., the tribune) in virtue of (**pro**) his power remove the people themselves in-accordance-with the custom of the Fathers, since the expression used ran as follows (*lit.*, ' it was spoken thus '), " if it seems good to you, depart, Quirites " '.

Conway in the *Oxford Text* writes **illam ipsam,** i.e. **plebem** object of **submouere,** for the MSS. **illum ipsum,** i.e. the **consul,** subject of **submouere,** used without an object.

Appius makes a debating point out of the courteous expression, **si . . . uidetur,** i.e. ' if you please ', to prove that the dispersal of a crowd depended, not on the power of the magistrate, but on the crowd's response to his polite request.

ll. 48–49. **facile perturbare poterat,** i.e. ' he had no difficulty in disconcerting '. **contemptim . . . disserendo,** ' in talking so contemptuously about his rights '.

There are many difficulties in this story. First what was this meeting? the **comitia curiata**? If so, had the tribunes at this time the right to convene it, preside, and introduce bills which, if passed, had the force of law? Was it a meeting of the **plebs,** the beginning of the **concilium plebis tributum**? If so, it had no constitutional sanction at this time, and it was not until 287 B.C. that its resolutions had the force of law. Moreover the tribunes could ask, not order, non-plebeians to withdraw. It is possible that in his account, Livy has been influenced by the position which the tribunate won in later Roman history.

l. 52. **uiolatus esset,** ' would have been manhandled '.

l. 53. **atrox,** adj. for adv. ' fiercely '.

ll. 54–55. **et concursus . . . fieret,** ' and did not (**ni**) a rush of men, an excited throng, take place from all the city into the forum '. Note: (i) **concitatae multitudinis,** in apposition with **hominum.** (ii) **fieret,** imperfect subj., not pluperf., because the action is felt to be continuous.

Translate: ' and at the same time (**et . . . et,** *lit.*, both . . . and) men in an excited throng kept rushing in from all over the city into the forum '.

l. 58. **negotio dato.** Translate as if it were **negotium dedisset,** ' given the job to ' = ' entrusted the job ', **ut . . . abducerent,** ' that they should get away ', i.e. ' of getting away '.

l. 59. **ipse,** ' (while) he himself . . .'.

l. 61. **darent,** indirect command, ' let them give time for their anger (to cool) '.

l. 62. **tempus,** acc. subject of **adempturum esse,** in acc. +infin. construction. **uim suam,** ' their power '. Note that **suam** refers to **illis,** not to **tempus** the subject, a legitimate use, as **suus** may be used to refer not only to the subject of a sentence (strict use) but also to any persons mentioned, provided that it is in an emphasised position.

CHAPTER 57

l. 2. **consul alter,** i.e. Appius Claudius.

l. 3. **Vbi,** connecting relative adverb: *lit.,* ' where ' = ' and there ' = ' and in this debate '.

l. 4. **in uicem,** *lit.,* ' in turn ', ' alternating ', can be taken as an adj., with **timor atque ira.**

l. 4. **uariassent,** *lit.,* ' had varied ', i.e. ' had produced divergent proposals (**sententias**) '.

ll. 4–6. quo . . . animi. Note: (i) quo magis, eo plus, 'the more . . . the more'. (ii) animi is the subject of both verbs. (iii) spatio interposito, 'time placed between ' = ' with the passing of time'. (iv) ab impetu, 'from impulsive action'.

l. 7. eius opera, 'by the service of him ' = ' thanks to him'.

l. 8. esset: subj. in causal clause, alleged reason, 'because (as they said) . . .'.

l. 8. ab Appio petitur; the verb is impersonal pass.: as usual we prefer personal + active: 'they begged Appius'.

ll. 9–10. in concordi ciuitate, 'in a community at-one-with-itself'.

ll. 10–12. dum . . . : acc. + infin.: ' (they said) that while . . .'.

ll. 10–11. ad . . . trahant, 'were pulling opposite ways'; lit., ' were pulling everything each to himself'.

l. 12. in medio, 'in those between the two parties'.

ll. 13–14. magis . . . quaeri, lit., 'it was more asked in whose control it (i.e. the state) was (rather) than that it be safe': i.e. ' men asked who was to control the state rather than sought to secure its safety'. Note, quaeri (impersonal pass.) governs both the indirect question and the ut clause (ut . . . sit).

l. 14. contra, adv., ' on the other hand'.

ll. 15–16. non consulem . . . , ' (it was) not the consul (who) . . . , (but) the senate (that) . . .'.

l. 17. leges, ' terms'.

l. 18. silentio, ' without opposition'.

CHAPTER 58

ll. 2–3. numero . . . fuerint is dependent upon Piso auctor est, ' Piso is the authority that . . .'. perinde ac, ' just as if'.

l. 6. inter, ' during'.

l. 7. uastauerant: subj., Volsci et Aequi.

l. 8. ad se receptum haberet, ' (the seceding plebeians) might have a place of refuge with them'.

ll. 8–9. **compositis rebus**, ' when harmony was restored '.

ll. 10–11. **Quinctio ... euenit,** ' Quinctius had the Aequi for his sphere of operations '.

l. 12. **esse,** historic infin.

l. 12. **liberior ... erat,** ' (but) it was less restrained (*lit.*, more unrestrained), because it was free from the controlling fetters of the tribunes '.

l. 13. **odisse,** historic infin.

l. 13. **se uictum ... ;** acc. and infin.: ' (he felt) that ...'.

ll. 14–15. **se ... esse,** ' that in-his-consulship when he had been chosen specially (**unicum**) to fight (**aduersus**) the power of the tribunes a law had been passed '.

l. 16. **nequaquam ... spe,** *lit.*, ' the hopes of the fathers (being) by no means so great ', i.e. ' when ... were not anything like as high '.

l. 19. **poterat:** subject is **exercitus. imbiberant:** subj. **milites.**

l. 21. **agere,** historic infin. So also **incedere** and **remittere** and the remaining infins. in this passage.

ll. 23–24. **si ... uellet ... adesset:** for the subj. in indefinite clauses, see the introduction, p. xv.

l. 23. **adhortator,** ' to encourage them '. See introduction, p. xvi.

l. 24. **sua sponte motam industriam,** ' the energy they had displayed of their own accord '.

l. 24. **praesenti,** ' to (him) present ', ' in his presence '.

l. 26. **inuictus odio plebeio,** ' which the hatred of the people had never mastered '.

l. 27. **omni ... prompta,** abl. absol., *lit.*, ' all strictness to no purpose brought forth ', i.e. ' having displayed all his strict methods ...'.

l. 30. **uocare,** ' he called (them) ...'.

CHAPTER 59

l. 1. **eorum,** *neuter,* ' of these facts '.

l. 2. **certamen animorum,** ' struggle of spirits ' = ' spirited struggle ': it is the object of **habiturum (esse).**

l. 5. **Appio, Fabio,** dats. of the person interested: ' But Appius found (the army) much more aggressive than F. (had done) '.

l. 6. **tantum,** ' only '.

l. 9. **extremi agminis,** ' of the rear-guard '.

l. 10. **tum . . . pugnandum,** *lit.,* ' then aggression for fighting was wrung (from them) ', i.e. ' then they were forced to be aggressive and fight '.

ll. 10–11. **uictor iam,** ' now victorious ' = ' in the moment of his victory '.

l. 12. **tantum,** ' only '.

l. 13. **alioqui . . .:** asyndeton, ' (but) that elsewhere . . .'.

l. 14. **quibus,** *neuter.*

l. 14. **animus** is the subject of **uellet: Appius** (easily understood from **animus)** of **aduocaret.**

l. 15. **aduocaret,** 'was-for-summoning'. Note this conative force.

l. 16. **ne utique,** ' that he should not on any account . . .'.

ll. 17–18. **cuius . . . esset,** ' for the whole force (of authority) lay in the general agreement to obey (*lit.,* was of men obeying) '.

ll. 18–20. **negare . . . :** acc. infin.: ' (the officers said) that . . .'.

l. 19. **passimque . . . postulantium,** ' and everywhere men could be overheard demanding '; *lit.,* ' the voices of (men) demanding were heard '.

ll. 21–22. **ingentis mali,** ' of a great disaster ', i.e. of utter defeat.

l. 23. **uictus,** i.e. Appius Claudius.

l. 24. **lucrarentur,** subject **milites;** the subjunctive is used because it gives Appius' reason for yielding. **tempus,** ' delay '.

l. 28. **ut,** ' as though '. **nouissimos,** ' the men in the rear '.

l. 29. **a quibus,** ' from them ', i.e. ' from the rear '. **ad primos,** ' to the van '. **perlatus,** ' spreading '.

l. 30. **eo,** ' such '.

ll. 32–33. **per . . . armorumque,** *lit.,* ' over the strewn mass of bodies and of arms ', i.e. ' over the bodies and weapons strewn in heaps '.

l. 35. **ex . . . cursu,** ' from their scattered and headlong flight '.

l. 36. **reuocando** = **reuocans;** introduction, p. xvi.

l. 37. **inuectus.** Make this deponent participle a main verb.

l. 38. **haud falso,** ' not falsely ' = ' with every justification '.

ll. 38–39. **proditorem . . . desertorem,** *lit.,* ' betrayer of . . . deserter of ', becomes ' that had betrayed . . . that had deserted . . .'. See introduction, p. xvi.

l. 40. **rogitans.** Begin a fresh sentence here, and take next the indirect question **ubi . . . essent.**

ll. 40–42. **inermes milites . . . uirgis caesos securi percussit;** ' he flogged[1] and beheaded[1] the soldiers without their arms, the standard bearers who had lost . . . , in addition (**ad hoc**) . . .'.

caesos percussit. For the use of the participle here and its English translation, cf. the note on Chap. 5, ll. 9–11.

Soldiers became ' double-ration ' soldiers as a reward for meritorious service in the field.

ll. 43–44. **cetera . . . lecti,** ' of the rest, every tenth man was chosen by lot for punishment '.

Note: (i) **cetera multitudo** is in apposition to the grammatical subject **decimus quisque:** (ii) **lecti** pl. logically, not grammatically, in agreement with **quisque.**

CHAPTER 60

l. 1. **contra ea,** *lit.,* ' against this '; i.e. ' as a contrast '. **in Aequis,** ' in the campaign against the Aequi '.

ll. 1–2. **inter . . . est. certatum est** is another example of the impersonal pass. Perhaps we could say: ' the consul and his men vied with one another in . . .'.

[1] Perhaps we ought to say: ' he ordered the flogging and beheading of . . .'

l. 2. **et,** ' both ', can be ignored.

l. 3. **quo** = **ut eo,** the **eo** going with **magis**: *lit.,* ' had brought it about (**effecerat**) that he rejoiced the more in (i.e., got the greater satisfaction from) his own temperament '.

l. 4. **tantae,** *lit.,* ' so great ', = ' perfect ' here.

ll. 6–7. **nec . . . praeda,** *lit.,* ' in no other campaign before, was booty driven from there more widely ', i.e. ' in no previous campaign had the Romans driven off booty from-that-country (**inde**) over a wider area '.

l. 8. **addebantur,** i.e. by the consul: **laudes,** ' words of praise '.

ll. 8–9. **haud minus quam,** ' no less than ' = ' as much as '.

ll. 13–15. **uaria . . . efficiunt:** the skeleton is: **comita tributa efficiunt annum exactum maxime insignem.** The order and emphasis of the Latin can be retained, if we turn into the passive: e.g. ' the year which had just ended with varying fortune in war . . . was made chiefly distinctive by the assembly by-tribes '.

ll. 15–16. **res . . . usu,** ' a matter more important in the victory (they had won) in the struggle they had undertaken (rather) than in (any) practical advantage '.

l. 16. **plus . . . ,** *lit.,* ' for more dignity was taken from the assembly itself by removing . . . , than (more) of strength was either added to the people or . . .', i.e. ' the loss of dignity to . . . was greater than the accession of strength to the people or the taking of it from the fathers '.

CHAPTER 61

l. 1. **excepit,** ' followed ' (intransitive).

l. 4. **cui . . . ,** ' against whom (as) the bitterest opponent . . . and (as) one-who-supported the cause of those who possessed public land as if he were the third consul (i.e. consul along with the other two) M.D. and Gn. S. appointed a day, (i.e. brought in an impeachment) '.

ll. 7–8. **ad iudicium populi,** ' to trial before the people '.

ll. 8–9. **plenus . . . irarum,** ' full of (i.e. bowed down) as he was,

222

by angry passions directed against himself and his father'.
suarum, paternarum are equivalent to objective genitives.

l. 9. **temere**, not in its common meaning of ' rashly ', but to be
taken closely with **non** =' hardly ', ' scarcely '. For this meaning,
cf. **nullus dies temere discessit,** ' hardly a day went by '. **pro ullo
aeque,** ' equally on behalf of any man ' =' as much on behalf . . .'.

l. 10. **propugnatorem . . . :** acc. +infin., ' (they felt) that . . .'.

ll. 11–12. **ad . . . tumultus,** i.e. **oppositum ad . . .** ' who-had-
firmly-stood against . . .'.

ll. 12–13. **modum . . . plebi,** ' one who had gone too far *(lit.,*
exceeded the limit) only in the fighting, was being thrown to the
anger of the people '.

l. 13. **unus e patribus,** ' alone amongst the fathers '.

l. 15. **pro nihilo habebat,** ' regarded as of no consequence '.

l. 17. **uestem mutaret.** See the note on Chap. 54, l. 14.

l. 17. **supplex,** adj. for adv., ' suppliantly '.

l. 18. **ne . . . quidem,** the **ne** strengthens the first negative **non,**
l. 16. See the note on Chap. 30, l. 15.

l. 19. **cum . . . esset,** ' although (it was) before the people (that)
he had to plead '.

ll. 22–23. **non minus reum quam consulem,** ' him (as) a defendant as much as . . . him (as) consul '.

l. 24. **quo.** The antecedent is **accusatorio spiritu,** ' in the
superior tone of an accuser in which '.

ll. 26–27. **ut ipsi diem prodicerent,** ' that they themselves
adjourned the trial '.

l. 27. **trahi** =**protrahi,** ' to be protracted ' =' to drag on '.

ll. 28–29. **ante . . . ueniret,** ' before, however, the appointed day
came '. Note the subj., cf. the introduction, p. xv.

ll. 29–30. **cuius laudationem,** ' his panegyric '.

l. 31. **supremum diem,** ' the last day ' =' the day of his funeral '.

ll. 32–33. **tam aequis auribus quam,** ' with ears as favourable
as ', i.e. ' with as much readiness as '.

l. 34. **frequens,** ' in large numbers '.

CHAPTER 62

ll. 4–5. **tempestas caelo deiecta,** ' a storm sent down from the heavens ' = ' a storm that dropped from the heavens ', *or* ' a torrential down-pour . . .'. Note the absence of the preposition with **caelo,** a use more common in poetry than in prose.

l. 5. **admirationem.** . . . The Latin order, object, verb, subject (**tranquilla serenitas reddita,** *lit.,* ' calm fine-weather restored ') can be retained by turning into the passive: ' their amazement was next increased . . . by the return of such calm fine-weather '.

ll. 6–7. **ut . . . fuerit,** ' that as if the camp were defended by some divine power, it was a-matter-of-religious-scruple to attack it a second time ', i.e. ' religious scruple forbade them . . .'.

ll. 11–12. **incendiis . . . exciti,** ' the Sabines (were) provoked when they had not only their farms but also the villages in which there were very many inhabitants destroyed by fire '; *lit.,* ' the S. provoked by the conflagrations . . .'.

l. 13. **cum . . . occurrissent.** Begin a fresh sentence here.

ll. 13–14. **ancipiti proelio digressi,** ' (and) after the indecisive fighting they retired (and) '.

l. 14. **rettulere,** ' they withdrew '.

l. 15. **satis,** ' a sufficient reason '.

l. 16. **integro bello,** abl. absol., ' the war intact ', i.e. ' havin done nothing to finish off the war '. **inde,** ' thence ', as often = ' from their country ', *or* ' from the Sabini '.

CHAPTER 63

ll. 3–4. **non . . . legis.** Note again the personal construction with **uidebatur.** We prefer impersonal: ' it did not seem . . .'.

ll. 4–6. **cum . . . cognitum est:** inverse **cum.** See the note on Chap. 10, ll. 37–39.

l. 6. **ea res,** ' this news '.

l. 7. **coacti,** ' being made to '. **educta . . . iuuentute.** Translate as main verb in the active.

l. 10. **nihil aliud . . . Romanis,** ' (having-done) nothing else but filled the Romans with groundless fears '.

l. 11. **citato agmine,** ' rapidly '.

l. 14. **rem . . . consulis,** ' the situation which was on the brink of disaster (*lit.*, having fallen forward) owing to the consul's lack of care '.

l. 16. **in urbem Antium.** Latin has apposition where we say ' of ': cf. **urbs Roma,** ' the city of Rome '.

l. 16. **ut tum res erant,** *lit.,* ' as things were then ' = ' for those days '.

l. 20. **tenent,** ' held (down) '.

l. 22. **utroque** with **consule,** ' each consul '.

CHAPTER 64

l. 1. **pacis,** partitive gen., dependent upon **aliquid.**

l. 2. **alias,** adverb, ' on other occasions '. **sollicitae,** in agreement with **pacis.**

l. 3. **irata,** ' in their anger '. **noluit,** ' refused '.

l. 4. **clientes.** See the note on Chap. 35, l. 18. The consuls were elected in the ' assembly-by-centuries ', **comitia centuriata,** in which the influence of the fathers and the wealthier classes predominated.

l. 7. **tranquilla** is grammatically in agreement with **initia:** in sense it goes with **annum.**

l. 8. **caedes et incendia:** we prefer: ' fire and slaughter '.

ll. 13–14. **populationem . . . fecit,** ' he devastated their country over so wide an area '.

l. 14. **multiplici,** i.e. than the booty the Sabines had driven off (l. 10 above).

l. 16. **et in Volscis . . . opera,** ' and indeed[1] in the campaign against the Volsci the Roman operations were outstandingly successful, owing to the services both of the commander and his men '.

---

[1] Cf. note on Ch. 11, l. 19.

ll. 17–18. **signis ... pugnatum** (est), 'there was a pitched battle'.

ll. 19–20. **quia ... erat**, *lit.*, 'because their few numbers were nearer to loss to-be-felt', i.e. 'because in their lack of numbers they felt their losses more keenly'.

l. 20. **gradum rettulissent.** See the note on Chap. 47, l. 8.

l. 20. **ni salubri mendacio**, *lit.*, 'had not by a salutory falsehood the consul ...'. i.e. 'had not a falsehood saved-the-day, one by which ...'.

l. 25. **uelut ... sumpta**, 'both sides resting by a kind of un-spoken truce'.

ll. 27–28. **hand dubitans ... abituros.** Note: (i) **dubitans** is sg. to agree with **ingens uis**. (ii) It is followed by acc. + infinitive—a construction which Livy uses as well as the more classical quin + subj. (iii) The subject of **senserint** is **Romani**; the object 'them', i.e. Volsci and Aequi.

ll. 30–31. **cum ... iussisset.** Drop the **cum** and make **iussisset** a main verb. Begin a fresh sentence at **Hernicorum** with 'Then'. **militem**, collective sg.

l. 32. **in stationem,** 'to (form) an out-post'.

l. 33. **in equos impositos,** 'whom he had mounted upon horses'.

l. 33. **canere,** 'to blow'.

l. 34. **sollicitum,** 'in anxious suspense'.

ll. 34–35. **reliquum noctis,** 'for the rest of the night'.

l. 36. **copia** also has the meaning 'power', 'chance', 'means'. Hence 'so that the Romans too had the chance of (some) sleep'.

l. 36. **Volscos....** Note once again the Latin order: object **Volscos**, subjects **species ...**, **fremitus ...**, finally the verb **tenuit** with **intentos** as predicate. It will be better to turn into the passive:

'The Volsci were kept alerted as for an enemy attack by the sight of ..., and by the stamping and neighing of horses which were maddened ...'.

ll. 37–38. **quos ... putabant,** 'whom they believed to be more numerous (than they were) and to be Romans'.

ll. 38–40. **et insueto . . . sonitu,** *lit.*, ' both an unaccustomed rider sitting (on them) and in addition the sound (of the trumpets) alarming their ears ', i.e. ' both by having an . . . and by the din . . . which . . .'.

CHAPTER 65

l. 3. **quamquam,** ' and yet '.

ll. 5–6. **post . . . fuit,** ' they withdrew safely in good order protected by the front ranks ', *lit.*, ' there was a safe withdrawal behind the first ranks . . .'.

l. 6. **ad iniquum locum;** ' the position was unfavourable, because the enemy were now above the Romans.

l. 7. **teneri = retineri,** historic infin.: ' were held back '.

l. 8. **agunt,** ' behaved '.

ll. 10–11. **uirtute . . . fidens,** ' for, while he could rely on the valour of his men, he had little confidence in the terrain '.

ll. 11–12. **clamorem . . . secuta,** ' and the deed followed the shout ', i.e. ' and their shout was immediately followed by action '.

ll. 12–13. **quo . . . euaderent,** ' that they might be lighter for the climbing the heights '. Note: **quo** replaces **ut** in a purpose clause which contains a comparative.

l. 13. **cursu subeunt,** ' they ran up '.

l. 13. **effusis: effundo** here means ' discharge '.

l. 15. **ingerit:** we say: ' (picked up and) threw '.

ll. 16–19. **sic . . . oneratum est, ni consul . . . excussisset,** ' thus the left wing of the R. was almost overwhelmed (and would have been), had not the consul . . . driven out their fear by shaming them '. For the conditional clause, cf. Chap. 10, l. 4.

ll. 17–19. **referentibus . . . ignauiam,** ' (to them) now retreating, (the consul) rebuking both their rashness, and their cowardice ': i.e. ' had not the consul, as they were beginning to retreat rebuked . . . (and) driven out . . .'.

l. 20. **ut,** ' when '. **uim . . . referebant,** ' they returned blow for blow '.

l. 22. **commouent aciem**, ' they set (their own) line in motion '.

ll. 22–23. **rursus . . . capto**, ' making again a (fresh) attack '.

ll. 23–24. **exsuperant . . . loci**, ' they made their way successfully up the hill '.

ll. 24–25. **iam . . . euaderent**, *lit.*, ' it was now near that they were emerging . . .', i.e. ' they were just about to emerge . . .'. Cf. Chap. 23, ll. 52–53.

l. 27. **incidere**, ' burst into '.

ll. 30–32. **nulla . . . animi**, *lit.*, ' (there being) no new onslaught (*abl. absol.*) of (them) attacking but because, right from the unsuccessful battle and the camp lost, their spirits had fallen '; i.e. ' although there had been no new onslaught or attack, but immediately after the unsuccessful battle and the loss of their camp the Volsci had lost all their spirit '.

VOCABULARY

(In the following vocabulary, only irregular verbs are given their principal parts in full. Otherwise the figures (1), (2), (3), (4), following a verb, denote that it is a regular example of that conjugation. No conjugation number is given in the case of -io verbs like capio. Numbers refer to chapter and section.)

As nearly all the names of characters in this book are of the second declension, they are not included in this vocabulary.

A. = Aulus.

a *or* **ab,** *prep. with abl.,* from, by; on.

abdico (1), *used reflexively,* abdicate.

abdo, -ere, -didi, -ditum (3), hide *(trans.).*

abduco, -ere, -duxi, -ductum (3), lead away.

abeo, -ire, -ii, -itum, go away, depart.

abhorreo (2), shrink from.

abicio, -ere, -ieci, -iectum, throw *or* fling away.

abigo, -ere, -egi, -actum (3), drive away.

absens, -ntis, absent.

absoluo, -ere, -ui, -utum (3), release; complete.

absterreo (2), frighten away.

abstineo, -ere, -tinui, -tentum (2), hold back.

absum, -esse, afui, am away *or* absent.

absumo, -ere, -sumpsi, -sumptum (3), destroy, kill.

abundo (1), overflow, am abundant.

abutor, -i, -usus (3) *dep.,* use up *(with abl.).*

ac *see* **atque.**

accedo, -ere, -cessi, -cessum (3), come to; am added.

accendo, -ere, -di, -sum (3), kindle, stimulate.

accido, -ere, -cidi (3), happen; fall upon *(with dat.).*

accingo, -ere, -nxi, -nctum (3), gird.

accio (4), send for.

accipio, -ere, -cepi, -ceptum, receive; suffer.

accusatio, -onis, *f.,* accusation.

accusatorius, -a, -um, of an accuser.

acer, -cris, -cre, sharp, keen, energetic; severe.

acerbitas, -atis, *f.,* harshness, severity.

acerbus, -a, -um, harsh, bitter.

aceruus, -i, heap.

acies, -iei, *f.,* line of battle.

acriter, *adv.,* keenly, fiercely.

actio, -onis, *f.,* business.

ad, *prep. with acc.,* to, up to; towards; by, near.

adcelero (1), hasten, quicken.

addo, -ere, -didi, -ditum (3), add.

addubito (1), doubt.

adduco, -ere, -duxi, -ductum (3), lead to; induce.

adeo, -ire, -ii, -itum, approach.

adeo, adv., to such a degree or extent.

adfecto (1), aim at.

adfero, -ferre, attuli, allatum, bring, offer; report (news).

adficio, -ere, -feci, -fectum, affect.

adfirmo (1), assert, maintain.

adfligo, -ere, -xi, -ctum (3), overthrow, shatter.

adgredior, -i, -gressus, dep., approach; attack.

adhibeo (2), call in; use, apply.

adhortatio, -onis, f., exhortation.

adhortator -oris, m., encourager.

adhortor (1), dep., encourage, exhort.

adicio, -ere, -ieci, -iectum, add.

adigo, -ere, -egi, -actum (3), bind (by an oath).

adimo, -ere, -emi, -emptum (3), take away.

adipiscor, -i, -eptus (3), dep., obtain; catch up.

aditus, -us, m., approach.

adiaceo (2), lie beside or next.

adiumentum, -i, n., help.

adiungo, -ere, -nxi, -nctum (3), join to.

adiutor, -oris, m., helper.

administratio, -onis, f., management.

admiratio, -onis, f., wonder.

admitto, -ere, -misi, -missum (3), commit; with equum, let go.

admodum, adv., very.

admoneo (2), make remember.

admoueo, -ere, -moui, -motum (2), bring up to.

adnitor, -i, -nisus (3), dep., strive.

adorior, -iri, -ortus (4), dep., attack; attempt (to do).

adprobo (1), approve.

adsiduus, -a, -um, persistent.

adsigno (1), allot.

adsuesco, -ere, -sueui, -suetum (3), grow accustomed (to).

adsum, -esse, -fui, am present or at hand; help (with dat.).

adsumo, -ere, -psi, -ptum (3), take to; admit.

adulescens, -entis, young; grown up: as noun, young man.

adultus, -a, -um, grown up.

adueho, -ere, -xi, -ctum (3), carry to; in pass., ride up.

aduenio, -ire, -ueni, -uentum (4), arrive, come up.

aduersarius, -i, m., opposer.

aduersor (1), dep., am against; oppose (with dat.).

aduersus, -a, -um, facing, opposite.

aduersus, prep., with acc., against.

aduocatus, -i, m., supporter.

aduoco (1), summon.

aduolo (1), hasten to.

aedes, -is, f., temple; in pl., house.

aedificium, -i, n., building.

aedifico (1), build.

aeger, -gra, -grum, sick, ill.

aegre, adv., hardly, with difficulty: aegre ferre, to be vexed or angry at.

aegritudo, -inis, f., vexation.

aeneus, -a, -um, of bronze.

aequalis, -e, equal: as noun, contemporary.

aequaliter, adv., equally.

Aequicus, -a, -um, of *or* with the Aequi.

aequo (1), make equal *or* level; equal.

aequus, -a, -um, even, level; favourable.

Aequus, -a, -um, of the Aequi; *as noun,* an Aequan.

aerarium, -i, *n.,* treasury.

aes, aeris, *n.,* bronze; money: **aes alienum,** debt.

aetas, -atis, *f.,* age.

aeternus, -a, -um, everlasting.

age, agedum, come!, come now!

ager, -gri, *m.,* field, land, territory.

agito (1), disturb, trouble; keep in suspense (48.7).

agmen, -inis, *n.,* column; army.

ago, -ere, egi, actum (3), drive, do; discuss, negotiate; urge.

agrarius, -a, -um, of land, agrarian.

agrestis, -is, *m.,* rustic, countryman.

Agrippa, -ae, *m.,* Agrippa (*Roman praenomen*).

aio, *defective vb.,* assert.

ala, -ae, *f.,* squadron (*of cavalry*).

alacritas, -atis, *f.,* enthusiasm.

alia, *adv.,* by another way.

alias, *adv.,* at another time.

alibi, *adv.,* in another place, elsewhere.

alieno (1), estrange.

alienus, -a, -um, of others.

alio, *adv.,* elsewhither.

alioqui, *adv.,* otherwise.

aliquamdiu, *adv.,* for some time.

aliquantus, -a, -um, of considerable amount.

aliquis, -qua, -quod, *adj.,* some, any.

aliquis, -qua, -quid, *pronoun,* some-one, something; anyone, anything.

aliquot, *indecl.,* many.

aliquotiens, *adv.,* at times.

aliter, *adv.,* otherwise.

alius, -a, -ud, other, another: **alii** . . . **alii,** some . . . others.

alo, -ere, alui, altum (3), nourish.

altaria, -ium, *n. pl.,* altar, altars.

alter, -era, -erum, another (*of two*); second.

alternus, -a, -um, alternate.

altus, -a, -um, high.

ambages, -ium, *f. pl., lit.,* roundabout ways; riddles.

ambigo, -ere (3), doubt.

ambio (4), canvass.

ambitio, -onis, *f.,* a seeking popularity.

ambitiosus, -a, -um, seeking popularity.

ambo, -ae, -o, both.

amens, -ntis, mad, out of one's mind.

amicus, -a, -um, friendly: *as noun,* friend.

amissio, -onis, *f.,* a losing, loss.

amitto, -ere, -misi, -missum (3), lose.

amnis, -is, *m.,* stream, river.

amoueo, -ere, -moui, -motum (2), move away.

amplector, -i, -xus (3), *dep.,* embrace.

amplus, -a, -um, great, honourable.

an, *conj.,* or (*in questions*).

anceps, -cipitis, double, on two sides; doubtful.

ango, -ere, -xi, -ctum (3), distress.

animaduerto, -ere, -ti, -sum, (3), notice; punish.

animus, -i, *m.,* mind; feeling; courage, spirit.

Anio, -enis, *m.,* Anio (tributary of the Tiber).

annales, -ium, *m. pl.,* chronicles.

annona, -ae, *f.,* corn supply; price of corn.

annus, -i, *m.,* year.

annuus, -a, -um, yearly.

anquiro, -ere, -quisiui, -quisitum (3), hold an enquiry.

ante, *prep. with acc.,* before; *adv.,* before, earlier.

antea, *adv.,* before.

antecedo, -ere, -cessi, -cessum (3), go before *or* in front.

antequam, *conj.,* before.

antesignani, -orum, *m. pl.,* front-rank fighters.

Antias, -atis, of Antium.

antiquus, -a, -um, ancient, old.

Antium, -i, *n.,* Antium.

Ap. = Appius.

aperio, -ire, -erui, -ertum (4), open.

aperte, *adv.,* openly.

apertus, -a, -um, open.

apparatus, -us, *m.,* preparation, pomp.

appareo (2), am clear.

apparitor, -oris, *m.,* servant.

appello (1), call; call upon.

appono, -ere, -posui, positum (3), join to.

apte, *adv.,* closely.

aptus, -a, -um, fitted, fit.

apud, *prep. with acc.,* among; to; in.

aqua, -ae, *f.,* water.

arbiter, -tri, *m.,* witness, outsider (37.3); arbitrator.

arbitrium, -i, *n.,* authority.

arbitror (1), *dep.,* think.

arceo, -ere, -ui, -ctum (2), ward off; keep away (23.12); prevent (5.9).

arcesso, -ere, -iui, -itum (3), fetch, summon.

ardeo, -ere, -si, -sum (2), burn.

ardor, -oris, *m.,* zeal, eagerness.

arduus, -a, -um, steep.

area, -ae, *f.,* level space.

Aricia, -ae, *f.,* Aricia.

Aricini, -orum, *m. pl.,* men of Aricia.

arma, -orum, *n. pl.,* arms, weapons.

armo (1), arm.

arripio, -ere, -ripui, -reptum, seize; arrest.

Arruns, -ntis, *m.,* Arruns.

ars, artis, *f.,* way; skill; strategy.

Arsius, -a, -um, of Arsia.

artus, -a, -um, narrow; scanty.

aruum, -i, *n.,* field.

arx, arcis, *f.,* citadel.

asper, -era, -erum, rough.

aspere, *adv.,* harshly.

asperitas, -atis, *f.,* harshness.

aspernor (1), *dep.,* reject.

asporto (1), carry away.

at, *conj.,* but.

atque, *conj.,* and.

atrox, -ocis, harsh, ruthless.

attineo, -ere, -tinui, -tentum (2), concern.

attonitus, -a, -um, astonished, thunderstruck.

auctio, -onis, *f.,* auction.

auctor, -oris, *m.,* supporter, promoter, advocate; author (42.1).

auctoritas, -atis, *f.,* authority, influence.

audacia, -ae, *f.,* daring.

audax, -acis, daring, bold.

audeo, -ere, ausus sum (2), *semi-dep.,* dare, venture.

audio (4), hear, listen to.

aufero, -ferre, abstuli, ablatum, carry or take away.

augeo, -ere, -xi, -ctum (2), increase.

aureus, -a, -um, golden.

auris, -is, f., ear.

Auruncus, -a, -um, of the Aurunci.

aut, conj., or: aut . . . aut, either . . . or.

autem, conj., however.

auxilium, -i, n., help: n. pl., auxiliary troops.

Auentinus, -i, m., the Auentine (hill).

auersus, -a, -um, turned away, on the other side.

auerto, -ere, -ti, -sum (3), turn away; divert (45.5).

auide, adv., eagerly.

auidus, -a, -um, eager (for).

auis, -is, f., bird.

auitus, -a, -um, of a grandfather.

auoco (1), summon.

auunculus, -i, m., (maternal) uncle.

barba, -ae, f., beard.

bello (1), make or wage war.

bellum, -i, n., war.

bene, adv., well, successfully.

beneficium, -i, n., service, boon.

benigne, adv., kindly.

benignus, -a, -um, kind, generous.

blandimentum, -i, n., favour.

bonus, -a, -um, good: bona, n. pl., goods.

brachium, -i, n., arm.

breui, adv., in a short time, soon.

breuis, -e, short.

breuiter, adv., briefly.

C. = Gaius.

cadauer, -eris, n., corpse.

cado, -ere, cecidi, casum (3), fall.

caedes, -is, f., killing, butchering (1.10).

caedo, -ere, cecidi, caesum (3), scourge; slay.

caelestis, -e, of or from heaven.

Caelius, -a, -um, Caelian.

caelum, -i, n., sky, heaven.

Caeno, -onis, f., Caeno (Volscian town).

Caeso, -onis, m., Caeso.

calamitas, -atis, f., misfortune.

calcar, -aris, n., spur.

calor, -oris, m., heat.

Campania, -ae, f., Campania.

campus, -i, m., plain.

cano, -ere, cecini, cantum (3), sing; prophesy (42.10).

capesso, -ere, -iui, or -ii, -itum (3), engage in.

capillus, -i, m., hair.

capio, -ere, cepi, captum, take captive.

Capitolium, -i, n., the Capitol.

captiuus, -i, m., a captive: also in fem.

capto (1), try to seize, catch.

caput, -itis, n., head; person; life; source (of stream, 38.1).

careo (2), (with abl.), am without; lose (23.5).

caritas, -atis, f., dearness, affection.

Carmentalis, -e, of Carmentis.

carnifex, -icis, m., executioner.

carnificina, -ae, f., torture-chamber.

carus, -a, -um, dear.

Cassius, -a, -ium, of the Cassii.

cassum, in, in vain.

Castor, -oris, m., Castor.

castra, -orum, n. pl., camp.

casus, -us, *m.*, fall; chance: casu, by chance.

causa, -ae, *f.*, cause, pretext; *abl.*, causā *as prep.*, for the sake of.

caueo, -ere, caui, cautum (2), take care *or* precautions against.

cauillor (1), *dep.*, mock, jest.

cedo, -ere, cessi, cessum (3), give way *or* ground; withdraw before (48.6) (*often with dat.*).

celebro (1), attend in large numbers.

celer, -eris, -e, swift.

ceno (1), dine.

censeo (2), think; give as an opinion; propose.

centuriatus, -a, -um, in centuries.

centurio, -onis, *m.*, centurion.

Ceres, -eris, *f.*, Ceres (*goddess of corn*).

certamen, -inis, *n.*, contest.

certatim, *adv.*, in rivalry.

certatio, -onis,*f.*, conflict, struggle.

certe, *adv.*, at any rate.

certo (1), strive, contend.

certus, -a, -um, certain, sure, fixed.

ceterum, *adv.*, but.

ceterus, -a, -um, the other, the rest.

cibus, -i, *m.*, food.

cicatrix, -icis, *f.*, scar.

cieo, -ere, ciui, citum (2), rouse, urge on; revive (47.1).

circa, *prep. with acc.*, round: *adv.*, round about.

Circeii, -orum, *m. pl.*, Circeii (*town*).

circum, *prep. with acc.*, around.

circumaro (1), plough around.

circumdo, -are, -dedi, -datum (1), put round.

circumeo, -ire, -ii, circuitum, go round.

circumfero, -ferre, -tuli, -latum, carry round; spread round about.

circumfundo, -ere, -fudi, -fusum (3), surround; *in pass.*, crowd round.

circummitto, -ere, -misi, -missum (3), send round.

circumscindo, -ere (3), tear off.

circumsedeo, -ere, -sedi, -sessum (2), besiege.

circumsisto, -ere, -stiti (3), stand round.

circumspecto (1), look round at.

circumsto, -are, -steti (1), stand round.

circumuenio, -ire, -ueni, -uentum (4), surround.

circus, -i, *m.*, circus.

citatus, -a, -um, at full speed.

cito (1), summon.

cito, *adv.*, quickly.

ciuilis, -e, between *or* of fellow-citizens.

ciuis, -is, citizen.

ciuitas, -atis, *f.*, citizenship; community, state.

clades *or* -is, -is,*f.*, defeat, destruction (13.1).

clam, *adv.*, secretly.

clamito (1), cry out.

clamo (1), shout, cry.

clamor, -oris, *m.*, shout.

clarus, -a, -um, famous.

classicum, -i, *n.*, trumpet.

Claudius, -a, -um, of the Claudii.

claudo, -ere, -si, -sum (3), shut up *or* in.

cliens, -ntis, *m.*, client.

cliuus, -i, *m.*, slope, hill.

Cluilius, -a, -um, of Cluilius.
Clusinus, -a, -um, of Clusium.
Cn. = Gnaeus.
coalesco, -ere, -alui, -alitum (3), unite.
coarguo, -ere, -ui (3), prove.
coemo, -ere, -emi, -emptum (3), buy up.
coeo, -ire, -ii, -itum, come together.
coepi, -isse, coeptus sum, began.
coerceo (2), hold in check, restrain.
coetus, -us, m., meeting.
cogito (1), ponder, plan.
cognatio, -onis, f., kinship.
cognatus, -us, m., kinsman.
cognomen, -inis, n., surname.
cognosco, -ere, -noui, -nitum (3), recognise; investigate (41.10).
cogo, -ere, coegi, coactum (3), compel.
cohors, -rtis, f., band, troop.
coitio, -onis, f., meeting.
Collatinus, -i, m., L. Tarquinius Collatinus.
collega, -ae, m., colleague.
collegium, -i, n., guild.
Collinus, -a, -um, Colline.
collis, -is, m., hill.
colo, -ere, colui, cultum (3),care for.
colonia, -ae, f., colony.
colonus, -i, m., settler.
columna, -ae, f., column.
comes, -itis, m., companion.
cominus, adv., hand to hand.
comis, -e, courteous.
comitas, -atis, f., courtesy, goodwill.
comiter, adv., courteously.
comitium, -i, n., the comitium; in pl., assembly; election.

comitor (1), dep., accompany.
commeatus, -us, m., supplies.
commilito, -onis, m., fellow-soldier.
committo, -ere, -misi, -missum (3), engage in, begin.
commodum, -i, n., advantage.
commodus, -a, -um, suitable.
commoueo, -ere, -moui, -motum (2), stir.
communio (4), fortify.
comparo (1), procure; compare.
compello, -ere, -puli, -pulsum (3), drive.
compesco, -ere, -pescui (3), restrain.
complector, -i, -plexus (3), dep., embrace.
compleo, -ere, -pleui, -pletum (2), fill.
complexus, -us (4), embrace.
comploratio, -onis, f., lamentation.
compono, -ere, -posui, -positum (3), arrange.
comprehendo, -ere, -di, -sum (3), seize.
comprimo, -ere, -pressi, -pressum (3), crush.
conatus, -us, m., attempt, effort.
concedo, -ere, -cessi, -cessum (3) yield, withdraw.
concieo, -ere, -ciui, -citum (2), rouse.
concilio (1), win over.
concilium, -i, n., assembly, meeting.
concito (1), stir up.
conclamo (1), call out or shout together.
concordia, -ae, f., harmony.
concors, -dis, at peace within.
concurro, -ere, -curri or -cucurri, -cursum (3), rush together.

VOCABULARY 235

concursus, -us, m., rush, charge.
condicio, -onis, f., term.
conditor, -oris, m., founder.
confero, -ferre, -tuli, -latum, bring
together.
confertus, -a, -um, crowded, dense.
confessio, -onis, f., confession,
acknowledgement.
confestim, adv., immediately.
conficio, -ere, -feci, -fectum, finish;
digest (32.10).
confido, -ere, -fisus sum (3), semi-
dep., rely upon (with dat.).
confirmo (1), encourage.
confligo, -ere, -flixi, -flictum (3),
meet in battle.
confugio, -ere, -fugi, flee to; take
refuge (in).
conglobo (1), band together.
conicio, -ere, -ieci, -iectum, throw.
coniectus, -us, m., a throwing.
coniunctus, -a, -um, united.
coniungo, -ere, -iunxi, -iunctum
(3), unite, join to.
coniunx, -iugis, c., husband, wife.
coniuratio, -onis, f., conspiracy.
coniuratus, -i, m., conspirator.
coniuro (1), conspire.
conligo, -ere, -legi, -lectum (3),
gather together.
conloquium, -i, n., conference.
conloquor, -i, -locutus (3) dep.,
talk with, converse.
conor (1), dep., try.
conqueror, -i, -questus (3), dep.,
complain loudly.
consceleratus, -a, -um, stained
with guilt.
conscientia, -ae, f., knowledge (of).
conscius, -i, m., accomplice.
conscribo, -ere, -scripsi, -scriptum
(3), enrol.
consecro (1), dedicate (to a god).

consensus, -us, m., agreement,
unanimity.
consentio, -ire, -sensi, -sensum
(4), agree.
consido, -ere, -sedi, -sessum (3),
take up one's position.
consilium, -i, n., counsel, plan, purpose; policy; advice.
consisto, -ere, -stiti, -stitum (3),
take one's stand or position.
consocio (1), unite.
conspectus, -us, m., sight.
conspicio, -ere, -spexi, -spectum,
catch sight of; see.
conspicor (1), dep., see; view.
conspiro (1), plot together.
constantia, -ae, f., firmness.
consterno (1), dismay, affright.
constituo, -ere, -stitui, -stitutum
(3), appoint, determine.
consto, -are, -stiti, -statum (3),
stand fast; am agreed (18.3);
take position (30.11).
consuetus, -a, -um, customary.
consul, -ulis, m., consul.
consularis, -is, m., an ex-consul.
consulatus, -us, m., consulship.
consulo, -ere, -ului, -ultum (3),
consult (with acc.); have regard
for, consult interests of (with
dat.).
consultatio, -onis, f., deliberation.
consulto (1), deliberate.
consultum, -i, n., decree.
consumo, -ere, -sumpsi, -sumptum
(3), consume.
consurgo, -ere, -surrexi, -surrec-
tum (3), rise, arise.
contagio, -onis, f., infection.
contaminatus, -a, -um, defiled.
contemno, -ere, -tempsi, -temptum
(3), despise, scorn.

contemptim, *adv.*, contemptuously.

contemptus, -a, -um, contemptible.

contendo, -ere, -di, -tum (3), hasten; fight; strive; vie.

conterreo (2), alarm, terrify.

conticesco, -ere, -ticui (3), quieten down.

continens, -ntis, continuous.

contingo, -ere, -tigi, -tactum (3), touch; defile.

continuatus, -a, -um, unbroken, continuous.

continuo (1), make continuous.

continuus, -a, -um, unbroken, continuous.

contio, -onis, *f.*, meeting; tribunal.

contra, *prep. with acc.*, against; *as adv.*, on the other hand.

contraho, -ere, -traxi, -tractum (3), collect; incur (23.14).

contrarius, -a, -um, opposite.

contumacia, -ae, *f.*, stubbornness.

contumaciter, *adv.*, stubbornly.

contumax, -acis, stubborn.

contumelia, -ae, *f.*, insult.

conueho, -ere, -uexi, -uectum (3), bring together.

conuena, -ae, *m.*, refugee.

conueniens, -ntis, agreeing with (*with dat.*).

conuenio, -ire, -ueni, -uentum (4), come together; *impersonally*, there is agreement.

conuerto, -ere, -ti, -sum (3), turn.

conuolo (1), fly together.

coorior, -iri, -ortus (4), rise up.

copia, -ae, *f.*, plenty; *in pl.*, forces, supplies.

Cora, -ae, *f.*, Cora (*a town*).

coram, *adv.*, openly.

Corbio, -onis, *f.*, Corbio (*a town*).

corbis, -is, *m.*, a basket.

Coriolanus, -i, *m.*, Coriolanus.

Corioli, -orum, *m. pl.* Corioli (*a town*).

cornicen, -cinis, *m.*, horn-blower.

cornu, -us, *m.*, horn; wing (*of an army*).

corona, -ae, *f.*, garland, chaplet.

corpus, -oris, *n.*, body; person.

corripio, -ere, -ripui, -reptum, reprove.

corrumpo, -ere, -rupi, -ruptum (3), spoil.

cotidianus, -a, -um, daily.

crastinus, -a, -um, by tomorrow.

creber, -bra, -brum, frequent.

creditor, -oris, *m.*, creditor.

credo, -ere, -didi, -ditum (3), believe; entrust (7.11; 45.10).

Cremera, -ae, *f.*, Cremera (*a town*).

creo (1), appoint, elect.

cresco, -ere, creui, cretum (3), grow.

crimen, -inis, *n.*, accusation, charge.

criminor (1), *dep.*, accuse; allege.

crudelis, -e, cruel.

cruentus, -a, -um, blood-stained.

Crustumeria, -ae, *f.*, (*or* -ium, -ii, *n.*), Crustumeria (*a town*).

Crustuminus, -a, -um, of Crustumeria.

cultor, -oris, *m.*, cultivator.

cum, *conj.*, when; though; since.

cum, *prep. with abl.*, with.

Cumae, -arum, *f. pl.*, Cumae (*a town*).

Cumanus, -a, -um, of Cumae.

cumulo (1), heap up, increase.

cunctatio, -onis, *f.*, delay.

cunctor (1), *dep.*, delay, hesitate.

cunctus, -a, -um, all.
cuneus, -i, *m.*, wedge.
cupiditas, -atis, *f.*, desire.
cupido, -inis, *f.*, desire.
cupio, -ere, -iui (-ii), -itum, desire.
cur, *adv.*, why.
cura, -ae, *f.*, care, attention.
curatio, -onis, *f.*, treatment.
curia, -ae, *f.*, senate.
curo (1), see *or* attend to; treat.
curro, -ere, cucurri, cursum (3), run,
cursus, -us, *m.*, running.
curulis, -e, curule.
custodia, -ae, *f.*, keeping watch.
custos, -odis, *c.*, guard.

damnatio, -onis, *f.*, condemnation.
damno (1), condemn.
damnum, -i, *n.*, loss.
de, *prep. with abl.*, (down) from;
about, of, for.
debello (1), finish a war.
debeo (2), owe; am to.
debilitas, -atis, *f.*, a crippling.
debitor, -oris, *m.*, debtor.
decedo, -ere, -cessi, -cessum (3),
withdraw.
decem, ten.
decerno, -ere, -crevi, -cretum (3),
fight; decree.
decet (2), *impers.*, it becomes.
decimus, -a, -um, tenth.
decipio, -ere, -cepi, -ceptum, deceive.
declino (1), swerve aside.
decoro (1), adorn.
decorus, -a, -um, fitting, seemly.
decretum, -i, *n.*, decree, decision.
decurro, -ere, -cucurri, *or* -curri,
-cursum (3), run down.
decus, -oris, *n.*, glory, distinction;
honour (7.4; 23.4).

dedecus, -oris, *n.*, dishonour.
dedicatio, -onis, *f.*, a dedication.
dedico (1), dedicate.
deditio, -onis, *f.*, surrender.
dedo, -ere, -didi, -ditum (3), surrender.
deduco, -ere, -duxi, -ductum (3).
lead down *or* away; plant (21.7).
defendo, -ere, -di, -sum (3), defend.
defero, -ferre, -tuli, -latum, bring
or carry down; report (4.6; 28.2).
deficio, -ere, -feci, -fectum, fail;
revolt.
defigo, -ere, -fixi, -fixum (3), fix
down.
defluo, -ere, -xi, -xum (3), flow *or*
slide down.
deformis, -e, ugly, hideous.
deformitas, -atis, *f.*, hideousness.
defungor, -i, -functus (3), *dep.*,
discharge fully (*with abl.*).
deicio, -ere, -ieci, -iectum, throw *or*
fling down.
dein, deinde, *adv.*, then.
deinceps, *adv.*, successively.
delectus, -a, -um, picked.
deliberabundus, -a, -um, deliberat-
ing.
deliberatio, -onis, *f.*, deliberation,
consultation.
deligo (1), bind fast.
deligo, -ere, -legi, -lectum (3),
choose.
demergo, -ere, -si, -sum (3), sub-
merge.
demigro (1), remove.
deminuo, -ere, -ui, -utum (3),
lessen.
demitto, -ere, -misi, -missum (3),
send down.
demo, -ere, dempsi, demptum (3).
take away.

demum, *adv.*, at last.

dens, dentis, *m.*, tooth.

depono, -ere, -posui, -positum (3), lay *or* put down.

depopulor (1), *dep.*, lay waste.

deposco, -ere, -poposci (3), demand, ask.

deprehendo, -ere, -prehendi, -prehensum (3), seize, catch.

derigo, -ere, -rexi, -rectum (3), direct.

descendo, -ere, -di, -sum (3), go *or* come down.

descisco, -ere, -ii, *or* -iui, -itum (3), go over.

deseco, -are, -cui, -ctum (1), cut down.

desero, -ere, -rui, -rtum (3), abandon.

desertor, -oris, *m.*, one who abandons.

desiderium, -i, *n.*, regret, longing for.

desilio, -ire, -silui, -sultum (4), leap down.

desisto, -ere, -stiti, -stitum (3), cease.

desperatio, -onis, *f.*, despair.

despero (1), despair.

destino (1), mark out.

destituo, -ere, -ui, -utum (3), place before.

desum, -esse, -fui, am wanting *or* lacking.

deterreo (2), prevent, deter.

detracto (1), shirk, refuse.

detraho, -ere, -traxi, -tractum (3), strip off.

detrudo, -ere, -si, -sum (3), dislodge.

deus, -i, *m.*, god.

deuinco, -ere, -uici, -uictum, defeat thoroughly.

deuolo (1), fly *or* hurry down.

dexter, -tera (-tra), -terum (-trum), right.

dextra, -ae, *f.*, right hand.

dico, -ere, dixi, dictum (3), say, speak; with diem, appoint a day.

dictator, -oris, *m.*, dictator.

dictum, -i, *n.*, saying.

dies, -ei, *m.*, day.

differo, -ferre, distuli, dilatum, postpone.

digero, -ere, -gessi, -gestum (3), set in order.

dignatio, -onis, *f.*, high position.

dignitas, -atis, *f.*, worth, position, dignity.

dignus, -a, -um, worthy (*with abl.*).

digredior, -i, -gressus (*dep.*), depart.

dilatio, -onis, *f.*, a putting off, postponement.

dilectus, -us, *m.*, levy.

dimicatio, -onis, *f.*, conflict, combat.

dimico (1), fight.

dimidium, -i, *n.*, half.

dimitto, -ere, -misi, -missum (3), send away *or* out.

dirigo, -ere, -rexi, -rectum (3), draw up.

diripio, -ere, -ripui, -reptum, plunder.

diruo, -ere, -ui, -utum (3), demolish, raze.

discedo, -ere, -cessi, -cessum (3), depart.

disciplina, -ae, *f.*, discipline.

discordia, -ae, *f.*, discord.

discors, -rdis, at variance.

discrimen, -inis, *n.*, struggle, danger.

discurro, -ere, -cucurri, *or* -curri,

-cursum (3), run in all directions.

discutio, -ere, -cussi, -cussum, shatter; bring to naught.

disicio, -ere, -ieci, -iectum, break up.

dispergo, -ere, -si, -sum (3), scatter.

displiceo (2), displease (*with dat.*).

dispono, -ere, -posui, -positum (3), post here and there.

dissero, -ere, -rui, -rtum (3), discourse.

dissipo (1), break up.

dissoluo, -ere, -solui, -solutum (3), break up, destroy.

dissuasor, -oris, *m.*, opponent.

distineo, -ere, -tinui, -tentum (2), hinder.

distraho, -ere, -traxi, -tractum (3), tear apart.

distribuo, -ere, -ui, -utum (3), distribute.

diu, *adv.*, for a long time.

diuturnus, -a, -um, lasting.

diues, -itis, rich, wealthy.

diuido, -ere, -si, -sum (3), divide.

diuinus, -a, -um, divine.

do, dare, dedi, datum (1), give.

doceo, -ere, docui, doctum (2), teach, tell.

dolor, -oris, *m.*, pain, resentment.

dolus, -i, *m.*, guile.

domesticus, -a, -um, of the family *or* home.

dominus, -i, *m.*, master.

domo, -are, -ui, -itum (1), tame.

domus, -us, *f.*, house, home: *loc.*, domi, at home.

donec, *conj.*, until.

dono (1), present with.

donum, -i, *n.*, gift.

dubito (1), doubt.

dubius, -a, -um, doubtful.

duco, -ere, -xi, -ctum (3), lead; consider; conduct (*of a funeral procession*).

dulcedo, -inis, *f.*, charm, attractiveness.

dum, *conj.*, while; provided that.

-dum, particle with **age, agite.**

dumtaxat, *adv.*, only.

duo, -ae, -o, two.

duplicarius, -i, *m.*, double-ration soldier.

duplico (1), double.

duumuir, -i, *m.*, a duumuir.

dux, ducis, *m.*, leader.

e, *see* ex.

ecce, behold.

Ecetrani, -orum, *m. pl.*, the Ecetrani.

edico, -ere, -xi, -ctum (3), proclaim.

edictum, -i, *n.*, proclamation, edict.

editus, -a, -um, rising.

edo, -ere, -didi, -ditum (3), give forth; show.

educo (1), bring up; (3), lead out.

effero (1), make wild *or* savage.

effero, -ferre, extuli, elatum, carry out; bury (8.8; 33.11): *in pass.*, am elated.

efficio, -ficere, -feci, -fectum, bring about.

effugio, -ere, -fugi, escape.

effundo, -ere, -fudi, -fusum (3), pour out.

effuse, *adv.*, in disorder.

effusus, -a, -um, scattered, in disorder.

egens, -ntis, in want.

egeo (2), am in want, need (*with abl.*).

ego, I.

egredior, -i, -gressus, *dep.*, go out, leave.

egregius, -a, -um, outstanding, exceptional.

eicio, -ere, -ieci, -iectum, cast out.

elatus, see effero

elicio, -ere, -cui, -citum, entice *or* draw out.

eligo, -ere, -legi, -lectum (3), choose out.

eludo, -ere, -si, -sum (3), mock, jeer.

emineo (2), stand out, am conspicuous.

emitto, -ere, -misi, -missum (3), send out, launch.

emo, -ere, emi, emptum (3), buy.

en, lo!, see!

enarro (1), narrate.

enim, *conj.*, for.

enimuero, *adv.*, truly.

eniteo (2), shine out, am conspicuous.

enitor, -i, -nixus, -nisus (3), *dep.*, force my way up.

eo, *adv.*, thither, there.

eo, ire, iui *or* ii, itum, go.

eodem, *adv.*, to the same place.

eques, -itis, *m.*, cavalryman, trooper.

equester, -stris, -stre, of the cavalry, cavalry (*as adj.*).

equitatus, -us, *m.*, cavalry.

erga, *prep. with acc.*, towards (*in relations other than motion*).

ergastulum, -i, *n.*, work-prison.

ergo, *adv.*, therefore, then.

erigo, -ere, -rexi, -rectum (3), cheer, encourage; excite; take uphill.

eripio, -ere, -ripui, -reptum, snatch away, rescue.

error, -oris, *m.*, uncertainty.

erumpo, -ere, -rupi, -ruptum (3), sally forth; break out (63.2).

escendo, -ere, -di, -sum (3), go *or* mount up.

Esquiliae, -arum, *f. pl.*, the Esquiline.

et, *conj.*, and, et ... et, both ... and.

etiam, *adv.*, even, also.

Etruscus, -a, -um, Etruscan; *as noun*, an Etruscan.

etsi, *conj.*, even if, although.

euado, -ere, -uasi, -uasum (3), come out, emerge (50.10; 65.6); climb.

euagor (1), *dep.*, move at large.

euanesco, -ere, -nui (3), lose force.

euenio, -ire, -ueni, -uentum (4), fall out *or* to.

euentus, -us, *m.*, issue, result.

euinco, -ere, -uici, -uictum (3), prevail, persuade (4.3).

ex, *or* e, *prep. with abl.*, out of, from, of; in accordance with.

exacerbo (1), embitter.

exactor, -oris, *m.*, exactor.

exaudio (4), hear.

excedo, -ere, -cessi, -cessum (3), go out, leave, withdraw; go beyond; (with modum) be excessive (2.2).

excellens, -ntis, outstanding.

excelsus, -a, -um, high, lofty.

excio (4), stir up; provoke (30.10; 42.3; 62.4).

excipio, -ere, -cepi, -ceptum, catch; overhear (4.5).

excito (1), rouse; spur on.

excurro, -ere, -cucurri *or* **-curri, -cursum** (3), run *or* rush out.

excutio, -ere, -cussi, -cussum, shake *or* drive out.

exemplum, -i, *n.*, precedent.

exeo, -ire, -iui, (-ii), -itum, go out, leave.

exerceo (2), make use of.

exercitus, -us, *m.*, army.

exigo, -ere, -egi, -actum (3), drive out; spend (*of time*), *espec. in* **exactus,** spent.

exiguus, -a, -um, small, scanty.

eximius, -a, -um, surpassing, excellent.

existimo (1), think, consider.

exitus, -us, *m.*, way out.

exolesco, -ere, -eui, -etum (3), weaken.

exoletus, -a, -um, out of date.

exonero (1), free from.

exordior, -iri, -orsus (4), *dep.*, begin.

exorior, -iri, -ortus (4), *dep.*, arise.

expedio (4), set free, make ready.

expeditus, -a, -um, light-armed.

expello, -ere, -puli, -pulsum (3), drive out.

experior, -iri, -pertus (4), *dep.*, put to the test; learn by experience.

expers, -rtis, without a share in.

expeto, -ere, -petiui, -petitum (3), seek after.

expleo, -ere, -pleui, -pletum (2), fill *or* make up.

explico (1), **-are, -cui, -itum** (1), deploy.

exploro (1), reconnoitre.

expono, -ere, -posui, -positum (3), set forth.

exposco, -ere, -poposci (3), ask *or* beg.

exprimo, -ere, -pressi, -pressum, (3), wring from.

exprobro (1), make a matter of reproach; reproach with.

expromo, -ere, -mpsi, -mptum (3), disclose.

expugno (1), take by storm.

exsecror (1), *dep.*, curse.

exsequiae, -arum, *f. pl.*, funeral procession.

exsequor, -i, -secutus (3), *dep.*, follow up, carry out.

exsilium, -i, *n.*, exile.

exsisto, -ere, -stiti, -stitum (3), arise.

exsoluo, -ere, -solui, -solutum (3), pay for.

exspectatio, -onis, *f.*, awaiting, expectation.

exspecto (1), wait for.

exspiro (1), expire.

exsul, -ulis, *m.*, an exile.

exsulo (1), am *or* live in exile.

exsulto (1), leap up.

exsupero (1), prevail over, surmount.

exta, -orum, *n. pl.*, entrails.

extemplo, *adv.*, immediately.

externus, -a, -um, foreign.

exterreo (2), terrify.

extorqueo, -ere, -torsi, -torsum (2), wrest from.

extorris, -e, banished.

extra, *prep. with acc.*, outside.

extraho, -ere, -traxi, -tractum (3), prolong; put off (23.13).

extremus, -a, -um, utmost: **ad extrema,** to a crisis.

extrinsecus, *adv.*, from without.

exuo, -ere, -ui, -utum (3), strip (*with abl.*).

Fabianus, -a, -um, of Fabius.
Fabius, -i, *m.,* (i) Q. Fabius Pictor (*see introduction* p. xiii), (ii) *as adj.,* of the Fabii *or* Fabius.
facies, -ei, *f.,* shape, face.
facile, *adv.,* easily.
facilis, -e, easy.
facinus, -oris, *n.,* deed.
facio, -ere, feci, factum, do, make.
factio, -onis, *f.,* party spirit *or* conflict.
factito (1), do, perform.
factum, -i, *n.,* deed, action.
facundus, -a, -um, eloquent.
fallax, -acis, deceitful, unreliable.
fallo, -ere, fefelli, falsum (3), disappoint (39.1); deceive (45.13); escape notice of.
falsus, -a, -um, false.
fama, -ae, *f.,* report.
fames, -is, *f.,* hunger.
familia, -ae, *f.,* household; estate, property (41.10).
familiaris, -e, private; *as noun,* friend.
far, farris, *m.,* spelt.
fascis, -is, *m.,* the fascis.
fastidio (4), take offence.
fastigium, -i, *n.,* rank, condition.
fateor, -eri, fassus (2), *dep.,* admit.
fatum, -i, *n.,* destiny.
faustus, -a, -um, of good omen.
fauor, -oris, *m.,* good-will, enthusiasm.
felicitas, -atis, *f.,* success.
felix, -icis, fortunate.
femina, -ae, *f.,* woman.
fenerator, -oris, *m.,* money-lender.
fere, *adv.,* almost.
Ferentina, -ae, *f.,* Ferentina (*stream*).
ferio (4), make (*a treaty*).

ferme, *adv.,* almost.
fero, ferre, tuli, latum, carry, win; report; propose; put up with.
ferociter, *adv.,* boldly.
ferox, -ocis, bold; haughty.
ferrum, -i, *n.,* iron; weapon.
fertilis, -e, fruitful.
feruidus, -a, -um, hot, impetuous.
fessus, -a, -um, tired, weary.
festus, -a, -um, festal, holy.
fides, -ei, *f.,* good faith (7.10); reliance; protection (55.7); pledge.
fido, -ere, fisus sum (3) (*semi-dep.*), trust, confide.
fiducia, -ae, *f.,* confidence.
fidus, -a, -um, trustworthy, reliable.
figo, -ere, -xi, -xum (3), fix, plant.
filius, -i, *m.,* son.
finio (4), finish.
finis, -is, *m.,* end; *in. pl.,* borders, territory.
finitimus, -a, -um, neighbouring; *as noun,* neighbour.
fio, fieri, factus sum, *semi-dep.,* am done *or* made; become, happen, take place.
firmo (1), strengthen.
firmus, -a, -um, strong.
flagitator, -oris, *m.,* one who clamours for.
flagitium, -i, *n.,* disgrace.
flagro (1), blaze up; am on fire.
flecto, -ere, -xi, -xum (3), prevail upon, win over.
fletus, -us, *m.,* weeping, wailing.
flumen, -inis, *n.,* river.
fluo, -ere, -xi, -xum (3), flow.
foculus, -i, *m.,* brazier, fire.
foedus, -a, -um, inauspicious, terrible, horrible, ignominious.

foedus, -eris, *n.*, treaty.
foris, *adv.*, abroad.
forma, -ae, *f.*, shape.
forsitan, *adv.*, perhaps.
forte, *adv.*, by chance.
fortis, -e, brave.
fortuito, *adv.*, by chance.
fortuna, -ae, *f.*, fortune.
forum, -i, *n.*, the forum.
fossa, -ae, *f.*, ditch.
foueo, -ere, foui, fotum (2), cherish, foster.
fragor, -oris, *m.*, crash.
frango, -ere, fregi, fractum (3), break, break down.
frater, -tris, *m.*, brother.
fraudo (1), cheat, defraud.
fremitus, -us, *m.*, roaring.
fremo, -ere, -ui, -itum (3), murmur; cry angrily.
frequens, -ntis, in large numbers.
frequenter, *adv.*, in large numbers.
frequentia, -ae, *f.*, crowd.
fretus, -a, -um, relying on (*with abl.*).
fructus, -us, *m.*, crop.
frumentator, -oris, *m.*, corn-buyer.
frumentum, -i, *n.*, grain, corn.
fruor, -i, fructus (3), *dep.*, have the advantage of (*with abl.*).
frustra, *adv.*, in vain.
frustror (1), *dep.*, deceive, elude.
frux, frugis, *f.*, fruit.
fuga, -ae, *f.*, flight.
fugio, -ere, fugi, (fugitum), flee, escape.
fugo (1), put to flight.
fumus, -i, *m.*, smoke.
fundo (1), found, establish.
fundo, -ere, fudi, fusum (3), pour; rout.

funestus, -a, -um, polluted by death; in mourning (47.10).
fungor, -i, functus (3), *dep.*, perform (*with abl.*).
funus, -eris, *n.*, funeral.
furca, -ae, *f.*, fork.
furo (3), am mad.
furor, -oris, *m.*, madness.

Gabinus, -a, -um, of Gabii.
gaudeo, -ere, gauisus sum (2), *semi-dep.*, rejoice, rejoice at.
gaudium, -i, *n.*, joy.
gener, -eri, *m.*, son-in-law.
gens, gentis, *f.*, clan, tribe, race.
genus, -eris, *n.*, kind; birth; class.
gero, -ere, gessi, gestum (3), manage, do; have *a feeling* (12.10); wage (*of war*); *in pass.*, happen, take place.
gigno, -ere, genui, genitum (3), give birth to.
gladius, -i, *m.*, sword.
glisco (3), grow.
globus, -i, *m.*, throng.
gloria, -ae, *f.*, glory, fame.
Gradiuus, -i, *m.*, title of Mars.
gradus, -us, *m.*, step, stride.
grando, -inis, *f.*, hail.
grassor (1), *dep.*, advance.
gratia, -ae, *f.*, influence, favour; popularity; gratitude.
gratuitus, -a, -um, unpaid.
gratus, -a, -um, pleasing, popular, grateful.
grauis, -e, heavy, serious, grave.
grauiter, *adv.*, heavily, seriously.

habeo (2), have, hold.
habito (1), inhabit, dwell.
habitus, -us, *m.*, condition.

haereo, -ere, -si, -sum (2), cleave, am fixed or impaled in (6 9)
haesito (1), stick
hasta, -ae, f , spear
haud, adv , not
hauddum, adv , not yet
hercule, interj , by Hercules
hereditas, -atis, f , inheritance
heres, -edis, c , heir or heiress
Hernicus, -a, -um, of the Hernici; as noun, a Hernician
hesternus, -a, -um, of yesterday
hic, adv , here
hic, haec, hoc, this, he, she, it, they
hinc, adv , hence, after this
hinnitus, -us, m , neighing
hodie, adv , today
homo, -inis, c , human being, man
honestus, -a, -um, honourable
honor or honos, -oris, m , distinction, honour, position, office
honoro (1), honour
hora, -ae, f , hour
horrendus, -a, -um, formidable
horreo (2), shudder at
horridus, -a, -um, rough, savage, uncouth (32 8)
hospes, -itis, m , host
hospitalis, -e, of a host
hospitium, -i, n , hospitality, guest-friendship (22 7)
hostilis, -e, of an enemy, hostile
hostiliter, adv , in hostile fashion
hostis, -is, m , enemy
humanus, -a, -um, human

iaceo (2), lie
iacio, -ere, ieci, iactum, throw
iacto (1), put forward, mention
iam, adv , now, already
Ianiculum, -i, n , the Janiculum

Ianus, -i, m , Janus, as common noun, archway
ibi, adv , there
icio or ico, -ere, ici, ictum, (strike) make (a treaty)
ictus, -us, m , blow
idem, eadem, idem, same
ideo, adv on that account
idus, -uum, f pl , the Ides
igitur, conj , therefore
ignarus, -a, -um, not knowing
ignauia, -ae, f , cowardice
ignauus, -a, -um, cowardly
ignis, -is, m , fire
ignominia, -ae, f , disgrace humiliation
ignominiosus, -a, -um, disgraceful, humiliating
ignoro (1), do not know
ignosco, -ere, -noui, -notum (3) forgive (with dat)
ignotus, -a, -um, unknown
ille, -a, -ud, that, he, she, it, they
illic, adv , in that place
illinc, adv , thence
imbibo, -ere, -bi (3), fix in my mind
immaturus, -a, -um, unripe, premature
immemor, -oris, unmindful of
immensus, -a, -um, vast
immerito, adv , undeservedly
immineo (2), am imminent
immitis, -e, fierce
immitto, -ere, -misi, -missum (3) send into or against
impedio (4), hinder
impello, -ere, -puli, -pulsum (3), drive, shake (20 11)
impensa, -ae, f , expenditure
impensus, -a, -um, high

imperator, -oris, *m* , commander-in-chief

imperatorius, -a, -um, of a commander

imperitus, -a, -um, inexperienced, unacquainted with

imperium, -i, *n* , command, authority

impero (1), command, order, demand

impetro (1), obtain, win

impetus, -us, *m* , attack

impiger, -gra, -grum, active, vigorous *adv* , impigre

implico, -are, -ui, -itum (1), entangle

imploro (1), entreat

impono, -ere, -posui, positum (3), put *or* lay upon

impressio, -onis, *f* , attack

improuidus, -a, -um, not foreseeing, rash (50 6)

improuiso, *adv* , unexpectedly

impubis, -e, immature

impune, *adv* , with impunity

impunitas, -atis, *f* , impunity

in, *prep with acc* , to into towards, against, *with abl* , in, at, on among

incautus, -a, -um, incautious,

incedo, -ere, -cessi, -cessum (3) advance strut (6 7), fall upon (7 1), befall

incendium, -i, *n* fire, conflagration

incendo, -ere, -di, -sum (3), kindle

inceptum, -i, *n* , attempt, beginning

incertus, -a, -um, uncertain, doubtful

incestum, -i, *n* , unchastity

incido, -ere, -cidi, -casum (3), fall in with (23 9), befall (27 2), arise among (27 5)

incido, -ere, -cidi, -cisum (3), cut off

incipio, -ere, -cepi, -ceptum, begin

incito (1), stir up, urge on

inclino (1), give way (20 11), *reflex* , fall back

inclitus, -a, -um, renowned

includo, -ere, -si, -sum (3), shut in, choke

incoho (1), begin

incolumis, -e, safe, unhurt

incommodus, -a, -um, troublesome

inconsulte, *adv* , unadvisedly

inconsultus, -a, -um, unadvisedly

increpo, -are, -crepui, -crepitum (1), rebuke, cast in teeth

incruentus, -a, -um, bloodless

incultus, -a, -um, untilled

incursio, -onis, *f* , raid

incurso (1), raid

incursus, -us, *m* , onset

incutio, -ere, -cussi, -cussum, strike into

inde, *adv* , thence, from *or* of that

index, -icis, *c* , informer

indicium, -i, *n* , information

indico (1) disclose

indico, -ere, -dixi, -dictum (3), declare

indigeo (2), need (*with abl*)

indignatio, -onis, *f* indignation

indignitas, -atis, *f* , unworthiness, shameful wrong

indignor (1), *dep* , am indignant

indignus, -a, -um, unfitting, unworthy

indo, -ere, -didi, -ditum (3), apply, bestow (13 1)

induco, -ere, -duxi, -ductum (3), bring or lead into; with in animum, resolve (5.7; 15.3).

indulgentia, -ae, f., tenderness, liberality (9.7).

indulgeo, -ere, -si, -sum (2), offer concessions.

industria, -ae, f., energy.

indutiae, -arum, f. pl., truce.

ineo, -ire, -iui, (-ii), -itum, enter, enter upon; win (27.3).

inermis, -e, unarmed.

inexorabilis, -e, inexorable.

inexpiabilis, -e, irreconcilable.

inexpugnabilis, -e, impregnable.

infeliciter, adv., unsuccessfully.

infelix, -icis, unlucky; unsuccessful.

infensus, -a, -um, hostile; enraged.

infero, -ferre, -tuli, illatum, bring in, inflict; arma or signa inferre, to advance, attack; gradum inferre, to advance; se inferre, to rush against.

inferus, -a, -um, below; superl., infimus, lowest.

infeste, adv., in a hostile manner.

infestus, -a, -um, hostile, attacking; dangerous (11.3); pointed at the foe (46.7).

infidus, -a, -um, disloyal.

infirmus, -a, -um, weak.

inflammo (1), set on fire.

infra, prep. with acc., below.

infrequentia, -ae, f., lack of numbers.

infringo, -ere, -fregi, -fractum (3), break.

infula, -ae, f., head-band.

ingenium, -i, n., nature, character; temperament.

ingens, -ntis, huge.

ingero, -ere, -gessi, -gestum (3), pour upon; (of taunts, 45.10).

ingratus, -a, -um, ungrateful.

ingredior, -i, -gressus, dep., enter.

inicio, -ere, -ieci, -iectum, throw or put into.

inimicus, -i, m., (personal) enemy.

iniquitas, -atis, f., difficulty.

iniquus, -a, -um, unfair, unfavourable.

initium, -i, n., beginning.

iniungo, -ere, -iunxi, -iunctum (3), impose.

iniuratus, -a, -um, having taken no oath.

iniuria, -ae, f., wrong.

iniussu, adv., without the orders (of).

inlecebra, -ae, f., enticement.

inlino, -ere, -leui, -letum (3), smear.

inlucesco, -ere, -luxi (3), grow light.

innocens, -ntis, innocent, guiltless.

innocentia, -ae, f., freedom from guilt.

inopia, -ae, f., scarcity, lack.

inops, -opis, without resource, helpless.

inquam (3), say.

Inregillum, -i, n., Inregillum (a town).

inrito (1), provoke; quicken (39.11).

inritus, -a, -um, of no effect, in vain.

inrumpo, -ere, -rupi, -ruptum (3), break or burst into.

inruptio, -onis, f., rush.

inscribo, -ere, -scripsi, -scriptum (3), inscribe.

insculpo, -ere, -psi, -ptum (3), engrave.

insectatio, -onis, *f.*, pursuing.

insector (1), *dep.*, censure.

insequor, -i, -secutus (3), *dep.*, follow.

inseruio (4), show consideration for.

insideo, -ere, -sedi, -sessum, sit upon.

insidiae, -arum, *f. pl.*, ambush; plot.

insidiator, -oris, *m.*, assassin.

insigne, -is, *n.*, mark.

insignis, -e, distinguished, conspicuous.

insitus, -a, -um, innate.

insolens, -ntis, arrogant.

insons, -ntis, guiltless.

insperatus, -a, -um, unexpected; ex insperato, unexpectedly.

instauratio, -onis, *f.*, a repetition *or* renewal.

instauro (1), repeat.

instigo (1), spur on.

instituo, -ere, -stitui, -stitutum (3), establish; institute.

insto, -are, -stiti (1), press on, urge; am close (*with dat.*) 51.2.

instruo,-ere,-xi,-ctum (3), draw up.

insuetus, -a, -um, unaccustomed, unusual.

insula, -ae,*f.*, island.

insulto (1), behave insolently.

insum, -esse, -fui, am in.

insuper, *adv.*, actually.

intactus, -a, -um, untouched.

integer, -gra, -grum, afresh.

intendo, -ere, -di, -tum *or* -sum (3), stretch; aim, direct.

intentus, -a, -um, eager for; attentive.

inter, *prep. with acc.*, among, between.

intercedo, -ere, -cessi, -cessum (3), pass; (*of time* 64.8).

intercessio, -onis, *f.*, intervention; veto.

intercessor, -oris, *m.*, vetoer.

intercido, -ere, -cidi (3), am lost (4.7; 8.5).

intercursus, -us, *m.*, intervention (29.4).

interdum, *adv.*, sometimes.

interea, *adv.*, meanwhile.

interficio, -ere, -feci, -fectum, kill.

intericio, -ere, -ieci, -iectum, put between.

interim, *adv.*, meanwhile.

interitus, -us, *m.*, destruction.

intermitto, -ere, -misi, -missum (3), break off.

interpono, -ere, -posui, -positum (3), put between.

interpres, -etis, *c.*, negotiator.

interpretatio, -onis, *f.*, interpretation.

interrumpo, -ere, -rupi, -ruptum (3), break asunder.

intersum, -esse, -fui, I am present (at) *or* take part in.

interuallum, -i, *n.*, space between, distance, interval.

interuenio, -ire, -ueni, -uentum (4), come between; intervene.

interuentus, -us, *m.*, a coming between.

intestinus, -a, -um, internal.

intra, *prep. with acc.*, within.

intro (1), enter.

introeo, -ire, -iui (-ii), -itum, enter.

intromitto, -ere, -misi, -missum (3), send in, admit.

introrsum, *adv.*, in depth.

intus, *adv.*, inside, within.

inultus, -a, -um, unavenged, un-punished.

inuado, -ere, -uadi, -uasum (3), fall upon, attack.

inueho, -ere, -uexi, -uectum (3), carry to *or* into; *in pass.*, ride into; *also in pass.*, attack, charge; inveigh against (59.9).

inuenio, -ire, -ueni, -uentum (4), come upon, find.

inuentor, -oris, *m.*, originator.

inuictus, -a, -um, unconquered.

inuideo, -ere, -uidi, -uisum (2), grudge.

inuidia, -ae, *f.*, hostility; un-popularity.

inuiolatus, -a, -um, inviolable.

inuisus, -a, -um, hateful.

inuitamentum, -i, *n.*, incitement.

inuitus, -a, -um, unwilling.

inuoco (1), summon.

ipse, -a, -um, self, myself *etc.*

ira, -ae, *f.*, anger.

irascor, -i, iratus (3), *dep.*, I grow angry.

iratus, -a, -um, angry.

is, ea, id, that; he, she, it; they.

iste, -a, -ud, that (*of yours*).

ita, *adv.*, in such a way; so, thus.

itaque, *conj.*, and so.

item, *adv.*, likewise.

iter, itineris, *n.*, march, way, journey; iter facere, to march.

iterum, *adv.*, again, for the second time.

iubeo, -ere, iussi, iussum (2), order, command, bid.

iudex, -icis, *c.*, judge.

iudicium, -i, *n.*, judgment, trial.

iugum, -i, *n.*, ridge.

iungo, -ere, -xi, -ctum (3), join; form (*as a tie*) (22.7).

Iunius, -a, -um, of the Junii.

Iuppiter, Iouis, *m.*, Jupiter.

iuro (1), swear.

ius, iuris, *n.*, right, claim; law.

ius iurandum, iuris iurandi, *n.*, oath.

iussu, *adv.*, by the command (of).

iuuenis, -is, *m.*, young man.

iuuentus, -utis, *f.*, youth; the fighting men.

iuuo, -are, iuui, iutum (1), help: *impers.*, it pleases.

K. = Caeso.

L. = Lucius.

labes, -is, *f.*, falling.

Labici, -orum, *m. pl.*, Labici (*a town*).

labo (1), totter; am unreliable (39.10).

labor, -oris, *m.*, toil, effort.

labor, -i, lapsus (3), *dep.*, slip, fall down.

lacero (1), tear to pieces.

lacesso, -ere, -iui, -itum (3), pro-voke, challenge.

lacrima, -ae, *f.*, tear.

lacus, -us, *m.*, lake.

laetitia, -ae, *f.*, joy.

laetus, -a, -um, glad; welcome.

laeuā, on the left.

laeuus, -a, -um, left.

lapis, -idis, *m.*, milestone.

largitio, -onis, *f.*, largess.

Lars, Lartis, *m.*, Lord, (*honorary title of Etruscan kings*).

lasciuia, -ae, *f.*, wantonness.

lasciuio (4), get out of hand.

late, *adv.*, widely.

Latinus, -a, -um, of Latium *or* the Latins; Latin: *as noun*, a Latin.

latio, -onis, *f.*, right of bringing.

Latium, -i, *n.*, Latium.

latro, -onis, *m.*, bandit.

latrocinium, -i, *n.*, banditry.

latus, -a, -um, wide.

latus, -eris, *n.*, side, flank.

laudatio, -onis, *f.*, funeral speech.

laudator, -oris, *m.*, he who praises (*in funeral oration*).

laudo (1), praise.

laurea, -ae, *f.*, laurel.

laus, laudis, *f.*, praise.

Lauinium, -i, *n.*, Lavinium (*a town*).

laxamentum, -i, *n.*, respite.

laxo (1), loosen.

laxus, -a, -um, loose.

lectica, -ae, *f.*, litter.

lectus, -i, *m.*, bed.

legatus, -i, *m.*, envoy.

legio, -onis, *f.*, levy.

lego, -ere, legi, lectum (3), gather up; choose.

lenio (4), soften, mitigate.

lenis, -e, gentle.

leniter, *adv.*, gently.

letum, -i, *n.*, death.

leuis, -e, light; **leuiter,** *adv.*, lightly.

leuitas, -atis, *f.*, instability.

leuo (1), lighten, relieve.

lex, legis, *f.*, law; *in pl.*, terms.

liber, -era, -erum, free.

liberalis, -e, generous.

liberaliter, *adv.*, generously.

liberator, -oris, *m.*, liberator.

liberi, -orum, *m. pl.*, children.

libero (1), set free.

libertas, -atis, *f.*, freedom, liberty.

libido, -inis, *f.*, caprice.

licentia, -ae, *f.*, licence.

licet (2), *impers.*, it is allowed.

lictor, -oris, *m.*, lictor.

limen, -inis, *n.*, threshold.

limus, -i, *m.*, mud.

lingua, -ae, *f.*, tongue.

littera, -ae, *f.*, letter (*of alphabet*); *in pl.*, letter, despatch.

litus, -oris, *n.*, shore.

loco (1), place, post.

locus, -i, *m.*, place, position; opportunity, room.

longe, *adv.*, (by) far.

longinquus, -a, -um, distant.

Longula, -ae, *f.*, Longula (*a town*).

longus, -a, -um, long.

loquor, -i, locutus (3), *dep.*, speak, say.

lucror (1), *dep.*, gain.

luctus, -us, *m.*, mourning.

ludibrium, -i, *m.*, mockery.

ludus, -i, *m.*, game.

lugeo, -ere, -xi, -ctum (2), mourn.

lux, lucis, *f.*, (day)light.

luxurio (1), run riot.

luxuriosus, -a, -um, uncurbed.

M. = Marcus.

M'. = Manius.

macies, -ei, *f.*, leanness.

maestitia, -ae, *f.*, sadness.

maestus, -a, -um, sad.

magis, *adv.*, more.

magister, -tri, *m.*, master.

magistratus, -us, *m.*, magistrate, magistracy.

magnifice, *adv.*, splendidly.

magnificus, -a, -um, grand.

magnitudo, -inis, *f.*, greatness.

magnus, -a, -um, great.

maiestas, -atis, *f.*, greatness, dignity.

Maius, -a, -um, of May.
malignitas, -atis, f., niggardliness.
male, adv., unsuccessfully.
malo, malle, malui, prefer.
malum, -i, n., evil; punishment.
mando (1), entrust.
mane, adv., in the morning.
maneo, -ere, -si, -sum (2), remain.
manifestus, -a, -um, clear.
manipulatim, adv., in companies.
manipulus, -i, m., maniple, company.
mano (1), spread.
mansuetus, -a, -um, gentle.
manus, -us, f., hand; action.
Mars, -rtis, n., Mars; war.
Martius, -a, -um, of Mars.
mater, -tris, f., mother.
materia, -ae, f., material; opportunity.
matrimonium, -i, n., marriage.
matrona, -ae, f., married woman, matron.
maturo (1), hasten; bring to a head (32.2).
maturus, -a, -um, ripe.
maxime, superl. adv., especially; very greatly.
maximus, -a, -um, superl. adj., greatest.
medium, -i, n., middle.
medius, -a, -um, middle.
membrum, -i, n., member.
memini, -isse, remember.
memor, -oris, mindful (of).
memorabilis, -e, memorable.
memoria, -ae, f., remembrance.
memoro (1), relate.
mendacium, -i, n., lie.
Menenianus, -a, -um, of Menenius.
mentio, -onis, f., mention.
mercator, -oris, m., merchant.

merces, -edis, f., pay, payment.
Mercurius, -i, m., Mercury.
mereo (2) and mereor (2) dep., earn, deserve.
meritum, -i, n., service.
messis, -is, f., harvest.
metuo, -ere, -ui, -utum (3), fear.
metus, -us, m., fear.
mico, -are, -ui (1), flash.
miles, -itis, m., soldier.
militaris, -e, of soldiers.
militia, -ae, f., military service: militiae, in the field.
milito (1), serve.
mille, thousand: pl., milia.
minaciter, adv., threateningly.
minae, -arum, f. pl., threats.
minax, -acis, threatening.
ministerium, -i, n., tool; service.
minitabundus, -a, -um, threatening.
minitor (1), dep., threaten.
minor (1), dep., threaten.
miraculum, -i, n., marvel; prodigy (7.2).
mire, adv., wonderfully.
miror (1), dep., wonder (at).
mirus, -a, -um, wonderful.
misceo, -ere, -scui, -xtum (2), mix, mingle: engage in (19.5).
miser, -era, -erum, wretched.
miseret (2), impers., pity.
miseria, -ae, f., wretchedness.
miseror (1), dep., pity.
missilis, -e, missile (as adj.).
mitigo (1), allay, appease.
mitis, -e, gentle.
mitto, -ere, misi, missum (3), send; adjourn (24.4).
mobilis, -e, fickle, unreliable.
moderate, adv., with restraint.
moderatio, -onis, f., control.

moderator, -oris, *m.*, controller.
moderatus, -a, -um, restrained.
modicus, -a, -um, moderate.
modo, *adv.*, only.
modus, -i, *m.*, way; measure, limit.
moenia, -ium, *n. pl.*, walls.
moles, -is, *f.*, mass; pier (5.4);
 effort.
molimen, -inis, *n.*, great importance.
molior (4), *dep.*, work for *or* at.
mollis, -e, feeble, pusillanimous
 (27.4).
momentum, -i, *n.*, determining
 cause.
moneo (2), warn, urge.
mons, -ntis, *m.*, hill.
monumentum, -i, *n.*, memorial.
mora, -ae, *f.*, delay.
morator, -oris, *m.*, a hinderer.
morbus, -i, *m.*, disease.
moribundus, -a, -um, dying.
morior, -i, mortuus, *dep.*, die.
moror (1), *dep.*, stay.
mors, -tis, *f.*, death.
mortalis, -e, mortal.
mortifer, -era, -erum, deadly;
 fatal.
mos, moris, *m.*, custom.
motus, -us, *m.*, agitation, disturbance.
moueo, -ere, moui, motum (2),
 move.
mox, *adv.*, soon.
Mucius, -a, -um, of Mucius.
mucro, -onis, *m.*, sword-point;
 sword.
muliebris, -e, of a woman *or*
 women.
mulier, -eris, *f.*, woman.
multa, -ae, *f.*, fine; penalty
 (52.5).

multiplex, -icis, many times as
 great.
multiplico (1), multiply.
multitudo, -inis, *f.*, crowd, large *or*
 superior numbers; populace.
multus, -a, -um, much, many.
munificus, -a, -um, liberal, bounti-
 ful.
munimentum, -i, *n.*, fortification.
munio (4), fortify.
munus, -eris, *n.*, duty.
murus, -i, *m.*, wall.
mutabilis, -e, changeable.
muto (1), change.
mutuus, -a, -um, reciprocal.

nam, *conj.*, for.
namque, *conj.*, for.
narro (1), relate.
nascor, -i, natus (3) *dep.*, am born
natura, -ae, *f.*, nature.
natus, -us, *m.*, birth.
nauis, -is, *f.*, ship.
nauo (1), do, perform.
ne, *conj.*, that . . . not, lest; ne
 . . . quidem, not even.
-ne, *interrogative particle.*
nec, *conj.*, and . . . not; nec . . .
 nec, neither . . . nor.
necdum, and not yet.
necessarius, -a, -um, necessary,
 needful.
necessarius, -i, *m.*, relative *or* close
 friend.
necesse, *indecl. adj.*, inevitable.
necessitas, -atis, *f.*, necessity.
neco (1), kill.
necopinatus, -a, -um, unexpected.
necto, -ere, -xui *or* -xi, -xum (3),
 commit (*to bondage*).
necubi, lest anywhere.
nefas, *indecl.*, wickedness; sin.

neglegens, -ntis, careless.
neglegenter, *adv.*, carelessly.
neglegentia, -ae, *f.*, carelessness.
neglego, -ere, -xi, -ctum (3), disregard.
nego (1), say ... not; refuse, deny.
negotium, -i, *n.*, business, trouble.
nemo, -inem, nullius, nemini, nullo, no-one.
nepos, -otis, *m.*, grandson.
nequaquam, by no means.
neque, *see* nec.
nequeo, -ire, -iui, am not able.
neuter, -tra, -trum, neither.
neu *or* neue, *conj.*, and (that) ... not.
nex, necis, *f.*, death.
nexus, -a, -um, in bondage.
ni, *conj.*, if not, unless.
nihil, *indecl.*, nothing.
nihilum, -i, *n.*, nothing.
nimis, *adv.*, too much, too.
nimium, *adv.*, too much, excessively.
nimius, -a, -um, too great, excessive.
nisi, *conj.* if not, unless; except.
nitor, -i, nisus *or* nixus (3), *dep.*, strive, strain.
nobilis, -e, high born.
nobilitas, -atis, *f.*, high-birth.
nocens, -ntis, guilty.
noceo (2), harm (*with dat.*).
nocturnus, -a, -um, by *or* at night.
nolo, nolle, nolui, am unwilling; refuse.
nomen, -inis, *n.*, name.
nominatim, *adv.*, by name.
nomino (1), name.
non, *adv.*, not.
nondum, *adv.*, not yet.

nonnihil, in some degree.
Norba, -ae, *f.*, Norba (*a town*).
noscito (1), recognise.
nosco, -ere, noui, notum (3), get to know; *in perf.* =know.
noster, -tra, -trum, our.
nouellus, -a, -um, newly acquired.
nouitas, -atis, *f.*, newness.
nouus, -a, -um, new, strange, revolutionary: *in superl.*, latest; last (42.2).
nox, noctis, *f.*, night.
noxa, -ae, *f.*, punishment.
noxia, -ae, *f.*, offence.
nubo, -ere, -psi, -ptum (3), marry
nudo (1), strip.
nullus, -a, -um, no, none.
numen, -inis, *n.*, (divine) will *or* power.
numero (1), count.
numerus, -i, *m.*, number.
nunc, *adv.*, now.
nunquam, *adv.*, never.
nuntio (1), announce.
nuntius, -i, *m.*, news; messenger.
nuptus, -a, -um, married.
nurus, -us, *f.*, daughter-in-law.
nusquam, *adv.*, nowhere.
nutrio (4), nourish.
nutus, -us, *m.*, nod.

ob, *prep. with acc.*, on account of.
obeo, -ire, -ii, -itum, perform.
obequito (1), ride towards.
obicio, -ere, -ieci, -iectum, throw in the way; hold in front.
obiaceo (2), lie amongst.
obliuiscor, -i, -litus (3), *dep.*, forget (*with gen.*).
oboedio (4), obey.
oborior, -iri, -ortus (4), *dep.*, arise, well up.

obsaepio, -ire, -psi, -ptum (4), bar.

obseruo (1), observe.

obses, -idis, c., hostage.

obsideo, -ere, -sedi, -sessum (2), besiege.

obsidio, -onis, f., siege, blockade.

obsisto, -ere, -stiti (3), put myself in the way or as a barrier.

obsitus, -a, -um, covered over.

obstinatus, -a, -um, resolute.

obsto, -are, -stiti, -statum (1), stand in the way; hinder (with dat.).

obstupefacio, -ere, -feci, -factum, amaze.

obtempero (1), obey.

obtestor (1), dep., implore.

obtineo, -ere, -tinui, -tentum (2), hold fast; secure, bring about.

obtrectatio, -onis, f., disparagement.

obtrunco (1), cut down.

obtundo, -ere, -tudi, -tusum (3), importune.

obuersor (1), dep., stand before.

obuerto, -ere, -uerti, -uersum (3), turn towards.

obuiam, adv., to meet (with dat.).

obuius, -a, -um, meeting; obuius sum, I meet (with dat.).

occasio, -onis, f., opportunity.

occidio, -onis, f., slaughter.

occido, -ere, -cidi, -casum (3), fall.

occido, -ere, -cidi, -cisum (3), kill.

occulo, -ere, -ului, -ultum (3), hide.

occumbo, -ere, -cubui, -cubitum (3), fall.

occupo (1), seize.

occurro, -ere, -curri, -cursum (3), encounter (with dat.).

occurso (1), run up to.

oculus, -i, m., eye.

odium, -i, n., hatred.

offendo, -ere, -di, -sum (3), displease.

offero, -ferre, obtuli, oblatum, present; reflexively and in pass., present myself, encounter; appear (47.4).

officio, -ere, -feci, -fectum, am harmful to (with dat.).

officium, -i, n., duty.

offundo, -ere, -fudi, -fusum (3), present.

omitto, -ere, -misi, -missum (3), let go, give up.

omnino, adv., altogether.

omnis, -e, all.

onero (1), burden, overwhelm.

onus, -eris, n., burden.

opera, -ae, f., work, service.

opinio, -onis, f., thought.

Opiter, -iteris, m., Opiter (Roman praenomen).

oppidanus, -i, m., townsman.

oppidum, -i, m., town.

oppono, -ere, -posui, -positum (3), set in the way or as a barrier.

opportunus, -a, -um, exposed.

opprimo, -ere, -pressi, -pressum (3), crush.

oppugno (1), attack.

(ops), opis, f., help; in pl., resources: summa ope, with the utmost effort.

opto (1), pray or long for.

opulentus, -a, -um, rich, powerful.

opus, -eris, n., work: opus est, there is need of (with nom. or abl.).

oratio, -onis, f., speech.

orator, -oris, m., spokesman, envoy.

orbis, -is, m., circle.

orbus, -a, -um, bereft.

254 LIVY, BOOK TWO

ordino (1), arrange.
ordo, -inis, *m.*, rank.
origo, -inis, *f.*, source, origin.
orior, -iri, ortus (4), *dep.*, arise.
oriundus, -a, -um, originating,
sprung (from).
ornatus, -us, *m.*, apparel.
oro (1), beg.
Ortona, -ae, *f.*, Ortona (*a town*).
os, oris, *n.*, face.
ostendo, -ere, -di, -sum *or* -tum
(3), shew.
ostento (1), display.
Ostia, -ae, *f.*, Ostia (*a town*).
otiose, *adv.*, without promptness.
otiosus, -a, -um, at leisure.
otium, -i, *n.*, peace; inaction.

P. = Publius.
pacatus, -a, -um, friendly.
paco (1), pacify.
paene, *adv.*, almost.
paenitet (2), *impers.*, repent.
palam, *adv.*, openly.
Palatium, -i, *n.*, the Palatine hill.
pallor, -oris, *m.*, pallor.
palor (1), *dep.*, straggle (26.3);
am dispersed (50.6).
paludatus, -a, -um, wearing a
general's cloak.
palus, -i, *m.*, stake.
pando, -ere, -di, passum (3),
spread out.
par, paris, equal, a match for
(16.4).
parens, -ntis, *c.*, parent; father.
pareo (2), obey (*with dat.*).
paries, -etis, *m.*, a wall.
pario, -ere, peperi, partum, bear,
produce; win, acquire.
pariter, *adv.*, equally.
parma, -ae, *f.*, round shield.

paro (1), prepare.
pars, partis, *f.*, part; direction.
particeps, -cipis, sharing in (*with
gen.*); *as noun*, a sharer.
participo (1), share.
partim, *adv.*, partly.
parum, *adv.*, not sufficiently, not
fully.
parumper, *adv.*, for a short time.
paruus, -a, -um, small.
passim, *adv.*, in all directions.
passus, -us, *m.*, pace, step.
pastor, -oris, *m.*, shepherd.
patefacio, -ere, -feci, -factum,
open.
pateo (2), am *or* stand open.
pater, -tris, *m.*, father: *m. pl.*, the
patricians.
paternus, -a, -um, of father.
patientia, -ae, *f.*, tolerance, en-
durance.
patior, -i, passus, *dep.*, suffer,
allow.
patria, -ae, *f.*, native land *or* city.
patricius, -a, -um, patrician.
patrius, -a, -um, of a father.
patronus, -i, *m.*, patron.
paucitas, -atis, *f.*, fewness.
paucus, -a, -um, few, little.
paulatim, *adv.*, little by little.
paulo, *adv.*, (by) a little.
paululum, *adv.*, just a little.
paulum, *adv.*, a little.
pauper, -eris, of scanty means.
paueo, -ere, paui (2), am in a panic.
pauidus, -a, -um, panic-stricken.
pauor, -oris, *m.*, panic.
pax, pacis, *f.*, peace.
pecco (1), sin, offend.
pectus, -oris, *n.*, breast.
peculium, -i, *n.*, property.
pecunia, -ae, *f.*, money.

pecus, -oris, *n.*, herd *or* flock.

pedes, -itis, *m.*, foot-soldier.

pedester, -tris, -tre, of infantry.

Pedum, -i, *n.*, Pedum (*a Latin town*).

pello, -ere, pepuli, pulsum (3), drive, drive out.

penates, -ium, *m. pl.*, household gods.

pendeo, -ere, pependi (2), depend upon.

pendo, -ere, pependi, pensum (3), pay.

penes, *prep. with acc.*, in the power of.

penetro (1), make my way.

per, *prep. with acc.*, through, over, during; by means of.

perago, -ere, -egi, -actum (3), accomplish.

percello, -ere, -culi, -culsum (3), strike, smite, overwhelm.

percipio, -ere, -cepi, -ceptum, perceive, hear.

percontor (1), *dep.*, ask.

percutio, -ere, -cussi, -cussum, strike.

perduco, -ere, -duxi, -ductum (3), lead *or* bring to.

perduellio, -onis, *f.*, high treason.

peregre, *adv.*, from abroad.

peregrinus, -a, -um, foreign; *as noun*, foreigner.

pereo, -ire, -ii, -itum, perish.

perexiguus, -a, -um, scanty.

perfero, -ferre, -tuli, -latum, carry through.

perficio, -ere, -feci, -fectum, finish; bring to an end.

perfuga, -ae, *m.*, deserter.

perfugio, -ere, -fugi, flee to, take refuge in.

perfugium, -i, *n.*, refuge.

perfundo, -ere, -fudi, -fusum (3), inspire with.

pergo, -ere, -rexi, -rectum (3), proceed.

periculosus, -a, -um, dangerous.

periculum, -i, *n.*, danger.

perimo, -ere, -emi, -emptum (3), destroy.

perinde, *adv.*, in the same manner.

permitto, -ere, -misi, -missum (3), entrust.

pernicies, -ei, *f.*, harm.

perniciosus, -a, -um, harmful.

peropportune, *adv.*, very opportunely.

peropportunus, -a, -um, very opportune.

perpello, -ere, -puli, -pulsum (3), drive.

perpetuus, -a, -um, unbroken; in perpetuum, for ever.

persequor, -i, -secutus (3), pursue; punish (6.3).

perseuero (1), persist.

persoluo, -ere, -solui, -solutum (3), pay (in full).

persuadeo, -ere, -suasi, -suasum (2), persuade (*with dat.*).

pertempto (1), test.

pertinacia, -ae, *f.*, obstinacy.

pertinax, -acis, obstinate.

pertineo (2), concern, affect.

perturbo (1), trouble, confuse.

peruado, -ere, -uadi, -uasum (3), spread through.

peruenio, -ire, -ueni, -uentum (4), arrive (at), reach.

peruinco, -ere, -uici, -uictum (3), carry my point.

pes, pedis, *m.*, foot.

pestilens, -ntis, poisonous.

pestilentia, -ae, *f.*, plague.
pestis, -is, *f.*, destruction.
peto, -ere, -iui, -itum (3), seek; aim at.
piaculum, -i, *n.*, (divine) punishment.
pignus, -eris, *n.*, pledge.
pilum, -i, *n.*, javelin.
pilus, -i, *m.*, a maniple, company.
Piso, -onis, *m.*, Piso (*Roman annalist*).
pius, -a, -um, pure, holy.
placatus, -a, -um, friendly.
placeo (2), please (*with dat.*).
placide, *adv.*, peacefully.
placidus, -a, -um, quiet, peaceful.
placo (1), appease.
planus, -a, -um, level.
plebeius, -a, -um, plebeian; of the people.
plebs *or* plebis, -is *or* -ei, *f.*, the people.
plenus, -a, -um, full, loaded with.
plerique, -aeque, -aque, *pl.*, very many, most.
ploratus, -us, *m.*, wailing.
poena, -ae, *f.*, penalty, punishment.
Polusca, -ae, *f.*, Polusca (*a town*).
Pometia Suessa, -ae, Suessa Pometia (*a town*).
pompa, -ae, *f.*, procession.
Pomptinum, -i, *n.*, the Pomptine district.
pono, -ere, posui, positum (3), put, place; pitch.
pons, -ntis, *m.*, bridge.
pontifex, -icis, *m.*, pontifex.
populabundus, -a, -um, laying waste.
popularis, -e, democratic, popular.

populatio, -onis, *f.*, plundering, ravaging.
populator, -oris, *m.*, plunderer.
populor (1), *dep.*, lay waste.
populus, -i, *m.*, people.
Porsenna, -ae, *m.*, Porsenna.
porta, -ae, *f.*, gate.
porticus, -us, *f.*, colonnade.
portorium, -i, *n.*, toll, duty.
posco, -ere, poposci (3), demand.
possessor, -oris, *m.*, holder.
possideo, -ere, -sedi, -sessum (2), have *or* hold.
possido, -ere, -sedi, -sessum (3), take possession of.
possum, posse, potui, am able.
post, *prep. with acc.*, and *adv.*, after, behind; afterwards.
postea, *adv.*, afterwards.
posterus, -a, -um, following, next: posteri, *m. pl.*, posterity.
postis, -is, *m.*, door-post, door.
postmodo *or* postmodum, *adv.*, afterwards.
postquam, *conj.*, when.
postremo, *adv.*, finally.
postremum, *adv.*, lastly.
postremus, -a, -um, last.
postulo (1), demand.
Postumus *or* -ius, -i, *m.*, Postumus *or* Postumius.
potens, -ntis, powerful.
potestas, -atis, *f.*, power, office.
potior (4), *dep.*, get possession of (*with abl.*).
potior, -oris, preferable.
potissimum, *adv.*, in particular.
potissimus, -a, -um, most preferable.
potius, *adv.*, preferably, rather.
prae, *prep. with abl.*, before, for.

praecaueo, -ere, -caui, -cautum
(2), take precautions.
praeceps, -cipitis, headlong.
praeceptum, -i, *n.*, instruction.
praecipito (1), throw *or* fall headlong.
praecipuus, -a, -um, special.
praeco, -onis, *m.*, herald.
praeda, -ae, *f.*, booty.
praedabundus, -a, -um, plundering.
praedator, -oris, *m.*, plunderer.
praedico (3), charge, command.
praedo, -onis, *m.*, plunderer.
praedor (1), *dep.*, plunder.
praefero, -ferre, -tuli, -latum,
carry before; *in pass.*, rush past.
praegredior ,-i, -gressus, *dep.*, go
in advance.
praemium, -i, *n.*, reward.
Praeneste, -is, *n.*, Praeneste.
praeparo (1), prepare beforehand.
praepropere, *adv.*, too hastily.
praeproperus, -a, -um, too hasty.
praesens, -ntis, present, immediate.
praesentia, -ae, *f.*, presence.
praesidium, -i, *n.*, defence, protection; garrison.
praesto, -are, -stiti, -statum (1),
guarantee; honour (28.7).
praesultator, -oris, *m.*, foremost
dancer.
praesum, -esse, -fui, am in command of (*with dat.*).
praeter, *prep. with acc.*, besides,
except.
praeterea, *adv.*, besides, moreover.
praetereo, -ire, -ii, -itum, go past;
pass by.
praeteritus, -a, -um, past.
praetermitto, -ere, -misi, -missum
(3), neglect.

praeterquam, *conj.*, except.
praetexta, -ae, *f.*, purple-bordered
(toga).
praetorium, -i, *n.*, consul's quar-
ters.
praeualens, -ntis, very strong.
praeuerto, -ere, -uerti (3), put
before.
pratum, -i, *n.*, meadow.
precatio, -onis, *f.*, praying.
preces, -um, *f. pl.*, prayers, entreaties.
precor (1), *dep.*, entreat.
premo, -ere, pressi, pressum (3),
press hard.
prendo, -ere, -di, -sum (3), seize,
lay hold of.
prenso (1), grasp.
pretium, -i, *n.*, price.
pridie, *adv.*, the day before.
primo, *adv.*, at first.
primores, -um, the leading men.
primum, *adv.*, for the first time.
primus, -a, -um, first; in primis,
especially.
princeps, -cipis, foremost; chief.
principium, -i, *n.*, beginning.
prior, -us, prioris, former, previous.
priscus, -a, -um, old-fashioned.
pristinus, -a, -um, former.
prius, *adv.*, before, sooner.
priusquam, *conj.*, before.
priuatim, *adv.*, personally.
priuatus, -a, -um, private, of individuals (49.1); *as noun*, a
private individual.
pro, *prep. with abl.*, before, in front
of; on behalf of, in accordance
with.
probabilis, -e, worthy of approval.
probrum, -i, *n.*, insult.

procedo, -ere, -cessi, -cessum (3), advance.

procella, -ae, *f.*, tempest.

proceres, -um, *m. pl.*, leading men.

procul, *adv.*, at a distance, far from.

Proculus, -i, *m.*, Proculus.

prodeo, -ire, -ii, -itum, come *or* go forth; advance.

prodico, -ere, -dixi, -dictum (3), say *or* appoint beforehand.

prodigium, -i, *n.*, warning sign.

proditio, -onis, *f.*, betrayal, treachery.

proditor, -oris, *m.*, betrayer, traitor.

prodo, -ere, -didi, -ditum (3), betray.

produco, -ere, -duxi, -ductum (3), lead *or* bring forward, parade.

proelium, -i, *n.*, battle.

profectio, -onis, *f.*, departure.

profecto, *adv.*, assuredly.

profero, -ferre, -tuli, -latum, bring out.

proficiscor, -i, -fectus (3), *dep.*, set out.

profiteor, -eri, -fessus (2), *dep.*, declare.

prohibeo (2), prevent.

proicio, -ere, -ieci, -iectum, fling away; abandon (27.11).

proinde, *adv.*, therefore, accordingly.

prolabor, -i, -lapsus (3), *dep.*, slip forward.

prolato (1), put off.

promiscuus, -a, -um, indiscriminate.

promissum, -i, *n.*, promise.

promitto, -ere, -misi, -missum (3), promise.

promo, -ere, -mpsi, -mptum (3), bring out.

promoueo, -ere, -moui, -motum (2), move forward.

promptus, -a, -um, ready.

promulgo (1), propose.

pronuntio (1), announce, proclaim.

prope, *prep. with acc., and adv.*, near; *as adv.*, nearly, almost.

propediem, *adv.*, soon.

propello, -ere, -puli, -pulsum (3), drive forth.

propere, *adv.*, speedily.

propinquus, -a, -um, near, neighbouring; *as noun*, kinsman.

propior, -ius, -oris, nearer.

propitius, -a, -um, propitious, favourable.

propius, *adv.*, nearer, too near.

propono, -ere, -posui, -positum (3), publish.

propositum, -i, *n.*, purpose.

proprius, -a, -um, one's own.

propter, *prep. with acc.*, by reason of, on account of; owing to.

propugnator, -oris, *m.*, defender.

proripio, -ere, -ripui, -reptum, *reflex. verb*, burst forth.

prosequor, -i, -secutus (3), *dep.*, attend, escort.

prosilio, -ire, -ui (4), leap *or* rush forward.

prosperus, -a, -um, successful.

prosum, -(d)esse, -fui, am of advantage to (*with dat.*).

protego, -ere, -texi, -tectum (3), protect.

protinus, *adv.*, right on.

proueho, -ere, -uexi, -uectum (3), carry forward.

prouideo, -ere, -uidi, -uisum (2), see beforehand, shew foresight.

prouincia, -ae, f., sphere of activity.
prouocatio, -onis, f., right of appeal.
prouoco (1), appeal.
prouolo (1), fly forward.
proximus, -a, -um, nearest, last, recent; as noun, kinsman.
pubes or puber, -eris, mature.
publice, adv., officially; by official decree.
Publicola, -ae, m., Friend of the people.
publicum, -i, n., the state coffer.
publicus, -a, -um, public.
pudicitia, -ae, f., chastity.
pudor, -oris, m., shame.
puerilis, -e, of children.
pugna, -ae, f., fighting, fight, battle.
pugno (1), fight.
pulcher, -chra, -chrum, fine.
pulso (1), beat, manhandle.
puto (1), think.

Q. =Quintus.
qua, adv., where, by which way; qua . . . qua, both . . . and.
quacumque, adv., by whatever way.
quadraginta, forty.
quadratus, -a, -um, square.
quaero, -ere, -siui, -situm (3), seek; miss (3.3); procure (43. 10).
quaestio, -onis, f., enquiry.
quaestor, -oris, m., quaestor.
qualis, -e, what kind of; (such) as.
qualis, -ecumque, of whatever kind.
quam, adv., and conj., as, than; how; with superl. adj., or adv., as . . . as possible.

quamdiu, adv., how long.
quamquam, conj., although; and yet.
quamuis, adv., and conj., however much; although.
quando (quandoquidem), conj., since.
quantum, adv., so far as.
quantus, -a, -um, how much, (as much) as: quanti, at what price.
quartus, -a, -um, fourth: adv., quartum, for the fourth time.
quasi, adv., as if.
quatenus, adv., up to what point.
quattuor, four.
-que, and; -que . . . et, both . . . and.
quemadmodum, adv., as.
querella, -ae, f., complaint.
queror, -i, questus (3), dep., complain.
qui, quae, quod, rel. pron., who, which, that.
qui, quae, quod, interrog. adj., which? what?
qui, quae, quod, indefin. adj., any.
qui, interrog. adv., how?
quia, conj., because.
quicumque, quae-, quod-, whoever, whatsoever.
quidam, quae-, quod-, a certain, certain one, one.
quidem, adv., indeed.
quies, -etis, f., rest; peace (15.5).
quiesco, -ere, -eui, -etum (3), keep quiet, calm down.
quietus, -a, -um, quiet.
quilibet, quae-, quod-, any you please.
quin, conj., that, that . . . not; because . . . not; as adv., why, nay.

quinque, five.

Quintilis, -e, of July.

quippe, *conj.*, for indeed; *as adv.*, certainly.

Quirites, -ium, *m. pl.*, citizens (*of Rome*).

quis, quis, quid, *interrog. pron.*, who? which? what?

quis, qua, quid, *indefin. pron.*, anyone, anything.

quisquam, quae-, quid-, anyone, anything.

quisque, quae-, quod-, each, every.

quisquis, quaequae, quodquod, *adj.*, quisquis, quidquid, *noun*, whoever, whatever.

quo, *adv.*, whither.

quo, *conj.*, that, because.

quoad, *conj.*, as long as, until.

quod, *conj.*, because.

quominus, *conj.*, so that . . . not.

quomodo, *adv.*, how?

quondam, *adv.*, once, formerly.

quoniam, *conj.*, since.

quoque, *adv.*, also.

quot, as many as, as.

rabies, -em, -e, *f.*, fury.

rapio, -ere, -ui, -tum, seize, carry off.

rarus, -a, -um, here and there.

rebellio, -onis, *f.*, outbreak of warfare.

rebello (1), renew hostilities.

recens, -tis, recent, fresh.

recenseo (2), review.

receptus, -us, *m.*, retreat.

recido, -ere, -cidi, -casum (3), sink.

recipero (1), get back, recover.

recipio, -ere, -cepi, -ceptum, recover; *reflexively*, withdraw.

recito (1), read out.

reconcilio (1), win back.

recreo (1), renew.

reddo, -ere, -didi, -ditum (3), give back, restore, deliver.

redeo, -ire, -ii, -itum, return.

redigo, -ere, -egi, -actum (3), pay in.

redimo, -ere, -emi, -emptum (3), ransom.

redintegro (1), renew.

reditus, -us, *m.*, return.

reduco, -ere, -duxi, -ductum (3), lead *or* bring back.

reductor, -oris, *m.*, restorer.

refero, -ferre, rettuli, relatum, bring *or* carry back: bring before.

refert, rettulit, *imperson.*, it is of importance.

reficio, -ere, -feci, -fectum, restore, renew.

refugio, -ere, -fugi, flee away.

refuto (1), drive back, oppose.

regia, -ae, *f.*, palace.

Regillus, -i, *m.*, lake Regillus.

regio, -onis, *f.*, district, region.

regius, -a, -um, princely, royal.

regno (1), reign.

regnum, -i, *n.*, royal power, monarchy.

rego, -ere, rexi, rectum (3), rule, guide.

reicio, -ere, -ieci, -iectum, refer; put *or* thrust away.

relatio, -onis, *f.*, proposal.

religio, -onis, *f.*, religious scruple *or* fear.

religiosus, -a, -um, of *or* with religious scruples.

relinquo, -ere, -liqui, -lictum (3), abandon, forsake.

reliquus, -a, -um, remaining, the rest, the rest of.

remedium, -i, *n.*, remedy.

remitto, -ere, -misi, -missum (3), send back; abate; not insist upon (59.6).

remoror (1), *dep.*, delay.

remoueo, -ere, -moui, -motum (2), withdraw.

remuneror (1), *dep.*, repay.

renouo (1), renew.

reor, reri, ratus (2), *dep.*, think.

repello, -ere, reppuli, -pulsum (3), drive back.

repentinus, -a, -um, sudden.

reperio, -ire, repperi, repertum (4), discover, find out.

repeto, -ere, -iui *or* -ii, -itum (3), seek again; ask for back.

repleo, -ere, -eui, -etum (2), fill up.

repono, -ere, -posui, -positum (3), place.

repraesento (1), fulfil instantly.

reprehenso (1), check continually.

reprimo, -ere, -pressi, -pressum (3), check.

res, rei, *f.*, thing, matter, affair, deed; *in pl.*, property.

res publica, rei publicae, *f.*, the state.

rescindo, -ere, -scidi, -scissum (3), cut *or* break down.

reses, -idis, remaining behind.

resido, -ere, -sedi, settle, abate.

resisto, -ere, -stiti, resist; make a stand (*with dat.*).

respectus, -us, *m.*, regard (for) *with gen.*

respicio, -ere, -spexi, -spectum, have regard for.

respiro (1), breathe.

respondeo, -ere, -di, -sum (2), answer; reply.

responsum, -i, *n.*, answer.

respuo, -ere, -ui (3), reject, refuse, spurn.

restituo, -ere, -ui, -utum (3), restore.

retardo (1), make slow.

retineo, -ere, -tinui, -tentum (2), hold *or* keep back.

retracto (1), handle again.

retraho, -ere, -traxi, -tractum (3), drag back.

retribuo, -ere, -ui, -utum (3), I repay.

retro, *adv.*, backwards.

retundo, -ere, rettudi, retusum (3), hold back, check.

reus, -i, *m.*, accused.

reueho, -ere, -uexi, -uectum (3), carry *or* bring back: *in pass.*, ride back.

reuertor, -i, *perfect in active form* reuerti, reuersus (3), *dep.*, return, turn back.

reuoco (1), restrain.

rex, regis, *m.*, king; *in pl.*, the princes.

ripa, -ae, *f.*, bank.

rite, *adv.*, with due observances, duly.

rixa, -ae, *f.*, quarrel, brawl.

robur, -oris, *n.*, strength.

rogatio, -onis, *f.*, proposal, bill.

rogito (1), ask repeatedly.

rogo (1), ask.

Roma, -ae, *f.*, Rome.

Romanus, -a, -um, Roman; *as noun*, a Roman.

ruber, -bra, -brum, red.

rudis, -e, untrained, unskilled.

rumor, -oris, *m.*, report, rumour.

rumpo, -ere, rupi, ruptum (3), break.

rursus, *adv.*, back again; again.

Sabinus, -a, -um, Sabine; *as noun*, a Sabine.
sacer, -cra, -crum, sacred.
sacerdos, -otis, *m.*, priest.
sacerdotium, -i, *n.*, priesthood.
sacramentum, -i, *n.*, the military oath.
sacrificium, -i, *n.*, sacrifice.
sacrificolus, -i, *m.*, sacrificer.
sacro (1), dedicate to a deity.
sacrosanctus, -a, -um, sacrosanct.
saepe, *adv.*, often.
saepio, -ire, -psi, -ptum (4), fence round; bar.
saeuio (4), rage, am wild.
saeuitia, -ae, *f.*, cruelty, savage temper, sternness.
saeuus, -a, -um, cruel, harsh, stern.
sal, -is, *m.*, salt.
saltem, *adv.*, at least.
salubris, -e, serviceable (30.1), (44.5).
saluus, -a, -um, safe.
sancte, *adv.*, solemnly.
sanctus, -a, -um, holy, sacred, inviolable.
sane, *adv.*, well, very.
sanguis, -is, *m.*, blood, bloodshed (64.5).
sanitas, -atis, *f.*, good sense.
sano (1), heal.
satelles, -itis, *m.*, attendant, guard.
satio (1), satisfy fully.
satis, *adv.*, enough, sufficiently.
satisfacio, -ere, -feci, -factum, satisfy, give satisfaction.
Satricum, -i, *n.*, Satricum (*a town*).
Saturnalia, -ium, *n. pl.*, the Saturnalia.
Saturnus, -i, *m.*, Saturn.
saucius, -a, -um, wounded.
saxum, -i, *n.*, stone, cliff.

Scaeuola, -ae, *m.*, Scaevola.
sceleratus, -a, -um, wicked.
scelus, -eris, *n.*, crime.
scio (4), know.
sciscitor (1), *dep.*, ask.
scortum, -i, *n.*, prostitute.
scriba, -ae, *m.*, secretary.
scribo, -ere, -psi, -ptum (3), write; enrol.
scutum, -i, *n.*, shield.
se *or* sese, himself, herself etc.
secedo, -ere, -cessi, -cessum (3), withdraw, secede.
secessio, -onis, *f.*, secession.
secreto, *adv.*, in private.
secundum, *prep. with acc.*, after.
secundus, -a, -um, second; favourable.
securis, -is, *f.*, axe.
secus, *adv.*, otherwise.
sed, *conj.*, but.
sedeo, -ere, sedi, sessum (2), sit.
sedes, -is, *f.*, seat, dwelling.
seditio, -onis, *f.*, division, strife.
seditiosus, -a, -um, factious.
sedo (1), settle.
seduco, -ere, -duxi, -ductum (3), withdraw.
sedulo, *adv.*, deliberately.
seges, -etis, *f.*, crop.
segnis, -e, inactive, idle.
segniter, *adv.*, idly.
sella, -ae, *f.*, seat.
semel, *adv.*, once.
semper, *adv.*, once.
senator, -oris, *m.*, senator.
senatus, -us, *m.*, senate.
senecta, -ae, *f.*, old age.
senectus, -utis, *f.*, old age.
senex, -is, *m.*, old man.
senior, -oris, older: *as noun*, elder.
sensim, *adv.*, gently, quietly.

sensus, -us, *m.*, feeling.
sententia, -ae, *f.*, opinion: proposal.
sentio, -ire, -si, -sum (4), feel, perceive.
sepelio, -ire, -iui, -itum (4), bury.
sequor, -i, secutus (3), *dep.*, follow; pursue.
Ser. = Seruius.
serenitas, -atis, *f.*, fine weather.
sermo, -onis, *m.*, talk; speech.
sero, -ere ,-ui, -rtum (3), join; contrive (18.10).
serus, -a, -um, late.
seruio (4), am in slavery.
seruitium, *n.*, slavery.
seruitus, -utis, *f.*, slavery.
seruo (1), save, keep, preserve.
seruus, -i, *m.*, slave.
seu, *conj.*, or if, or; seu . . . seu, whether . . . or.
sextans, -ntis, *m.*, sixth part of an as.
si, *conj.*, if.
sic, *adv.*, so, thus.
Sicilia, -ae, *f.*, Sicily.
Siculus, -a, -um, Sicilian.
sicut, *adv.*, like, as.
Signia, -ae, *f.*, Signia (*a town*).
signifer, -feri, *m.*, standard- bearer.
significo (1), indicate.
signum, -i, *n.*, standard; signal; statue.
silentium, -i, *n.*, inaction.
silua, -ae, *f.*, forest.
Siluanus, -i, *m.*, Silvanus.
similis, -e, like.
simul, *adv.*, at the same time.
simulatio, -onis, *f.*, pretence.
simulo (1), pretend.
sine, *prep. with abl.*, without.
singuli, -ae, -a, each individually, one (at a time).

sinister, -tra, -trum, left.
sino, -ere, siui, situm (3), allow.
sisto, -ere, stiti, statum (3), halt.
siue, *see* seu.
socer, -eri, *m.*, father-in-law.
societas, -atis, *f.*, alliance.
socius, -i, *m.*, ally.
sodalis, -e, comrade.
soleo, -ere, solitus sum (2) *semi-dep.*, am accustomed.
solidus, -a, -um, complete.
solitus, -a, -um, customary.
sollemnis, -e, regular, customary; *in neut. pl.*, formalities, customary rites.
sollicito (1), stir up, irritate (15.2); excite (42.6).
sollicitudo, -inis, *f.*, anxiety.
sollicitus, -a, -um, anxious, troubled.
solum, -i, *n.*, soil.
solum, *adv.*, only.
solus, -a, -um, alone.
solutus, -a, -um, unrestrained, unrestricted (3.2); free.
soluo, -ere, -ui, -utum (3), loose, set free (from).
somnium, -i, *n.*, dream.
somnus, -i, *m.*, sleep.
sonitus, -us, *m.*, sound.
sordidatus, -a, -um, in mourning dress.
soror, -oris, *f.*, sister.
sors, -rtis, *f.*, lot.
sortior (4), *dep.*, draw lots.
sospes, -itis, safe.
Sp. = Spurius.
spatium, -i, *n.*, space; time.
species, -ei, *f.*, look, phantom (36.4); vision (59.5).
spectaculum, -i, *n.*, show; sight.
spectator, -oris, *m.*, spectator.

spectatus, -a, -um, tested, proved; established (7.9).

specto (1), look at.

sperno, -ere, spreui, spretum (3), despise; reject, spurn.

spero (1), hope, hope for; expect, look forward to.

spes, -ei, *f.*, hope, expectation.

spiculum, -i, *n.*, dart.

spiritus, -us, *m.*, spirit, pride.

spolio (1), strip.

spolium, -i, *n.*, spoil.

sponte sua, of his (their) accord.

squalor, -oris, *m.*, dirt.

statim, *adv.*, at once.

statio, -onis, *f.*, post, outpost.

statiuus, -a, -um, stationary: *n. pl., as noun,* stationary camp.

statua, -ae, *f.*, statue.

statuo, -ere, -ui, -utum (3), set up, determine.

status, -us, *m.*, position, condition.

stimulo (1), goad, spur on.

stimulus, -i, *m.*, goad; incentive.

stipendium, -i, *n.*, pay; tax, tribute.

stirps, -is, *f.*, parent stock.

sto, -are, steti, statum (1), stand.

strages, -is, *f.*, mass.

stramentum, -i, *n.*, straw.

strepitus, -us, *m.*, din.

strepo, -are, -ui, (1), ring out (45.5).

struo, -ere, -xi, -ctum (3), build, devise, prepare.

studium, -i, *n.*, zeal, enthusiasm, effort.

stupeo (2), I am beside myself.

suadeo, -ere, -si, -sum (2), advise, urge (*with dat.*).

sub, *prep. with acc., or abl.,* under, beneath, close to.

subdo, -ere, -didi, -ditum (3), put under.

subeo, -ire, -ii, -itum, undergo; enter (42.1).

subicio, -ere, -ieci, -iectum, put under.

subigo, -ere, -egi, -actum (3), subdue.

subitus, -a, -um, sudden.

subiectus, -a, -um, lying under *or* near; adjacent to.

sublicius, -a, -um, of piles.

submitto, -ere, -misi, -missum (3), let down, lower; tone down (61.5).

submoueo, -ere, -moui, -motum (2), remove, make withdraw.

subrogo (1), cause to be elected.

subsidiarii, -orum, *m. pl.*, reserve troops.

subsidium, -i, *n.*, help, aid; reserves.

subtraho, -ere, -traxi, -tractum (3), withdraw.

subueho, -ere, -uexi, -uectum (3), bring up.

succedo, -ere, -cessi, -cessum (3), succeed.

successus, -us, *m.*, success.

succurro, -ere, -curri, -cursum (3), come into the mind.

sudor, -oris, *m.*, sweat.

Suessa, -ae, *f.*, Suessa Pometia.

sufficio, -ere, -feci, -fectum, elect in place of; am strong enough (8.4).

suffragium, -i, *n.*, vote.

suggero, -ere, -gessi, -gestum (3), append.

sum, esse, fui, am.

summa, -ae, *f.*, sum.

summus, -a, -um, highest; utmost.

sumo, -ere, -mpsi, -mptum (3), take; inflict (*of punishment*).
sumptus, -us, *m.*, expense.
super, *prep. with acc.*, in addition to; *with abl.*, upon, concerning; *as adv.*, more.
superbe, *adv.*, arrogantly.
superbia, -ae, *f.*, arrogance, tyranny.
superbus, -a, -um, arrogant, tyrannical.
superincido (3), fall upon from above.
superior, -ius, -oris, higher; victorious.
supero (1), overcome; surpass.
superstes, -stitis, surviving.
supersum, -esse, -fui, survive; am in abundance (42.9).
superus, -a, -um, above.
superuacuus, -a, -um, superfluous.
superuenio, -ire, -ueni, -uentum (4), come upon the scene.
suppeto, -ere, -petiui, -petitum (3), am sufficient for.
suppleo, -ere, -pleui, -pletum (2), make up (*the number*).
supplex, -icis, humble, suppliant; *as noun*, a suppliant.
suppliciter, *adv.*, suppliantly.
supplicium, -i, *n.*, death penalty.
supprimo, -ere, -pressi, -pressum (3), put a stop to, suppress.
supra, *prep. with acc.*, above.
supremus, -a, -um, last.
surdus, -a, -um, deaf.
suscipio, -ere, -cepi, -ceptum, undertake.
suspensus, -a, -um, uncertain, anxious.
suspicio, -onis, *f.*, suspicion.

suspicio, -ere, -spexi, -spectum, look up to; *p.p.p.* suspectus, mistrusted, suspected.
sustento (1), sustain; keep alive (34.4); hold in check (44.9).
sustineo, -ere, -tinui, -tentum (2), support; hold out against.
suus, -a, -um, his, her etc., own.

T. =Titus.
tabes, -is, *f.*, plague, infection.
tacite, *adv.*, silently.
tacitus, -a, -um, silent; unexpressed.
talis, -e, such.
tam, *adv.*, to such a degree, so.
tamen, *adv.*, yet, however.
tamquam, *adv.*, just *or* like as; as if.
tandem, *adv.*, at length; *in questions*, pray.
tantum, *adv.*, to such an extent; only.
tantummodo, *adv.*, only.
tantus, -a, -um, so great.
tarde, *adv.*, slowly.
tardus, -a, -um, slow.
Tarquinianus, -a, -um, of the Tarquins.
Tarquiniensis, -e, of Tarquinii; *as noun*, native of Tarquinii.
Tarquinius, -i, *m.*, Tarquin; *in pl.*, the Tarquins; *as adj.*, of the Tarquins.
tego, -ere, -xi, -ctum (3), cover, protect.
tellus, -uris, *f.*, earth; the Earth-goddess.
telum, -i, *n.*, weapon, missile.
temere, *adv.*, blindly; haphazardly.
temeritas, -atis, *f.*, rashness.

tempero (1), refrain from (23.10); use restraint (52.5).

tempestas, -atis, *f.,* weather, storm.

templum, -i, *n.,* enclosure, platform; temple.

tempto (1), try, test.

tempus, -oris, *n.,* time.

teneo, -ere, tenui, tentum (2), hold, keep; *reflexive,* remain (in).

tenor, -oris, *m.,* course.

tentorium, -i, *n.,* tent.

tenuis, -e, slight; mean.

tergiuersor (1), *dep.,* shilly-shally.

tergum, -i, *n.,* back; rear.

terni, -ae, -a, three each.

tero, -ere, trivi, tritum (3), waste.

terra, -ae, *f.,* earth, land.

terreo (2), frighten.

territo (1), frighten.

terror, -oris, *m.,* fear, alarm.

tertius, -a, -um, third.

testis, -is, *m.,* witness.

testor (1), *dep.,* call to witness.

Tib. =Tiberius.

Tiberinus, -i, *m.,* god of the Tiber.

Tiberis, -is, *m.,* Tiber.

timeo (2), fear.

timor, -oris, *m.,* fear.

titulus, -i, *m.,* term.

tollo, -ere, sustuli, sublatum (3), raise; remove; destroy.

tonitrus, -us, *m.,* thunder.

torreo, -ere, torrui, tostum (2), scorch, burn.

tot, *indecl.,* so many.

totiens, *adv.,* so often, as often.

totus, -a, -um, whole.

trado, -ere, -didi, -ditum (3), hand over *or* down.

traduco, -ere, -duxi, -ductum (3), lead across *or* by.

traho, -ere, -xi, -ctum (3), draw; protract; derive (5.10).

traicio, -ere, -ieci, -iectum, put across.

trames, -itis, *m.,* path.

trano (1), swim across.

tranquillus, -a, -um, quiet, calm.

trans, *prep. with acc.,* across.

transeo, -ire, -ii, -itum, cross.

transfero, -ferre, -tuli, -latum, transfer.

transfigo, -figere, -fixi, -fixum (3), pierce through.

transfuga, -ae, *m.,* deserter.

transfugio, -ere, -fugi, desert.

transgredior, -i, -gressus, *dep.,* cross.

transilio (4), jump over.

transitio, -onis, *f.,* desertion.

transuersus, -a, -um, athwart, across.

Trebium, -i, *n.,* Trebium (*a town*).

trecenti, -ae, -a, three hundred.

trepidatio, -onis, *f.,* confusion, excitement.

trepido (1), am in confusion *or* excited, *or* agitated.

trepidus, -a, -um, frightened, panic-stricken.

tres, tria, three.

triarii, -orum, *m. pl.,* veteran troops.

tribulis, -e, tribesman.

tribunal, -alis, *n.,* platform, tribunal.

tribunicius, -a, -um, of a tribune.

tribunus, -i, *m.,* tribune.

tribus, -us, *f.,* tribe.

tributum, -i, *n.,* property-tax.

tributus, -a, -um, by tribes.

triennium, -i, *m.,* space of three years.

trifariam, *adv.*, in three places.
triginta, thirty.
tristis, -e, harsh, stern; sad.
triumpho (1), celebrate a triumph.
triumphus, -i, *m.*, triumph, triumphal procession.
trucido (1), butcher, massacre.
trux, -cis, fierce.
tu, you.
tubicen, -cinis, *m.*, trumpeter.
tueor (2), *dep.*, guard, protect.
Tullius, -i, *m.*, Tullius.
tum, *adv.*, then.
tumultuose, *adv.*, in confusion.
tumultuosus, -a, -um, agitating.
tumultus, -us, *n.*, disturbance, confusion, uproar.
tunc, *adv.*, then.
turba, -ae, *f.*, crowd.
turbator, -oris, *m.*, disturber.
turbo (1), throw into confusion.
turbulentus, -a, -um, troubled, stormy.
turma, -ae, *f.*, troop (of horse).
turpis, -e, disgraceful.
turpiter, *adv.*, disgracefully.
Tusculanus, -a, -um, of Tusculum.
Tuscus, -a, -um, Tuscan, Etruscan; *as noun*, a Tuscan, Etruscan.
tutela, -ae, *f.*, protection.
tutor (1), *dep.*, defend.
tutus, -a, -um, safe.
tuus, -a, -um, your.
tyrannus, -i, *m.*, tyrant.

ubi, *adv.*, where, when.
ulciscor, -i, ultus (3) *dep.*, avenge, take vengeance on, punish.
ullus, -a, -um, any.
ultimus, -a, -um, utmost, desperate; direst (43.3).
ultor, -oris, *m.*, avenger, punisher.

ultra, *adv.*, further.
ultro, *adv.*, actually, taking the initiative, unasked.
una, *adv.*, together.
unde, *adv.*, whence.
undique, *adv.*, from *or* on all sides.
unicus, -a, -um, singular.
uniuersus, -a, -um, all, in a body; the whole of.
unquam, *adv.*, ever.
unus, -a, -um, one.
unusquisque, unaquaeque, unumquodque, each one.
urbanus, -a, -um, of the city.
urbs, -bis, *f.*, city (*often* = Rome).
urgeo, -ere, ursi (2), press hard.
usquam, *adv.*, anywhere.
usque, *adv.*, right on.
usura, -ae, *f.*, interest.
usurpo (1), make use of.
usus, -us, *m.*, advantage.
ut, *adv. and conj.*, as, when; *with subj.*, in order that, that.
uter, utra, utrum, which (*of two*)?
uterque, utraque, utrumque, each (*of two*), both.
utique, assuredly.
utor, -i, usus (3), *dep.*, use (*with abl.*).
utrimque, *adv.*, on *or* from both sides.
utroque, *adv.*, in both directions.
uxor, -oris, *f.*, wife.

uaco (1), am free *or* exempt from.
uado (3), go.
uadum, -i, *n.*, shoal, shallow.
uagor (1), *dep.*, move about.
uagus, -a, -um, moving.
ualeo (2), am strong *or* effective.
ualidus, -a, -um, strong.
ualles, -is, *f.*, valley.

uallum, -i, n., rampart.
uanus, -a, -um, false, fruitless.
uarie, adv., in various ways.
uario (1), vary.
uarius, -a, -um, diverse, varying.
uastatio, -onis, f., devastation.
uasto (1), lay waste.
uastus, -a, -um, waste, desolate.
uates, -is, m., seer, prophet.
uaticinor (1), dep., prophesy.
-ue, enclitic, or.
uehemens, -ntis, stormy, violent,
  forcible.
uehiculum, -i, n., conveyance.
Veiens, -ntis, m., of Veii: as noun,
  a native or soldier of Veii.
uel, adv., even.
Veliternus, -a, -um, of Velitrae.
uello, -ere, uolsi, uolsum (3), tear
  down.
uelo (1), envelop.
uelut, adv., like as, like as; so to
  speak, as though.
uena, -ae, f., vein.
uendo, -ere, -didi, -ditum (3), sell.
uenenum, -i, n., poison.
ueneo, -ire, -ii, -itum, am sold.
uenia, -ae, f., mercy, forgiveness.
uenter, -tris, m., belly.
uerber, -eris, m., scourging.
uerbero (1), scourge.
uerbum, -i, n., word.
uerecundia, -ae, f., respect.
uero, adv., in truth, indeed.
uerso (1), agitate (45.5); in pass.,
  move, am.
uertex, -icis, m., summit.
uerto, -ere, -ti, -sum (3), turn,
  change.
uerum, -i, n., truth.
uerus, -a, -um, true; adv., uere.
uerutum, -i, n., javelin.

Vestalis, -e, of Vesta.
uester, -tra, -trum, your.
uestibulum, -i, n., door.
uestigium, -i, n., trace.
uestis, -is, f., dress.
Vetelia, -ae, f., Vetelia (a town).
ueto, -are, -ui, -itum (1), forbid.
uetus, -eris, old.
uetustas, -atis, f., age.
uexo (1), harass.
uia, -ae, f., way, road.
uiator, -oris, m., officer.
uicis, no nom., f., change, alternation; in uicem, in turn,
  mutually.
uictor, -oris, m., victorious, victor.
uictoria, -ae, f., victory.
uictus, -us, m., sustenance.
uicus, -i, m., village.
uidelicet, adv., evidently.
uideo, -ere, uidi, uisum (2), see;
  in pass., seem, appear.
uigeo (2), am vigorous.
uigil, -is, m., sentry.
uigilia, -ae, f., watch.
uiginti, twenty.
uilis, -e, cheap.
uilla, -ae, f., country house; farm.
uincio, -ire, -nxi, -nctum (4), bind.
uinco, -ere, uici, uictum (3), conquer; prevail.
uinc(u)lum, -i, n., bond, chain,
  fetter.
uindex, -icis, c., champion.
uindico (1), avenge, punish.
uindicta, -ae, f., rod.
uinea, -ae, f., mantlet.
uinum, -i, n., wine.
uiolens, -ntis, fierce.
uiolentia, -ae, f., ferocity.
uiolo (1), outrage, assail, defile.
uir, uiri, m., man.

uirga, -ae, f., rod.
uirginitas, -atis, f., virginity.
uirgo, -inis, f., virgin, girl.
uis, acc. uim, abl. ui, f., violence,
force, might; mass (of people);
in pl., uires, -ium, strength.
uita, -ae, f., life.
uito (1), avoid.
uiuidus, -a, -um, vigorous.
uiuo, -ere, uixi, uictum (3), live.
uiuus, -a, -um, living.
uix, adv., scarcely, hardly.
uociferor (1), dep., cry aloud.
uoco (1), call, summon.
Volero-onis, m., Volero.
Volesus, -i, m., Volesus.
uolgo (1), make common or general.
uolgo, adv., commonly, openly.
uolgus, -i, n., the (common) people.

uolnero (1), wound.
uolnus, -eris, n., wound.
uolo, uelle, uolui, wish, consent.
Volscus, -a, -um, of or with the
Volsci; as noun, a Volscian.
uoltus, -us, m., look, expression.
uoluntarius, -a, -um, self-ap-
pointed.
uoluntas, -atis, f., will, wish.
uoluptas, -atis, f., pleasure; in pl.,
good things (32.9).
uoluo, -ere, -ui, -utum (3), roll;
ponder.
uos, you (plural).
uotum, -i, n., prayer, wish.
uoueo, -ere, uoui, uotum (2),
vow.
uox, uocis, f., voice, cry, utterance;
in pl., shouts, cries.